Developing Teachers' Assessment Capacity

Given the academic benefits of assessment-driven teaching, and the growing accountability context of educational systems around the world, there is a rapidly developing need to educate teachers in effectively using assessments to promote, monitor, and report on student learning. However, assessment has historically been a neglected area in teacher education programmes, and empirical research has consistently shown assessment as an area of challenge for many teachers. While there is an increased focus across teacher education and professional literature on enhancing the assessment capacity of educators, there remains little empirical research on innovative and data-based strategies to effectively achieve this goal. The purpose of this book is to consolidate existing research on assessment education and to provoke innovative and effective approaches to educating teachers and teachers-in-training about assessment. Given the dearth of relevant research, this book also considers the matter of retention and extension of initial assessment learning into teaching careers. Combined, the chapters in this book provide a foundation for novel thinking about developing teachers' assessment capacity from pre-service to in-service contexts.

The chapters in this book were originally published as a special issue of *Assessment in Education: Principles, Policy & Practice*.

Christopher DeLuca is an Associate Professor in Educational Assessment at the Faculty of Education, Queen's University, Kingston, Canada. His research examines the complex intersections of curriculum, pedagogy, and assessment as operating within evolving frameworks of educational accountability and standards-based teaching and learning. His work focuses primarily on developing and enhancing educators' assessment capacity to better support positive student learning experiences and outcomes.

Sandra Johnson has extensive experience in teaching, research, and assessment. She has served on government advisory committees on assessment, and provided assessment support and training for several international projects. She is a founding director of Assessment Europe, a founding member and Fellow of the Association for Educational Assessment – Europe, an Honorary Research Fellow in the University of Bristol's Graduate School of Education, and an Honorary Member of the European Educational Research Association's Network 9 (Assessment, Evaluation, Testing and Measurement).

Developing Teachers' Assessment Capacity

Edited by
Christopher DeLuca and Sandra Johnson

LONDON AND NEW YORK

First published 2018
by Routledge
2 Park Square, Milton Park, Abingdon, Oxon, OX14 4RN, UK

and by Routledge
711 Third Avenue, New York, NY 10017, USA

Routledge is an imprint of the Taylor & Francis Group, an informa business

© 2018 Taylor & Francis

All rights reserved. No part of this book may be reprinted or reproduced or utilised in any form or by any electronic, mechanical, or other means, now known or hereafter invented, including photocopying and recording, or in any information storage or retrieval system, without permission in writing from the publishers.

Trademark notice: Product or corporate names may be trademarks or registered trademarks, and are used only for identification and explanation without intent to infringe.

British Library Cataloguing in Publication Data
A catalogue record for this book is available from the British Library

ISBN13: 978-1-138-49303-2

Typeset in MinionPro
by diacriTech, Chennai

Publisher's Note
The publisher accepts responsibility for any inconsistencies that may have arisen during the conversion of this book from journal articles to book chapters, namely the possible inclusion of journal terminology.

Disclaimer
Every effort has been made to contact copyright holders for their permission to reprint material in this book. The publishers would be grateful to hear from any copyright holder who is not here acknowledged and will undertake to rectify any errors or omissions in future editions of this book.

Contents

Citation Information   vii

Introduction: Developing assessment capable teachers in this age of accountability   1
Christopher DeLuca and Sandra Johnson

1   Student teachers' appraisal of the importance of assessment in teacher education and self-reports on the development of assessment competence   7
Christoph Schneider and Rainer Bodensohn

2   Exploring the challenge of developing student teacher data literacy   27
Bronwen Cowie and Beverley Cooper

3   Integrating assessment for learning in the teacher education programme at the University of Oslo   44
Lisbeth M. Brevik, Marte Blikstad-Balas and Kirsti Lyngvær Engelien

4   Assessment for equity: learning how to use evidence to scaffold learning and improve teaching   65
Mary F. Hill, Fiona Ell, Lexie Grudnoff, Mavis Haigh, Marilyn Cochran-Smith, Wen-Chia Chang and Larry Ludlow

5   A rubric to track the development of secondary pre-service and novice teachers' summative assessment literacy   85
Frances Edwards

6   Professional controversies between teachers about their summative assessment practices: a tool for building assessment capacity   108
Lucie Mottier Lopez and Raphaël Pasquini

CONTENTS

7 Standards of practice to standards of evidence: developing assessment capable teachers 130
Claire Wyatt-Smith, Colette Alexander, Deanne Fishburn and Paula McMahon

8 Scaling up, *writ small*: using an assessment for learning audit instrument to stimulate site-based professional development, one school at a time 151
Zita Lysaght and Michael O'Leary

9 Developing teachers' capacities in assessment through career-long professional learning 170
Kay Livingston and Carolyn Hutchinson

Index 189

Citation Information

The chapters in this book were originally published in the *Assessment in Education: Principles, Policy & Practice*, volume 24, issue 2 (May 2017). When citing this material, please use the original page numbering for each article, as follows:

Introduction
Developing assessment capable teachers in this age of accountability
Christopher DeLuca and Sandra Johnson
Assessment in Education: Principles, Policy & Practice, volume 24, issue 2 (May 2017)
pp. 121–126

Chapter 1
Student teachers' appraisal of the importance of assessment in teacher education and self-reports on the development of assessment competence
Christoph Schneider and Rainer Bodensohn
Assessment in Education: Principles, Policy & Practice, volume 24, issue 2 (May 2017)
pp. 127–146

Chapter 2
Exploring the challenge of developing student teacher data literacy
Bronwen Cowie and Beverley Cooper
Assessment in Education: Principles, Policy & Practice, volume 24, issue 2 (May 2017)
pp. 147–163

Chapter 3
Integrating assessment for learning in the teacher education programme at the University of Oslo
Lisbeth M. Brevik, Marte Blikstad-Balas and Kirsti Lyngvær Engelien
Assessment in Education: Principles, Policy & Practice, volume 24, issue 2 (May 2017)
pp. 164–184

CITATION INFORMATION

Chapter 4
Assessment for equity: learning how to use evidence to scaffold learning and improve teaching
Mary F. Hill, Fiona Ell, Lexie Grudnoff, Mavis Haigh, Marilyn Cochran-Smith, Wen-Chia Chang and Larry Ludlow
Assessment in Education: Principles, Policy & Practice, volume 24, issue 2 (May 2017) pp. 185–204

Chapter 5
A rubric to track the development of secondary pre-service and novice teachers' summative assessment literacy
Frances Edwards
Assessment in Education: Principles, Policy & Practice, volume 24, issue 2 (May 2017) pp. 205–227

Chapter 6
Professional controversies between teachers about their summative assessment practices: a tool for building assessment capacity
Lucie Mottier Lopez and Raphaël Pasquini
Assessment in Education: Principles, Policy & Practice, volume 24, issue 2 (May 2017) pp. 228–249

Chapter 7
Standards of practice to standards of evidence: developing assessment capable teachers
Claire Wyatt-Smith, Colette Alexander, Deanne Fishburn and Paula McMahon
Assessment in Education: Principles, Policy & Practice, volume 24, issue 2 (May 2017) pp. 250–270

Chapter 8
Scaling up, writ small: using an assessment for learning audit instrument to stimulate site-based professional development, one school at a time
Zita Lysaght and Michael O'Leary
Assessment in Education: Principles, Policy & Practice, volume 24, issue 2 (May 2017) pp. 271–289

Chapter 9
Developing teachers' capacities in assessment through career-long professional learning
Kay Livingston and Carolyn Hutchinson
Assessment in Education: Principles, Policy & Practice, volume 24, issue 2 (May 2017) pp. 290–307

For any permission-related enquiries please visit:
http://www.tandfonline.com/page/help/permissions

INTRODUCTION

Developing assessment capable teachers in this age of accountability

Over the past two decades, a global movement towards accountability in education has emerged. This movement is marked by government demands for ever higher academic standards and commensurate student achievement throughout education systems, and the proliferation of student assessments at all levels – classroom, district, state, national and international (Nichols & Harris, 2016; Stobart, 2008). Accountability has become the prevailing watchword, with teacher assessment capability (and assessment literacy) now considered a fundamental competency for all educators (Popham, 2009; Xu & Brown, 2016). Educational policies and professional standards throughout the world call for educators to integrate assessments throughout instruction to support, monitor and report on student learning, and to use summative forms of assessment to document and demonstrate achievement of educational standards (DeLuca, LaPointe-McEwan, & Luhanga, 2016; Gotch & French, 2014). The accountability movement is supported by educational research that confirms assessment-based teaching as a potentially effective educational strategy to improve student achievement (e.g. Black & Wiliam, 1998; Hattie, 2009).

Stressing the importance of assessment literacy, James Popham (2009, p. 4) notes 'educators' inadequate knowledge in assessment can cripple the quality of education. Assessment literacy is seen as a sine qua non for today's competent educator'. Likewise, Johnson (2011, p. 121), in the context of summative assessment for system monitoring, observes that 'the increasing politicisation of assessment over recent decades has strengthened [the] need for a high degree of assessment literacy among practitioners and others involved in the business of education'. DeLuca and Bellara (2013) further comment that as the landscape of educational assessment changes to include accountability mandates and standards-based teaching but also student-centred pedagogies and student-directed assessments, 'there is a continued need to shift pre-service assessment education experiences that prepare teachers to embrace multiple purposes and practices of assessment in schools' (p. 367).

Despite these widespread calls for assessment capable teachers, research indicates that teachers generally maintain low levels of assessment knowledge and skills, with beginning teachers particularly unprepared for assessment in schools (DeLuca & Klinger, 2010; MacLellan, 2004). This persistent finding is unsurprising as assessment has historically been a neglected area of study in teacher education programmes, at least in Anglophone countries (La Marca, 2006; Shepard, Hammerness, Darling-Hammond, & Rust, 2005; Stiggins, 1999; Taras, 2007). Moreover, current teacher education models maintain several challenges for supporting teacher candidates' and initial teachers' developing conceptions and practices of assessment. The often short and fragmented (i.e. on-campus versus practicum) structure of teacher education programmes, diversity of instructors and variability in their approaches to assessment, and competing learning priorities limit the consistency and prominence of effective assessment education within initial preparatory programmes (DeLuca & Volante, 2016; Taras, 2007). Instructors' own levels of assessment capability might also, in some cases, be lacking.

Once in field, and especially within their first five years, beginning teachers work to establish confidence across their practice with explicit professional learning in assessment not always accessible or available. Instead, practising teachers tend to learn about assessment through collaboration and discussions with colleagues, and adapt to in-school assessment routines and cultures. However, how effective this learning is – how similarly and how consistently teachers are able to apply criteria-based standards of judgement when evaluating evidence of student learning and achievement – is rarely systematically researched, even in high-stakes assessment contexts (Johnson, 2013).

Accordingly, we situate this special issue amid these professional learning challenges and with the aim to present cutting-edge research into assessment education – to provoke innovative and effective approaches to supporting teacher assessment capability from pre-service to in-service. To this end, this collection includes nine articles from a variety of different countries: Australia and New Zealand, along with Germany, Ireland, Norway, Scotland and Switzerland. Combined, the articles discuss opportunities for enhancing teacher education programming at institutional and system levels.

Innovative approaches to pre-service assessment education are described in seven of the papers: Brevik, Blikstad-Balas and Engelien; Cowie and Cooper; Edwards; Hill and colleagues; Mottier Lopez and Pasquini; Schneider and Bodensohn; and Wyatt-Smith and colleagues. Across these papers, we see a consistent emphasis on encouraging teacher candidates to cultivate their understandings of assessment by using critical reflective practices rooted in Assessment for Learning (AfL) principles to support their own development. This recursive form of learning (i.e. learning assessment by using assessment for your own learning) is counter-intuitive for many teacher candidates who are initially preoccupied with the assessment of students, as evidenced in the Norwegian study. Through ongoing criterion-referenced self-assessment and the interrogation of controversial assessment incidences, these papers advocate for the active use of assessment strategies in the development of assessment capable teachers. The paper by Wyatt-Smith and colleagues further extends this argument by invoking the need for systemic cohesion across sites of assessment education. In particular, the authors describe a process of aligning learning criteria across universities and external agencies to enable a consistent message and collective effort in supporting initial teacher learning in assessment. The final two papers, by Lysaght and O'Leary on one hand, and Livingston and Hutchinson on the other, focus on teachers' continuing professional development once in-service. Both papers invite us to consider the factors and structures that enable continued assessment education once teachers are in career, and pose significant questions that challenge conventional notions of professional development.

Christoph Schneider and Rainer Bodensohn, in their paper 'Student teachers' appraisal of the importance of assessment in teacher education and self-reports on the development of assessment competence', describe an empirical study focused on teacher candidates' perceptions towards assessment learning in their pre-service programme in Germany. This country context is particularly interesting as assessment has traditionally featured alongside curriculum and pedagogy in initial teacher education programmes in many German universities; hence teacher candidates are able to comment on the relative importance and valuing of assessment in relation to other programme content. In Schneider and Bodensohn's study, over 900 teacher candidates rated the importance of each of the official assessment standards that underpinned their training programme, and recorded the frequency with which they believed they behaved in accordance with the standards in practicum situations. Their analyses revealed that teacher candidates perceive assessment as a distinct domain and assign high rating to the importance and value of this domain in pre-service education programmes. We position this article first in this special issue as a baseline for thinking about pre-service and in-service assessment education. Clearly, the topic is one valued by teacher candidates and therefore deserves purposeful attention and planning.

In 'Exploring the challenge of developing student teacher data literacy', Bronwen Cowie and Beverley Cooper reiterate the need for more informed teacher data use, including advocacy for formative assessment and the need for teachers to account for student learning within the

New Zealand context. In this paper, Cowie and Cooper point to challenges, relevant in their contexts and others, related to developing teacher candidates' and teachers' assessment and data literacy. Specifically, they argue that a dominant impediment is the fact that teachers might not have a sufficient prior grounding in basic mathematics and statistics to fully use data in meaningful ways. The paper reports lecturer, teacher candidate and school leader views of the role and requirements of data literacy using data from a larger New Zealand study into how to foster student-teacher mathematical thinking for the breadth of teacher professional work. Their findings suggest a concern and opportunity to develop assessment and data literacy through mathematical and statistical understandings. For us, this suggests that assessment education is not a stand-alone topic; rather it has relevant cognates in curriculum and pedagogy, and pre-requisites in areas of mathematics, statistics and the psychology of learning.

In their contribution from Norway, 'Integrating assessment for learning in the teacher education programme at the University of Oslo', Lisbeth Brevik, Marte Blikstad-Balas and Kirsti Engelien focus on a newly revised master's level teacher education programme, in which AfL principles have been purposefully integrated. With almost 150 teacher candidates involved in the research, this case study described through lecture notes, student videos, and student exam papers aimed to examine how AfL was used in the service of teacher candidate learning. An important finding from the study was that teacher candidates appeared more concerned with assessing their students' learning than assessing themselves and their own developing assessment capability. Accordingly, this study reminds us that teacher candidates are primarily focused on their students' growth and development, and that as teacher educators, we need to create the conditions through which they begin to focus simultaneously on their own development. If teacher candidates and teachers can see value in using AfL to support their own learning, they are more likely to appreciate assessment as an effective pedagogical approach with their classroom students. Hence, learning to assess is just as much about teacher candidates' use of assessment for professional learning as it is about classroom assessment.

Mary Hill and colleagues, in their paper 'Assessment for equity: learning how to use evidence to scaffold learning and improve teaching', examine evidence regarding the assessment learning of 27 pre-service teachers in New Zealand, who were following a new Master of Teaching programme designed to prepare participants to address persistent inequitable outcomes of designated student groups in the country. The assessment curriculum was integrated across all courses and in-school experiences as one of six 'interconnected facets of practice for equity'. Drawing on questionnaire data, interpretive analyses of assignments and focus group interviews, the study found that the programme combined theory and practice to build the assessment understanding and competence needed to address equity issues. The authors argue that this successful outcome was facilitated by incorporating the assessment curriculum into each course and intertwining university and school experiences, supported by a consistent focus on addressing equity throughout. Building on previous teacher education literature, this study provides further empirical evidence for a comprehensive and cohesive approach to assessment education, where candidates explore assessment alongside other critical topics in a coherent view of teacher education programming. Such an approach requires collaboration amongst faculty members to map the terrain of teacher learning, and establish complementary learning opportunities that build teacher candidates' competencies and confidence in assessment and teaching.

In another contribution from New Zealand, 'A rubric to track the development of secondary pre-service and novice teachers' summative assessment literacy', Frances Edwards notes that in order to assess student learning dependably teachers need to be able to call on specialised assessment knowledge and skills, and that these develop over time through ongoing teacher learning and experience. The author presents the SALRubric, an instrument specially constructed to track the development of secondary science teachers' summative assessment literacy. The rubric covers 10 dimensions across three categories drawn from the literature and context-specific empirical evidence: knowledge of assessment, understanding the context for assessment and recognising the impact of assessment. The paper goes on to describe an application of the rubric in New Zealand, during which an increasing level of sophistication in teachers' summative assessment literacy was observed over 20 months, albeit in a 'nuanced manner' for individual teachers. Implications of the use of the rubric are discussed in terms of summative assessment literacy practice and development.

The recent introduction of new regional curricula into the country, with a concomitant requirement for teachers to assess their students with reference to them, sets the context for the research described in Lucie Mottier Lopez and Raphaël Pasquini's contribution from Switzerland: 'Professional Controversies between Teachers about their Summative Assessment Practices: A Tool for Building Assessment Capacity'. The authors overview two collaborative research projects carried out in French-speaking Switzerland, that observed controversies in action having to do with the identification of appropriate pass marks for self-developed tasks and tests, i.e. standard setting. One project involved primary teachers and was based on a form of social moderation, while secondary teachers participated in the second project that referenced a model of curriculum alignment. The findings supported the potentially constructive role of professional controversies in building teachers' summative assessment capacity, and suggest the value of exploring alternative pedagogical approaches to assessment education. As such, we argue that future research should extend the repertoire of pedagogies for effective assessment education that enable teacher educators to more readily engage teacher candidates in new learning about assessment.

In their contribution from Australia, 'Standards of practice to standards of evidence: developing assessment capable teachers', Claire Wyatt-Smith, Colette Alexander, Deanne Fishburn and Paula McMahon describe a project that began in response to a national context of increasing emphasis on standards and accountability. The project had a three-part commitment at its core. The first was to undertake a comprehensive audit and analysis of all teacher education programmes in the state of Queensland. This audit established the approaches and practices universities relied on when preparing assessment capable pre-service teachers. The second was to take account of multiple perspectives and approaches in initial teacher education, to integrate data into how beginning teachers are prepared to source and use evidence for improving learning and teaching. The third was to develop new principles, policies and practices for reviewing and moderating teacher education programmes against professional standards. The paper proposes a move beyond the discourse of professional standards of practice towards a complementary discourse of standards of evidence. Through this work, we see the value of inter-agency collaboration and the role for standards-based education in ensuring consistency and possibilities for teacher preparation.

From the professional in-service context, Zita Lysaght and Michael O'Leary in the Republic of Ireland carried out an empirical study involving completion of a self-assessment questionnaire by 594 practising teachers drawn from 42 primary schools. The study confirmed the urgent need for high-quality professional development to build teachers' assessment capability. However, fiscal considerations obviated any possibility of financial support for a national programme of in-service assessment development. In their paper, 'Scaling Up, *Writ Small*: Using an Assessment for Learning Audit Instrument to Stimulate Site-Based Professional Development, One School at a Time', the authors offer the results of their study, and describe a strategy of drilling down to one in-school approach (i.e. Design-Based Implementation Research) to reflect on the importance of site-based collaborative professional development between researchers, teachers and others, as a mechanism for addressing teachers' needs in a manner that also supports other participants' professional interests.

In a complementary way, the work of Kay Livingston and Carolyn Hutchinson in Scotland takes a long view of career development while recognising the importance of balancing teachers' individual learning priorities with systemic professional learning supports. Their paper, 'Developing teachers' capacities in assessment to promote pupil learning through career-long professional learning', provides us with a comprehensive description of how various levels of an education system can work to provide options for teacher-driven professional learning. The authors specifically explore how teachers understand assessment in relation to their students' learning, the curriculum and their pedagogical choices, and how teachers' capacity to use assessment to improve students' learning can be developed through career-long professional learning (CLPL). Ultimately, Livingston and Hutchinson wrestle with a persistent challenge for in-school professional learning by considering how teachers' learning can be implemented and sustained both locally and nationally.

Interestingly, across pre-service and in-service contexts of assessment education there are consistent findings that effectively support teacher assessment capability. First, learning to assess involves teachers driving their learning by selecting priorities that are meaningful to them, their career stage and their context of work. It also involves actively integrating and practising assessment principles within their own professional learning so that they become intimately familiar with assessment processes and how they operate to support learning. Second, learning to assess involves aligning learning goals with professional development criteria and monitoring teacher learning through evidence-based self-assessments and feedback from knowledgeable others. Lastly, learning to assess involves multiple stakeholders. Aligning priorities across stakeholders is a challenge but a clear necessary step in providing meaningful opportunities for teacher learning at university, school and system levels.

As we continue to promote assessment as a fundamental competency for teachers in the twenty-first century, the papers in this collection argue for additional empirical research in assessment education. Among the pressing topics for future research are the need to examine (a) models for universities to build meaningful learning partnerships with local schools, education bodies and accreditation agencies in the service teacher learning; (b) the design of coherent teacher education programmes that put assessment learning to work in relation to other fundamental teacher competencies and complex educational contexts; (c) diverse pedagogical approaches to engage teachers in learning about assessment; and (d) teacher candidates' and teachers' prioritisation and valuing of assessment within their own professional development. Within this era of increased educational accountability, there is clearly an urgent and global need to support teachers' work and learning in assessment. The papers in this collection demonstrate the value and power of quality research and teacher education in addressing this need.

References

Black, P., & Wiliam, D. (1998). *Inside the black box*. London: King's College.
DeLuca, C., & Bellara, A. (2013). The current state of assessment education: Aligning policy, standards, and teacher education curriculum. *Journal of Teacher Education, 64*, 356–372.
DeLuca, C., & Klinger, D. A. (2010). Assessment literacy development: Identifying gaps in teacher candidates' learning. *Assessment in Education: Principles, Policy & Practice, 17*, 419–438.
DeLuca, C., LaPointe-McEwan, D., & Luhanga, U. (2016). Teacher assessment literacy: What is it and how do we measure it? *Educational Assessment, Evaluation, and Accountability, 28*, 251–272.
DeLuca, C., & Volante, L. (2016). Assessment for learning in teacher education programs: Navigating the juxtaposition of theory and praxis. *Journal of the International Society for Teacher Education, 20*, 19–31.
Gotch, C. M., & French, B. F. (2014). A systematic review of assessment literacy measures. *Educational Measurement: Issues and Practice, 33*, 14–18.
Hattie, J. (2009). *Visible learning: A synthesis of over 800 meta-analyses relating to achievement*. London: Routledge.
Johnson, S. (2011). *Assessing learning in the primary classroom*. London: Routledge.
Johnson, S. (2013). On the reliability of high-stakes teacher assessment. *Research Papers in Education, 28*, 91–105.
La Marca. P. (2006, June). *Assessment literacy: Building capacity for improving student learning*. Paper presented at the National Conference on Large-Scale Assessment, Council of Chief State School Officers, San Francisco, CA.

DEVELOPING TEACHERS' ASSESSMENT CAPACITY

MacLellan, E. (2004). Initial knowledge states about assessment: Novice teachers' conceptualizations. *Teaching and Teacher Education, 20*, 523–535.

Nichols, S. L., & Harris, L. R. (2016). Accountability assessment's effects on teachers and schools. In G. Brown, & L. R. Harris (Eds.), (pp. 40–56). *Handbook of human and social conditions in assessment*. New York, NY: Routledge.

Popham, W. J. (2009). Assessment literacy for teachers: Faddish or fundamental? *Theory Into Practice, 48*, 4–11.

Shepard, L., Hammerness, K., Darling-Hammond, L., & Rust, F. (2005). Assessment. In L. Darling-Hammond & J. Bransford (Eds.), *Preparing teachers for a changing world: What teachers should learn and be able to do* (pp. 275–326). San Francisco, CA: Jossey-Bass.

Stiggins, R. J. (1999). Evaluating classroom assessment training in teacher education programs. *Educational Measurement: Issues and Practice, 18*, 23–27.

Stobart, G. (2008). *Testing times: The uses and abuses of assessment*. Milton Park: Routledge.

Taras, M. (2007). Assessment for learning: Understanding theory to improve practice. *Journal of Further and Higher Education, 31*, 363–371.

Xu, Y., & Brown, G. (2016). Teacher assessment literacy in practice: A reconceptualization. *Teaching and Teacher Education, 58*, 149–162.

Christopher DeLuca

Sandra Johnson

Student teachers' appraisal of the importance of assessment in teacher education and self-reports on the development of assessment competence

Christoph Schneider and Rainer Bodensohn

ABSTRACT
Competence in assessment has been identified as a key feature in teachers' professional success. However, assessment competence is a complex field, comprising capacity in both summative and formative assessment. Hence, a detailed view on how student teachers perceive assessment is the focus of this study. Based on an official catalogue of assessment standards, over 900 student teachers repeatedly rated the importance of the standards and the frequency with which they behaved in accordance with the standards in practicum situations. Analyses revealed that (a) students perceived assessment competence as a contextual entity distinguishable from other domains, (b) while they assigned high importance ratings to assessment standards in general, standards concerned specifically with external evaluation were seen as relatively unimportant, and (c) they perceived a rise in their own assessment competence during their teacher education. Taken together, this suggests that in the student view assessment competence is important and develops over time.

Introduction

In contemporary literature on educational assessment in general and on teachers' assessment practice in particular, there is no doubt that assessment capacity, or assessment competence as we refer to it in this paper, is a key feature for successfully enacting the teaching profession. Assessment in educational settings is a complex issue, characterised by some dichotomies or contrasting aims. As Berry and Adamson (2011) summarise, assessment can, for example, follow a formative or summative approach, be formal or informal, focus on high-stakes testing vs. low-stakes assessment accompanying pupils' learning processes, apply criterion-based, social or ipsative frames of reference; assessment outcomes can be communicated by means of numerical expression (marks) or in verbal reports, etc.

In an effort to systematise this complex field, DeLuca, LaPointe-McEwan and Luhanga have recently (2016) identified a number of main themes of assessment by reviewing systematisations of assessment standards mainly originating from English-speaking countries.

DEVELOPING TEACHERS' ASSESSMENT CAPACITY

These main themes are: assessment purposes (e.g. summative vs. formative assessment), assessment processes (basically the 'tools' of assessment), communication of assessment results, issues of fairness and ethics (including, for example, knowledge about and awareness of observational bias), measurement theory (the 'hard facts' on psychometric testing) and assessment for learning (AFL, i.e. explicitly making use of assessment techniques in supporting pupils' learning). On a meta-level, the theme that teachers should be provided with learning opportunities that allow the development of assessment competence is added to the list. Although there is some variability in the relative weighting of these themes (a) across standards catalogues reviewed and (b) across recent decades, this list provides an overall framework of the issues with which assessment is concerned. With respect to the two main purposes of assessment (selection based on summative assessment vs. providing a basis for learning support by formative assessment), DeLuca et al. (2016) note a clear trend in recent years towards highlighting the importance of formative assessment as opposed to summative assessment. This trend has also become visible in reforms of assessment education in many countries throughout the last decades (Berry, 2011).

Yet, in contrast to detailed consideration of all facets and tasks which assessment encompasses in practice, formal learning opportunities specifically designed to develop future teachers' assessment competence in the form of specific lectures or courses within teacher training programmes are often scarce or even non-existent (cf. Leighton, Gokiert, Cor, & Heffernan, 2010; Popham, 2004). In consequence, the status quo of teachers' assessment literacy leaves much to be desired (cf. DeLuca et al., 2016). On the other hand, there is empirical evidence that specific assessment courses within teacher training are effective in enhancing student teachers' confidence in their own assessment capacity (DeLuca & Klinger, 2010) and in deepening understanding of assessment (DeLuca, Chavez, & Cao, 2013).

A theoretical or scientific consensus on the elements that assessment encompasses is, however, only one side of the coin. While the multifaceted nature of assessment activities, and the competences related to these, have been extensively described, it does not necessarily follow that (future) practitioners (i.e. both student teachers and teachers in service) would 'naturally' adopt all the various viewpoints. The question of practitioners' internalisation of all aspects of assessment along with associated implications for professional action has rarely been addressed in research. In this context, a number of questions can be raised: Do practitioners perceive different assessment activities and related competences as one entity within a wider framework of professional pedagogical action? Are practitioners willing to comply with expectations based on a set of assessment skills which they must be able to enact in professional practice? Do future practitioners feel that their assessment competence is increasing as they progress through their teacher training? This paper seeks to offer answers to these questions based on quantitative student teacher surveys in a German teacher training context.

Due to the fact that the teaching profession and teacher education in Germany are characterised by some unique features, a brief description is provided in the next section. This is followed by an overview of the set of professional competences embodied in the national standards for teacher training, which serves as the theoretical framework for our empirical study of the student view of assessment competence. The assessment courses that are regular components in teacher training in Germany will then be briefly illustrated. As the study reported in this paper is embedded into the wider context of the KOSTA (acronym for COmpetence and STAndard Orientation in Teacher Education) project, KOSTA's aims will also be presented along with some salient findings.

Outline of the German teacher education system and of the teaching profession in Germany

In an international comparison, the German status quo of teacher education and of the teaching profession is characterised by some unique features. The following section is limited to an excerpt which is relevant for the scope of this paper and does not claim to concisely depict all aspects. Full information on the legislation and the structures of the German teacher education system can be derived from KMK (2015).

First, teacher education is regulated by the *Länder*[1] legislation under the responsibility of the respective Ministries of Education. The involvement of a state representative in accreditation procedures for Bachelor's or Master's teacher education programmes guarantees state responsibility for content requirements. Second, obtaining teaching certification for different school types requires enrolment in different teacher education programmes. In consequence, student teachers have to decide on a specific teacher career relatively early in the course of their teacher education, typically after the first two years of university training. Excluding vocational schooling, these programmes lead to certification for teaching in either primary schools (ISCED 1), lower track secondary schools up to grade 10 (ISCED 2), academic track secondary schools (Gymnasium) up to grade 13 (ISCED 2 and ISCED 3), and special needs education schools (no unique ISCED equivalent). Third, teacher training is generally divided into two subsequent stages, successful completion of the first stage being an entry requirement for the second stage. The first stage is a BA/MA programme, typically lasting four years at a university or an equivalent higher education institution, enriched by periods of in-school practicums. The second stage (preparatory service), encompassing 12 to 24 months of in-school training, is in the hands of ministry-run teacher training institutes, and terminates with full teacher certification (state examination). The first stage compulsorily encompasses studies in at least two content domains (i.e. the subjects the candidate will later teach in school) as well as in educational sciences. It is thought to provide the theoretical foundations for the chiefly practice-oriented second stage. Fourth, once teacher candidates have obtained full certification at the end of the preparatory service, they may apply for a post in school service. After the first two to three years in service, teachers must pass a first examination of their teaching skills, typically carried out by the local school principal. If successful, they generally receive the status of lifelong civil servants. Thus, individual teachers are in no way threatened by appraisals of their work with respect to their employment conditions. With some variation between the ISCED types, teacher salaries in Germany are well above the OECD average in both absolute and relative terms, while the teaching workload is slightly higher than the OECD mean (OECD, 2013). Fifth, teachers are expected to engage in tertiary teacher education offerings at a volume of typically five working days per year, with free choice of courses to follow.

Binding standards for teacher education on a national level

While legislation on education matters in general, and on the organisation of teacher education, is in the hands of the *Länder* in Germany, *the Standing Conference of the Ministers of Education and Cultural Affairs of the Länder in the Federal Republic of Germany (Kultusministerkonferenz, KMK)* is the national authority concerned with implementing nationwide standards on educational matters in order to ensure cross-*Länder* comparability

DEVELOPING TEACHERS' ASSESSMENT CAPACITY

Table 1. Contents of the KMK standards of teacher training (2004/2014): eleven competences pertaining to four broad competence domains.

Competence domain **'Teaching'**

C1: Teachers plan their lessons diligently and behave professionally in the classroom
C2: Teachers support pupil learning by providing adequate learning opportunities; they motivate students and encourage them to use the learning contents for transfer purposes
C3: Teachers promote pupils' self-regulated learning and working

Competence domain **'Education'**

C4: Teachers are familiar with their pupils' social and cultural living conditions; in the school context, teachers influence students' individual development
C5: Teachers impart values and norms; they support pupils' self-directed judging and behaviour
C6: Teachers find pathways for resolving difficulties and conflicts in school and in the classroom

Competence domain **'Assessment'**

C7: Teachers diagnose pupils' prerequisites for learning and learning processes; they support individual pupils and counsel learners and their parents
C8: Teachers assess pupils' learning outcomes by means of transparent evaluation criteria

Competence domain **'Innovation'**

C9: Teachers are well aware of their profession's particular demands; they understand their profession as a public appointment with a high level of responsibility and commitment
C10: Teachers understand their profession as a lifelong learning task
C11: Teachers contribute to the planning and implementation of school development projects and programmes

Note: These are non-official translations for illustrative purposes within the scope of this paper.

of graduation at all educational levels. This facilitates mobility of both pupils and teaching staff across *Länder* boundaries. Based on an expert's report by Terhart (2002) expressing normative considerations, the KMK (2004/2014) has issued binding *Standards for Teacher Training in the Educational Sciences,* which encompass the four broad competence domains of 'Teaching', 'Education', 'Assessment' and 'Innovation'.[2] These standards constitute an exhaustive description of professional (pedagogical) competences that all teachers are assumed to possess upon obtaining teaching certification. *Länder* legislation must then guarantee that all competences described therein are developed in their teacher education programmes. The four domains of competence are based on eleven competence descriptions, as shown in Table 1.

Assessment competence within the KMK's standards

While the KMK's competences C7 and C8 (see Table 1) explicitly encompass assessment competence, some elements of C10 (pertaining to the 'Innovation' domain) may, in a wider sense, be additionally filed under assessment competence. Table 2 offers an exemplary overview of elements of assessment competence as represented in the KMK's (2004/2014) standards.

Following the strong tradition of the field of 'Pedagogical Diagnostics' (a term introduced by the influential German educationalist Karlheinz Ingenkamp in 1968; cf. Ingenkamp, 1985) as a pillar of school pedagogy in Germany, issues of (a) recognition and handling of diversity, (b) formative assessment, (c) counselling of pupils and parents, and (d) research orientation (i.e. the ability and the willingness to keep up with current findings of educational research relevant to the teaching profession) are regarded as 'natural' constituents of assessment competence. Comparing the KMK standards to similar collections from the Anglo-Saxon context (e.g. Brookhart, 2011; JCSEE, 2015; review by DeLuca et al., 2016),

10

DEVELOPING TEACHERS' ASSESSMENT CAPACITY

Table 2. KMK standards of teacher training (2004/2014) indicative of assessment competence (excerpts).

C7: Teachers diagnose pupils' prerequisites for learning and learning processes; they support individual pupils and counsel learners and their parents

Teacher graduates ...

... are familiar with concepts of heterogeneity and diversity and know how to handle individual learning prerequisites in teaching in diverse classrooms.

... recognise pupils' learning potentials, learning obstacles and learning progress.

... know the principles of formative assessment in the classroom and are capable of harmonising (pupils') learning prerequisites and (the curriculums') desired learning outcomes.

... know principles and approaches in counselling pupils and parents and adequately apply these approaches in practice.

C8: Teachers assess pupils' learning outcomes by means of transparent evaluation criteria

Teacher graduates ...

... know different approaches in educational assessment, including their advantages and disadvantages, and apply them adequately in constructing tasks.

... are familiar with different frames of reference [social, criterion-related and ipsative] in appraising pupils' achievement and apply them appropriately.

... know about the charged relationship of supportive vs. selective functions of educational assessment.

... adequately apply scoring techniques.

... give feedback and substantiate evaluation and assessment outcomes in addressee's language while providing perspectives for future learning.

... utilise assessment outcomes as a source of feedback in teaching.

C10: Teachers understand their profession as a perpetual learning task

Teacher graduates ...

... know and make use methods of internal and external evaluation for purposes of developing and ensuring instructional quality.

... receive and appraise findings from educational research and integrate these into professional action.

Note: These are non-official translations for illustrative purposes within the scope of this paper. The choice of excerpts from the KMK's standards strives to illustrate the full scope, but is inevitably less detailed than the original.

there are some apparent differences concerning concepts as well as language use. For example, the concept of 'Assessment for Learning' (AFL), which has been intensively discussed on an international scale (e.g. Berry & Adamson, 2011; Black, 2015; Black & Wiliam, 1998; Tigelaar & Beijaard, 2013), is not *expressis verbis* referred to in the German standards. This does not imply, however, that formative assessment is a neglected issue in the German context. On the contrary, 'Pedagogical Diagnostics', as a main teaching area in school pedagogy, has always been inherently concerned with 'taking the right decisions in the interest of the learner' (Ingenkamp & Lissmann, 2008, p. 14; translation by the authors), a notion which comes very close to 'the most valued aim, that of developing the learning capacity of [...] students' (Black, 2015, p. 163)[3]. As this basic notion, and the need for formative assessment in the classroom to be embedded therein, has not been questioned for decades in the German context; German educationalists have not in any substantial way contributed to the international ongoing debate on AFL. Likewise, though the term 'feedback' appears in the KMK standards as such, it has a wider connotation than simply communicating achievement-related information to students. Rather, issues of counselling pupils and their parents with a wider pedagogical scope are traditionally treated as inherent aspects of assessment in the German context. The rationale behind the close link between assessment and counselling is that the teacher has the most comprehensive view on a pupil's learning behaviour and achievement outcomes. Thus, not only providing feedback on outcomes but also communicating with individual pupils, parents, and potentially third parties in order to elaborate solutions aiming at ameliorating the individual pupil's learning is regarded as one component of teachers' assessment competence. A further issue, not explicitly addressed in

11

international standard catalogues, is teachers' research orientation. However, this notion bears some close resemblance to the recently discussed concept of teachers' data literacy (Cowie & Cooper, 2017, in this issue).

In spite of all differences in the terminology on assessment in an educational context, there is certainly a high degree of congruence in conceptual understanding of assessment. With the possible exception of counselling and research orientation, all of the elements of assessment competence in the KMK's standards (see Table 2) can be heuristically allocated inside the assessment themes outlined by DeLuca et al. (2016).

Elements of assessment in German teacher education curricula

As the KMK's standards are compulsory for teacher education at a national level, *Länder* legislation has to guarantee their implementation. This ensures that, amongst other domains, teacher candidates' assessment competence is represented in a substantial way in all teacher education programmes. However, legislative structures and ways of communicating formal requirements differ considerably between the *Länder*, impeding direct comparisons of teacher education curricula. Exemplarily, the BA teacher education curriculum in the *Land* of *Rhineland-Palatinate* (where the present study was carried out) includes a compulsory study module on 'Diagnostics, Diversity, Adaptive Teaching and Inclusion' at the secondary teacher education level (ISCED 2 and ISCED 3). Therein, assessment competence is explicitly addressed in a central lecture on 'Pedagogical Diagnostics' focusing on the theoretical foundations of assessment. In addition, it is covered in a more practice-oriented course including teacher students' practical training in planning and enacting assessment tasks. As the module ends with a central exam covering all its aspects, student teachers are obliged to learn about assessment in depth.

Evaluation of student teachers' competence development in a German university: outline of the KOSTA project

The approach of KOSTA follows the basic model of a chain of effects in teacher education (Galluzzo & Craig, 1990) which continues to be strongly referred to in German teacher education literature (e.g. Frey, 2014; Terhart, 2002). In this chain of effects, student teachers' 'Training Experiences' (in teacher education) are thought to causally influence their 'Performance Competencies', which in turn have an effect on their 'Pupils' Learning Experiences' and, finally, on 'Pupil Outcomes'. In KOSTA specifically the first link of this chain (i.e. the effect of training on competences) is subject to empirical analysis.

For purposes of monitoring the competence development of all students in the teacher education programmes at one German university with a strong focus in teacher education, students compulsorily participated in surveys in a longitudinal design. In the KOSTA project, students periodically self-rated their competences in the domains proposed by the KMK (2004/2014).

As the term 'competence' has been used with a wide variety of meanings and thus lacks conceptual clarity (see Bodensohn, 2003), it is necessary to briefly outline the competence concept underlying the KOSTA project. Here, the concept of action competence in the teaching profession is applied in the sense of Weinert (2001) and Oser (2013), treating competence as a set of facets including, most importantly, social behaviour:

DEVELOPING TEACHERS' ASSESSMENT CAPACITY

> All knowledge types together (content knowledge, pedagogical knowledge, management knowledge, knowledge of learning psychology, etc.) fall short of constituting competence. Though all this is a prerequisite to competence and influences competence, the competence itself additionally requires practical training in application. [...] All studies assessing knowledge, knowledge types and their application in critical situations (in a 'what should be done, if ...' manner) do not model competence but rather the knowledge base for the competence. (Oser, 2013, p.7, translation by the authors)

In this understanding, a person would only be accredited to possess a certain competence if he or she displayed or applied relevant behaviour in practice. Following the same rationale, KOSTA assesses competence by self-ratings of the frequency with which such behaviour occurred[4]. Whether self-ratings constitute valid indicators of a person's competence has been subject to debate (e.g. Hartig & Jude, 2007). Overall, self-report data have been found to be mediocre estimators of true conditions whenever 'hard' data are at hand. In a meta-analysis on the validity of self-ratings on intelligence, for example, these were only loosely correlated ($r = .33$) to intelligence test scores (Freund & Kasten, 2012). In the domain of teachers' competences, however, no such 'hard' data are available. Alternative approaches in competence assessment (e.g. standardised tests, expert's ratings, observational or behavioural ratings, vignettes, portfolio analyses) do all have their strengths and weaknesses; yet none of these approaches may claim to provide 'hardest' or 'reference' data. The validity of self-ratings in competence assessment is thus a relative matter. It is, for example, doubtful whether experts' ratings would yield a more valid picture of a teacher candidate's competence than self-ratings (e.g. Howard, 1990).

As an integral part of the study programmes in teacher education, KOSTA served three-fold aims: first, students anonymously received individual feedback on strengths and weaknesses in their self-reported profile of competences in relation to their peers (mean profile of all students in the cohort) by entering a unique code into an online tool. Second, data aggregated over cohorts or study programmes were published in reports and served as feedback to teacher educators and the University Directorate. Third, regular collections of data from each semester were combined into longitudinal datasets for the purpose of scientific analysis of student teachers' competence development.

To bring the KMK's relatively abstract standard descriptions and the concept of action competence underlying the KOSTA approach together, standard descriptions had to be translated into units of observable behaviour providing the item basis for student teachers' self-ratings. First, in a bottom-up approach, a group of advanced student teachers was instructed to recall key situations and demands within the in-school practicums they had completed, and to assign those to the eleven areas of competence pertaining to the four KMK competence domains (Table 1). Next, a group of educational researchers screened the students' proposals in a top-down manner, formulated items and evaluated their embedding into a theoretical background in educational literature. These procedures resulted in a set of five to eight items adjacent to each of the 11 competence descriptions, giving a total of 65 items. In the logic of the initial bottom-up approach starting off from practical situations and demands, it is not guaranteed that each aspect of the KMK standards was depicted in a specific item. Rather, the items derived represent a collection of demands of practical and in-job situations in which the standards would come to life.

Within the first weeks of the teacher education programme, students completed an entry survey (t0) that included sociodemographic variables, measures of study motivation, personality (part of the Big Five[5]), self-efficacy beliefs, and personal competences. At two

DEVELOPING TEACHERS' ASSESSMENT CAPACITY

48. I relate my ratings on pupils' achievement to previously defined learning goals.								
a	Which overall importance do I assign to this competence?	(1) very important ... (6) completely unimportant	1	2	3	4	5	6
b	How often did I apply this competence?	(1) very often ... (6) never	1	2	3	4	5	6
c	How well did the university train me towards this competence?	(1) very well ... (6) not at all	1	2	3	4	5	6

Figure 1. KOSTA sample item from the 'Assessment' competence domain.

measurement points, each following a two to four weeks[6] long in-school practicum during the Bachelor's programme (t1, typically after 1½ to 2 years of studies, and t2, near the end of the Bachelor's programme, with a time interval of 1 to 1½ years between t1 and t2), students self-rated their competences, with the practicum providing the source for reflection.

In the KOSTA surveys, instrumentation was identical at t1 and t2. On each occasion, students completed the 65 behaviour-related items described above. Each item had to be answered from three different perspectives: First, students rated the overall importance of the standard (importance aspect); second, the frequency with which they had acted in accordance with the standard inside the in-school practicum they had just completed (frequency of application aspect, i.e. the competence self-rating) and third, the perceived quality of university training specifically towards this standard (quality of training aspect). A sample item from the 'Assessment' domain is displayed in Figure 1.

As the German scale of school marks runs from 1 (very good) to 6 (insufficient), six-point-ratings were obtained in this format salient to all students. For later purposes of data analysis, however, scores were recoded so that a high numerical score corresponds to a high rating. In order to minimise acquiescence effects and to encourage self-critical evaluation, students were given written consent that their ratings were treated fully anonymously and would in no way influence marks, examinations or evaluations of their performance. KOSTA started in 2007 and was concluded in 2014. Data collected from students beginning their studies before 2009 form the KOSTA I database including 429 cases with full longitudinal data. From 2009 onwards, full data are available for 931 cases, forming the KOSTA II database, on which the latent variable analyses reported in this paper are based. Additionally, in a qualitative study, student teachers were asked for their perceptions of the strengths and weaknesses of the teacher education programme they were enrolled in (see Bodensohn, Weresch-Deperrois, & Kajdas, 2012).

Previous findings from the KOSTA project

Analyses based on the KOSTA I database followed three overall directions. First, at the level of the four broad competence domains of 'Teaching', 'Education', 'Assessment' and

'Innovation', a shift in competence between t1 and t2 was evaluated by means of Latent Change Models (LCM) for 'frequency of application'. Whereas students self-reported a significant shift in competence in the 'Teaching' and 'Innovation' domains, no such shift was observed in the 'Education' domain (Schneider & Bodensohn, 2014). Unfortunately, due to poor goodness of fit of the latent variable model, no robust results could be obtained for the 'Assessment' domain [7]. Findings generally reveal that while students are apparently able to enhance their teaching skills in the course of pre-service teacher training, the development of educational competence may be a task which is more difficult to accomplish.

The second line of analyses was concerned with the question of whether a high perceived 'quality of training' in the four domains had an effect on the self-ratings of 'frequency of application'. In latent variable structural equation modelling (SEM), high perceived quality of training displayed had a significant effect on self-reported competence in all domains (Schneider & Bodensohn, 2014). Thus, at least in the eyes of student teachers themselves, high quality teacher education does, indeed, have an important effect on the development of professional competence; this finding is centrally opposed to arguments typically provided by those advocating deregulation in teacher education (cf. Cochran-Smith & Fries, 2001; Darling-Hammond, 2006).

In a third stage of analyses, the question of whether students' personality features (as assessed at t0) would be able to predict later competence development between t1 and t2 was explored. Of the variables in the analyses, self-efficacy beliefs (SEB) turned out to be the dominant predictor for a shift in competence in all domains under observation (Schneider, Bodensohn & Foerster, 2014). More than other personality traits (e.g. Extraversion or Conscientiousness) or intrinsic motivation, SEB appears to be a key predictive factor for the development of professional competence during teacher training. This finding is in line with meta-analytical evidence on the dominant role of SEB in predicting university students' academic performance (Richardson, Abraham, & Bond, 2012).

Research questions related to assessment competence

Although KOSTA is a project designed to monitor student teachers' development in all relevant domains of professional competence, KOSTA data permit a focus on assessment competence. Specifically, available data may shed light on students' perceptions and self-ratings of those behavioural elements that comprise assessment capacity in practice. Here, analyses focused on three aspects. First, normatively gathered collections of elements pertaining to assessment competence (i.e. the collections of assessment standards outlined above) are not necessarily perceived as a contextual entity by student teachers. Empirical analyses of student teachers' views of the importance of standards pertaining to different domains of competence are hypothesised to reveal that assessment competence is, indeed, perceived as an entity distinguished from other domains. The *first research question* thus to be raised is whether the normatively proposed four-domain structure of teachers' professional competence holds true in the student teachers' importance ratings; in other words, if student teachers look at their competences in the same way as experts would. This structural equality, or, boldly speaking, the sharing of a common language in addressing competences is, for example, an important prerequisite in providing student teachers with individual feedback on their assessment capacity.

Next, as noted earlier, assessment competence is a complex field with a wide range of facets. Consequently, it encompasses a great number of activities and routines that teachers will face and must be able to master in their everyday work. The inclusion of all these elements in extensive collections of standards does not imply that student teachers have internalised the normatively proposed elements of assessment competence and would be willing to comply with the expectation to apply relevant behaviour in practice. Thus, the *second research question* is concerned with the importance ratings student teachers would assign to the distinct standards comprising assessment competence. In examining importance at the item level, both the absolute magnitude of the importance ratings and the relative positioning of these ratings must be considered, the latter in order to identify aspects of assessment competence which may be seen as subordinate and may be rather neglected in professional practice.

Due to problems in modelling, students' competence development (i.e. a longitudinal shift in frequency of application) in the 'Assessment' domain was not analysed on the basis of KOSTA I data. Based on empirical remodelling of this domain, using the much larger KOSTA II database, these analyses became feasible. The *third research question* is concerned with whether student teachers' self-reported assessment competence was increasing through the course of their pre-service studies. Because student teachers, under German legislation, are supposedly provided with sufficient learning opportunities in educational assessment, a significant shift could be expected.

Methods

The KOSTA II sample

All subjects were enrolled in pre-service teacher education study programmes leading to a Bachelor's degree (Bachelor of Education) at the University of Koblenz-Landau, Campus Landau in southwestern Germany (*Land Rhineland-Palatinate*). Subjects took up their studies from 2009 onwards and completed participation in the surveys up to 2014. They were obliged to participate in the surveys upon entering university training and twice after an in-school practicum (for more information on design and variables assessed refer to the 'Outline of the KOSTA project' section above). For purposes of latent variable analysis, only subjects with complete longitudinal data were included (931 student teachers; 21% male; mean age at t0: 20.6 years, SD: 3.9). At the university, three different teacher education programmes were offered: N_{prim} = 481 (51.7%) students were enrolled in a primary school teachers' (ISCED 1) programme, N_{sec} = 260 (27.9%) in two different secondary teachers' programmes (ISCED 2 and ISCED 2/3; see above) and $N_{special}$ = 190 (20.4%) students in a special needs education teacher programme (as opted for at t0). Note that these proportions are the status quo at the university under observation and are not representative of the national population of student teachers. Nevertheless, the different programmes included in the data-set are each represented by a subsample of substantial size. For the purpose of determining the importance ratings assigned to the single standards (*second research question*), all available data gathered at t1 (2020 student teachers) were inspected.

Preliminary study on the empirical structure of the 'Assessment' competence domain

As outlined above, problems in latent variable modelling in the 'Assessment' domain prevented analysis of competence development in this domain. Unlike in the other three

DEVELOPING TEACHERS' ASSESSMENT CAPACITY

Table 3. Three factor solution yielded by principal axis factoring of nine items in the 'Assessment' competence domain (varimax-rotated factor loading matrix).

Item wording	F1	F2	F3
47: I stipulate and then respect transparent evaluation criteria	**.74**	.21	.25
48: My evaluations refer to learning outcomes defined beforehand	**.62**	.21	.28
42: I make use of different methods in evaluating achievement	**.58**	.33	.17
44: In evaluating achievement, I adequately combine a social and an individual perspective	**.50**	.34	.34
38: I recognise individual learning prerequisites and learning progresses	.16	**.68**	.18
43: I support pupils according to their individual prerequisites and needs	.29	**.60**	.24
39: In designing my lessons, I make use of the insights gained by my diagnostic competence	.37	**.48**	.15
45: I am aware that teachers' evaluations may be subjective	.23	.18	**.72**
46: I take into account that evaluations and expectations influence the learning process	.35	.29	**.62**

Note: (a) Primary factor loadings are printed in boldface, (b) English item wordings are ad hoc translations of the German original for the purpose of illustration.

competence domains, where the normatively proposed structure of competences smoothly led to indicators performing well in latent variable analysis, empirical remodelling of the items in the 'Assessment' domain became necessary. In order to derive adequate indicators, t1 data for 2020 student teachers on the 'frequency of application' aspect of all eleven 'Assessment' items were submitted to exploratory factor analyses (principal axis factoring, orthogonal varimax rotation). Judging by KMO = .910, the data-set was highly adequate for analysis. In a number of subsequent analysis steps, three orthogonal factors were extracted, accounting for 52.4% of the item variance. Two items expressing elements of counselling competence (40: 'Concerning a pupils' disciplinary or learning problems, I cooperate with the parents' and 41: 'In counselling, I refrain from subjective evaluations') were excluded from analysis as they (a) led to overall factor structures not allowing for straightforward interpretations and (b) failed to load on a common factor[8]. The remaining nine items, in contrast, formed three well interpretable factors (see Table 3) to be named as F1 (4 items): 'Assessment Techniques', F2 (3 items): 'Recognition of Heterogeneity' and F3 (2 items): 'Awareness of Observational Bias'.

Scale reliabilities (Cronbach's α) calculated on the items loading on each of the factors were satisfactory at .81, .70 and .74, respectively. It is obvious that nine items or standards on the behaviour level (alone) are not able to cover the full scope of all elements of assessment competence as shown in Table 2. Yet, the three orthogonal factors that emerged are interpretable in terms of meaningful aspects of assessment competence as perceived by student teachers. Furthermore, they performed well as manifest indicators of a latent assessment competence variable in subsequent analysis.

Data analysis procedures

In order to test the *first research question* of whether the normatively proposed structure of four broad competence domains ('Teaching', 'Education', 'Assessment' and 'Innovation') can be replicated empirically, confirmatory factor analysis (CFA) was applied. The *second research question* of student teachers' was concerned with the degree of compliance with or internalisation of the single elements of assessment competence (i.e. the importance ratings of the single standards). Here, the descriptive statistics on the respective importance ratings were inspected. In order to examine the hypothesis of a longitudinal shift in students' self-rated assessment competence (*third research question*), a LCM with mean structures

DEVELOPING TEACHERS' ASSESSMENT CAPACITY

(cf. Geiser, 2010) was applied to the 'frequency of application' responses (cf. Schneider & Bodensohn, 2014). All latent variable analyses were carried out with the Mplus 7.31 software (Muthén & Muthén, 2015), using the default full information maximum likelihood (FIML) procedure for missing data estimation.

Results

Working on the *first research question* of whether the normatively proposed structure of teachers' professional competence (KMK, 2004/2014) encompassing four competence domains holds true in student teachers' perception of the importance of the single standards pertaining to those four domains, four structural models with differing implications were tested against each other. Latent variables representing the four domains were modelled by a set of three manifest indicators each[9]. By means of CFA, four models were compared:

(1) a general factor model assuming that all indicators load on one latent construct to be named 'teacher's general professional competence',

(2) a model of four orthogonal latent competence domains where latent factor correlations were restricted to zero,

(3) a model of four oblique latent competence domains where factor correlations were set free, and

(4) a model of four latent competence domains with a second-order general factor accounting for the first-order factors' covariances.

Whereas model 1 would suggest that teacher candidates perceive teacher competence as an 'all but one' construct, and thus would not be able to meaningfully distinguish between the four domains, model 2 would imply that the four domains are unrelated to one another (e.g. that there is no mutual relation between teaching competence and assessment competence). Model 3, assuming four interrelated, yet distinguishable, areas of competence comes closest to the basic idea of the KMK's structuring of teachers' professional competence, while model 4 would imply that, after all, the four distinct domains are but aspects of a higher order general construct. In order to decide which of the proposed models fits the data best, the models' RMSEA, CFI, TLI, sRMR and AIC indices[10] were compared. Model fit parameters are displayed in Table 4.

Judging by all criteria, model 1 did not fit the data well. Thus, the data did not support the hypothesis that student teachers would perceive professional competence as one global construct with no meaningful subdomains. Model 2, which would be indicative of four domains of competence that are not perceived as interrelated, displays fit properties far beyond the boundaries of acceptability and can be ruled out. Model 3, in contrast, fits the data quite well, while introducing a second-order general factor in model 4 does not lead to an increase in model fit as compared to model 3. Hence, there is no advantage in assuming that, even if the four competence domains form distinct constructs, a higher order general

Table 4. Goodness of fit for the CFA models on the 'importance' aspect ratings.

	X^2	df	RMSEA	TLI	CFI	sRMR	AIC
M1: General factor model	819.5	54	.123	.848	.976	.056	14109.2
M2: Four orthogonal factors	2269.9	54	.210	.560	.640	.368	15559.7
M3: Four correlated factors	277.3	48	.072	.949	.963	.034	13579.0
M4: Second-order factor model	291.5	50	.072	.948	.961	.035	13589.3

DEVELOPING TEACHERS' ASSESSMENT CAPACITY

Table 5. Descriptive statistics for the importance ratings of assessment standards (item level).

Standards originating from the 'Assessment' domain	M	SD
38: I recognise individual learning prerequisites and learning progresses	5.51	.98
39: In designing my lessons, I make use of the insights gained by my diagnostic competence	5.14	.78
42: I make use of different methods in evaluating achievement	5.09	.90
43: I support pupils according to their individual prerequisites and needs	5.33	.78
44: In evaluating achievement, I adequately combine a social and an individual perspective	4.93	.88
45: I am aware that teachers' evaluations may be subjective	5.07	.94
46: I take into account that evaluations and expectations influence the learning process	5.07	.83
47: I stipulate and then respect transparent evaluation criteria	5.05	.93
48: My evaluations refer to learning outcomes defined beforehand	4.88	.93
Standards originating from the 'Innovation' domain	M	SD
56: I use evidence from educational research in my own work	4.43	1.03
61: I use evidence from research on teaching and learning in planning and conducting projects	4.49	.93
62: In teaching and in school, I make use of evaluation techniques and instruments	4.43	1.01
63: I use evaluation results to optimise my teaching and behaviour in school	4.49	1.00

Note: Ratings on a six-point-scale (recoded) ranging from 1 'completely unimportant' to 6 'very important'.

professional competence factor would be 'behind' the first-order competence domains. In summary, the comparison of the four models indicates that, indeed, student teachers do look at teachers' professional competence in the same way as is normatively proposed.

To answer the *second research question* concerning the degree to which the student teachers were willing to comply with standards of assessment competence, the importance ratings for single items were reviewed. In addition to the KOSTA items within the 'Assessment' domain itself, those items from the 'Innovation' domain expressing aspects of a widened understanding of assessment competence (e.g. making use of the outcomes of in-school evaluations or large-scale-assessments in optimising teaching) were included in the analysis. Following the rationale that each standard should at least be regarded as 'important', all items with importance ratings falling short of a score of 5 on a six-point scale ranging from 1 (completely unimportant) to 6 (very important) were seen as problematic. The results of the descriptive analysis of the student teachers' importance ratings of assessment standards on the single-standard level (second research question) are reported in Table 5. In absolute terms, all assigned importance ratings exceed the theoretical scale mean of 3.5. Thus, none of the standards fails to be seen as at least 'quite' important. In relative terms, though, the four standards originating from the 'Innovation' domain fall substantially short of a rating of 5, which indicates that they are perceived as less than 'important'. Furthermore, these standards receive the very lowest importance ratings out of all 65 KOSTA items (not reported in this paper). Thus, elements of research orientation and of taking note of evaluation techniques and results ranged at the bottom of these student teachers' willingness to comply with professional standards.

Lastly, addressing the *third research question* concerning a gain in self-perceived assessment competence over the course of the teacher education programme, a LCM with mean structures was calculated (see Figure 2). In this model, the three indicators identified in the preliminary analysis again formed the latent assessment competence variable. In order to ensure contextual stability in the latent variable, factorial invariance (between t1 and t2) was assumed. To account for stable indicator-specific variance components, correlated uniqueness paths were allowed (cf. Marsh, Byrne, & Yeung, 1999). The specific parameter of interest within the LCM was the mean parameter of the latent change variable (ΔAC); evidence for student teachers' average gain in assessment competence would be provided if the latter parameter was found to be statistically different from zero.

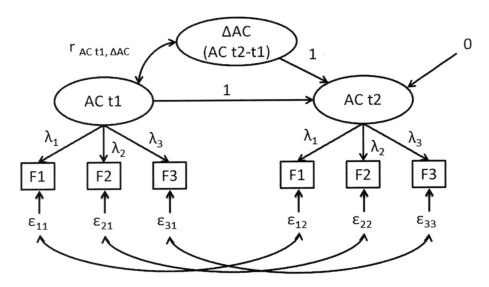

Figure 2. Structure of the latent change model for the latent assessment competence variable.
Note: AC: 'assessment competence'; F1 to F3 are indicators calculated as mean scores of the items pertaining to the three components of assessment competence identified in the preliminary study.

Fit statistics reveal that this model is adequate to describe the data (X^2 = 36.6, df = 9, RMSEA = .057, TLI = 978, CFI = .987, sRMR = .033). At a magnitude of .072, the mean parameter of the latent change variable (ΔAC)[11] is significantly greater than zero (S.E. = .035, $p < .042$). Thus, while the shift in self-reported assessment competence is not to be referred to as a big effect in absolute terms, there is still evidence for an overall gain in the student teachers' development in this area.

Discussion

Summary and implication of findings

In the CFA on the structure of student teachers perceptions of professional competence (*first research question*), the model of four distinguishable, yet correlated, domains of competence ('Teaching', 'Education', 'Assessment' and 'Innovation') was found to fit the data better than models assuming a general factor of teacher competence. Thus, the student teachers' conceptions of areas of competence appear to be in line with the normatively proposed systematisation of competences as expressed in the KMK's (2004/2014) standards for teacher training. Specifically, this result implies that in the students' view, too, assessment competence is one contextual entity for which student teachers are able to reflect upon their own competence. This structural finding has important implications, as the sharing of the notion of four distinct domains of competence is a prerequisite, e.g. for providing student teachers with feedback specifically on their competence in any specific domain.

The *second research question* was concerned with student teachers' compliance with standards (i.e. with expectations of which competences they must possess upon obtaining teaching certification) in the assessment competence domain. In absolute terms, all standards were characterised as important (rather than unimportant) by the students. Our data thus reveal that on average, student teachers had internalised standards in the assessment domain and would, in consequence, be willing to comply with the standards in practice.

In a relative view, however, the importance ratings associated with some specific standards fell remarkably short of the criterion that all standards should be regarded as 'important'. While all standards originating from the KMK's 'Assessment' domain (i.e. those items representing assessment techniques, recognition of diversity and awareness of observational bias[12]) received high importance ratings, issues of evaluation and research orientation in particular were perceived as relatively unimportant by the student teachers. As in-service teachers have been reported to display sceptical or at least ambivalent attitudes towards large-scale assessments or external evaluations (e.g. Demmer, 2010; Kanders & E., 2006; Leighton et al., 2010), our findings suggest that students in teacher education share this scepticism as well. Judging by the relative pattern of importance ratings assigned to the different assessment standards, student teachers may tend to feel that their key tasks are in-classroom assessment activities, and that there may be some psychological factors impeding compliance with evaluation demands 'from outside'. Such factors include a perceived loss of control, lack of insight into the aims and benefits of 'external' evaluations, the perception of unremunerated extra workload, or objections to receiving feedback as a potential threat to self-esteem (Behnke & Steins, 2015).

In the German context, our finding that issues of external evaluation are seen as relatively unimportant by student teachers also carries a connotation somewhat different from what it would imply in English-speaking countries. The mediocre results of German school students in international large-scale assessments (PISA and TIMSS) in the early 2000s received great attention in the public debate and in the media, and led to a number of policy reform strands, including the implementation of regular intra- and interstate monitoring of pupils' learning outcomes by standardised testing. Results (in particular at the level of *Länder* comparisons) are vividly discussed not only amongst educational researchers and policy-makers, but also in the mass media. That said, school or teacher accountability is nevertheless a less urgent concern in Germany as compared to many other countries. Due to their status as civil servants, teachers in Germany are in no way threatened in their employment status if their pupils' outcomes are poor. Furthermore, in their view the evaluation-based feedback they receive has much less impact on their work than teachers from other countries report in TALIS (Barfknecht & von Saldern, 2010). Likewise, at the school level, pupils' poor performance normally does not lead to 'hard' consequences, such as shutting down schools. In this light, student teachers' low ratings of the importance of external evaluation have an extra nuance: knowing that pupils' achievement outcomes do not severely impact on teachers' personal working conditions may also contribute to a rather indifferent attitude towards evaluation matters in general. These organisational features of the German school system make it even more necessary to strengthen student teachers' related competences in specific courses within teacher education offerings. Following this line of argument, elements of research orientation[13], or 'data literacy' in teacher education, may also contribute to widen the understanding of evidence-based optimisation of teaching practices on both an individual and a system level.

In summary, as Leighton et al. (2010) concluded, assessment literate teachers 'must understand not only classroom assessment but, also, large-scale-tests' (p. 19), specifically developing competences related to summative assessment and external evaluation is a major concern. Thus, our findings point to a deficit in student teachers' assessment education. In line with the argument provided by Drechsel and Prenzel (2012), explicitly enhancing student teachers' knowledge on the philosophy, aims, contents and methodology of large-scale assessments (possibly along with a basic understanding of empirical research in education) may be a prominent challenge in enhancing student teachers' assessment competence.

Finally, the *third research question* was concerned with whether student teachers felt that their assessment competence, operationalised by the frequency with which they displayed competence-relevant behaviour in in-school practicums, was rising during the course of their teacher education. Here, we were able to find a significant effect, indicating that there was some positive dynamics in the development of student teachers' assessment competence. Given that the students in our sample had undergone university instruction in educational assessment, the significant shift suggests that what was learned in theory did contribute to an increase in action competence in the assessment domain in a practicum setting. Nevertheless, with our design it was not possible causally to relate this rise in competence to the *quality* of assessment courses attended. In summary, the observed shift in the student teachers' self-ratings implies that assessment-related competences did develop during enrolment in teacher education – a finding in line with earlier research findings (DeLuca & Klinger, 2010; DeLuca et al., 2013).

Limitations and directions for further research

One limitation of our study is that within the very wide scope of KOSTA, striving to monitor student teachers' development of professional competence in all domains, assessment competence in particular is depicted by relatively few items. Although structural analysis of the assessment-related items in the preliminary factor analysis yielded three meaningful and practice-relevant facets of assessment competence, these facets do not by any means cover the full scope of themes in assessment education as described in DeLuca et al. (2016). One obvious desideratum is thus to measure assessment competence in a more fine-grained way by developing and administering more detailed instruments. Given the differences in addressing assessment issues in teacher education programmes between Anglo-Saxon countries and Germany, it might also be highly interesting to carry out cross-cultural studies in a common design in order to determine the exact impact of the legislative or country-specific features on the development of assessment competence.

Furthermore, as our data suggest a particular relative deficit in student teachers' perceived importance of competence elements related to external evaluation or large-scale assessment studies, a more detailed exploration of those competence elements designed to unveil the precise nature of these deficits would be required. If there was more detailed evidence on what exactly leads student teachers to cultivate relatively aloof attitudes towards external evaluation (and, in the same vein, towards a more research-oriented or evidence-based perspective on teaching and learning), attempts at specifically altering these attitudes might be tested in intervention studies. To achieve this, 'experimentally' including more teaching content on these issues in courses on assessment may be a promising approach.

Notes

1. In the Federal Republic of Germany, there are 16 *Länder* (federal states).
2. Note that the KMK's definitions of competence domains (i.e. the specific set of standards subsumed under each of the four domains) are referred to as 'Teaching', 'Assessment' etc. In contrast, content areas will be addressed as teaching competence, assessment competence, etc., when not related specifically to the KMK domains.

DEVELOPING TEACHERS' ASSESSMENT CAPACITY

3. Of note, Black (2015) states that this principle has *not* been seen as an inherent feature of educational assessment, but rather as in opposition to the aims of summative assessment. Hence, formative assessment, or AFL, is introduced as a means to widen the concept of educational assessment itself.

4. In KOSTA we did not ask student teachers about the *quality* of the application of competence-relevant behaviour, but merely about the *frequency*. Teacher candidates at this relatively early stage of their teacher education (i.e. the first practicums) cannot realistically be expected to (already) behave or perform in a successful way (quality aspect). It may, however, be expected that they are aware of the standards for professional teaching behaviour (as expressed in the items) and that they attempt to behave in these ways. At this early stage thus, the frequency of attempt itself is seen as an indicator for competence.

5. The Big Five model of five stable personality traits covers personality features beyond intellectual ability, *viz.* 'Neuroticism' (or, reversely, 'Emotional Stability'), 'Extraversion', 'Conscientiousness', 'Openness to Experience', and 'Agreeableness' (e.g. McCrae & John, 1992). In the KOSTA project, only the first three of these traits, found to have an impact on success in the teaching profession in earlier studies, were assessed by means of the 'Teacher Personality Adjectives Scale' (Brandstätter & Mayr, 1994).

6. As study regulations varied amongst different teacher education programmes and over time, there was some variation in the duration of the practicums.

7. Whereas latent variable modelling in three of the four domains was feasible on the basis of the sets of items serving as manifest indicators (each item pertaining to the KMK's normatively proposed eleven competence descriptions, see Table 1), the modelling strategy failed for the 'Assessment' domain. To overcome this serious shortcoming, items in the 'Assessment' domain were later submitted to empirical re-analysis of KOSTA II data with the aim of identifying indicator variables adequate for latent variable modelling. Results from this pre-analysis are reported as a preliminary study below.

8. Given that assessment and feedback in an educational context go hand in hand, there is good reason to understand counselling competence as one aspect of a broader assessment competence (as is done in the KMK's 'Assessment' standards). Therefore, some items on counselling were included in KOSTA. On the other hand, empirical evidence suggests that counselling and assessment competence are only loosely correlated in the .20 range (Klug, Bruder, Keller, & Schmitz, 2012). Assuming both aspects to be indicative of a common construct in numerical analysis may thus be a misspecification.

9. In the 'Teaching', 'Education' and 'Innovation' domains, indicators were calculated as scale means of all items pertaining to the respective competences as proposed by the KMK (2004/2014), e.g. the KMK competences 1–3 as displayed in Table 1 formed the indicators underlying the latent 'Teaching' competence variable. In the 'Assessment' domain, the three indicators generated in the preliminary exploratory factor analysis were used.

10. RMSEA = Root Mean Square Error of Approximation, TLI = Tucker-Lewis Index, CFI = Comparative Fit Index, sRMR = Standardised Root Mean Square Residual, AIC = Akaike Information Criterion; for more information on these indices and their interpretation see for example Hu and Bentler (1999) or Schermelleh-Engel, Moosbrugger, and Müller (2003).

11. Unstandardized estimate; the value reported refers to the original item metrics (six-point scale).

12. These were the facets of assessment competence identified in the preliminary structural analysis – see methods section.

13. While research orientation is not addressed in catalogues of assessment competence in an international context (cf. DeLuca et al., 2016), it is explicitly included in the KMK (2004/2014) standards (see Table 2).

Disclosure statement

No potential conflict of interest was reported by the authors.

References

Barfknecht, T., & von Saldern, M. (2010). Evaluation und Feedback der Lehrkräfte [Evaluation and feedback of teachers]. In M. Demmer & M. von Saldern (Eds.), *"Helden des Alltags": Erste Ergebnisse der Schulleitungs- und Lehrkräftebefragung (TALIS) in Deutschland* (pp. 94–115). Münster: Waxmann.

Behnke, K., & Steins, G. (2015). Widerstand von Lehrkräften gegenüber Evaluationen: Eine psychologische Betrachtung [Teachers' resistance against evaluations: A psychological view]. *Lernende Schule, 18*, 9–12.

Berry, R. (2011). Assessment reforms around the world. In R. Berry & B. Adamson (Eds.), *Education in the Asia-Pacific Region: Issues, concerns and prospects: Vol. 14. Assessment Reform in Education. Policy and Practice* (pp. 89–102). Dordrecht: Springer. doi:10.1007/978-94-007-0729-0_7

Berry, R., & Adamson, B. (2011). Assessment reform past, present and future. In R. Berry, & B. Adamson (Eds.), *Education in the Asia-Pacific Region: Issues, concerns and prospects: Vol. 14. Assessment Reform in Education. Policy and Practice* (pp. 3–14). Dordrecht: Springer. doi:10.1007/978-94-007-0729-0_1

Black, P. (2015). Formative assessment – an optimistic but incomplete vision. *Assessment in Education: Principles, Policy & Practice, 22*, 161–177. doi:10.1080/0969594X.2014.999643.

Black, P., & Wiliam, D. (1998). Assessment and classroom learning. *Assessment in Education: Principles, Policy & Practice, 5*, 7–74. doi:10.1080/0969595980050102.

Bodensohn, R. (2003). Die inflationäre Anwendung des Kompetenzbegriffs fordert die bildungstheoretische Reflexion heraus [Inflationary use of the term 'competence' calls for its theoretical reflection]. *Empirische Pädagogik, 17*, 256–271.

Bodensohn, R., Weresch-Deperrois, I., & Kajdas, J. (2012). *Evaluation an der Schnittstelle zur Schulpraxis 2009 – 2011* [Evaluations at the interface to school practice]. Retrieved from Universität Koblenz-Landau http://www.uni-landau.de/schulprakt-studien/120711_Zwischenbericht_KOSTA.pdf

Brandstätter, H., & Mayr, J. (1994). Die "Lehrer-Persönlichkeits-Adjektivskalen" (LPA): Ein Instrument zur Selbsteinschätzung berufsrelevanter Persönlichkeitsmerkmale [The "Teacher Personality Adjectives Scale": A self-rating instrument on personality traits relevant for the profession]. In J. Mayr (Ed.), *Studien zur Bildungsforschung & Bildungspolitik: Vol. 11. Lehrer/in werden* (pp. 231–247). Innsbruck: Österr. Studien-Verl.

Brookhart, S. M. (2011). Educational assessment knowledge and skills for teachers. *Educational Measurement: Issues and Practice, 30*, 3–12. doi:10.1111/j.1745-3992.2010.00195.x.

Cochran-Smith, M., & Fries, M. K. (2001). Sticks, stones, and ideology: The discourse of reform in teacher education. *Educational Researcher, 30*, 3–15. doi:10.3102/0013189X030008003.

Cowie, B., & Cooper, B. (2017, in this issue). Exploring the challenge of developing student teacher data literacy. *Assessment in Education: Principles, Policy & Practice, 24*, 147–163. doi:10.1080/0969594X.2016.1225668

Darling-Hammond, L. (2006). Constructing 21st-century teacher education. *Jorunal of Teacher Education, 57*(10), 1–15. doi:10.1177/0022487105285962

DEVELOPING TEACHERS' ASSESSMENT CAPACITY

DeLuca, C., Chavez, T., & Cao, C. (2013). Establishing a foundation for valid teacher judgement on student learning: the role of pre-service assessment education. *Assessment in Education: Principles, Policy & Practice, 20*, 107–126. doi:10.1080/0969594X.2012.668870.

DeLuca, C., & Klinger, D. A. (2010). Assessment literacy development: Identifying gaps in teacher candidates' learning. *Assessment in Education: Principles, Policy & Practice, 17*, 419–438. doi:10.1080/0969594X.2010.516643.

DeLuca, C., LaPointe-McEwan, D., & Luhanga, U. (2016). Teacher assessment literacy: A review of international standards and measures. *Educational Assessment, Evaluation and Accountability, 28*, 251–272. doi:10.1007/s11092-015-9233-6.

Demmer, M. (2010). Evaluation, Beurteilung und Feedback aus Sicht von Schulleitungen und Lehrkräften: Ausgewählte Aspekte der TALIS-Befragung [Evaluation and feedback as seen by school principals and teachers. Selected findings from TALIS]. In W. Böttcher (Ed.), *Evaluation, Bildung und Gesellschaft. Steuerungsinstrumente zwischen Anspruch und Wirklichkeit* (pp. 241–257). Münster: Waxmann.

Drechsel, B., & Prenzel, M. (2012). Was Lehrkräfte über internationale Vergleichsstudien wissen und in der Aus- und Weiterbildung erfahren sollten [What teachers should know about international large scale assessments and what they should learn in teacher education]. In C. Kraler, H. Schnabel-Schüle, M. Schratz, & B. Weyand (Eds.), *Kulturen der Lehrerbildung. Professionalisierung eines Berufsstands im Wandel* (pp. 123–140). Münster: Waxmann.

Freund, P. A., & Kasten, N. (2012). How smart do you think you are? A meta-analysis on the validity of self-estimates of cognitive ability. *Psychological Bulletin, 138*, 296–321. doi:10.1037/a0026556

Frey, A. (2014). Kompetenzmodelle und Standards in der Lehrerbildung und im Lehrerberuf [Models of competence and standards in teacher education and in the teaching profession]. In E. Terhart, H. Bennewitz, & M. Rothland (Eds.), *Handbuch der Forschung zum Lehrerberuf* (2nd ed., pp. 712–744). Münster, NY: Waxmann.

Galluzzo, G. R., & Craig, J. R. (1990). Evaluation of preservice teacher education programs. In W. R. Houston, M. Haberman, & J. Sikula (Eds.), *Handbook of research on teacher education. A project of the association of teacher educators* (pp. 599–616). New York: Macmillan Publishing Company.

Geiser, C. (2010). *Datenanalyse mit Mplus: Eine anwendungsorientierte Einführung* [Data analysis with Mplus: A practice-oriented introduction]. Wiesbaden: Springer.

Hartig, J., & Jude, N. (2007). Empirische Erfassung von Kompetenzen und psychometrische Kompetenzmodelle [Empirical assessment and psychometric models of competence]. In J. Hartig & E. Klieme (Eds.), *Möglichkeiten und Voraussetzungen technologiebasierter Kompetenzdiagnostik* (pp. 17–36). Bonn: BMBF.

Howard, G. S. (1990). On the construct validity of self-reports: What do the data say? *American Psychologist, 45*, 292–294.

Hu, L., & Bentler, P. M. (1999). Cutoff criteria for fit indexes in covariance structure analysis: Conventional criteria versus new alternatives. *Structural Equation Modeling: A Multidisciplinary Journal, 6*(1), 1–55. doi:10.1080/10705519909540118

Ingenkamp, K. (1985). *Lehrbuch der pädagogischen Diagnostik* [Textbook on pedagogical diagnostics] (1st ed.). Weinheim: Beltz.

Ingenkamp, K., & Lissmann, U. (2008). *Lehrbuch der pädagogischen Diagnostik* [Textbook on pedagogical diagnostics] (6th ed.). Weinheim: Beltz.

Joint Committee on Standards for Educational Evaluation. (2015). *The classroom assessment standards for PreK-12 teachers.* Retrieved from https://www.amazon.com/Classroom-Assessment-Standards-PreK-12-Teachers-ebook/dp/B00V6C9RVO/ref=sr_1_1?s=digital-text&ie=UTF8&qid=1442331481&sr=1-1&keywords=classroom+assessment+standards

Kanders, M., & Rösner, E. (2006). Das Bild der Schule im Spiegel der Lehrermeinung: Ergebnisse der 3. IPS-Lehrerbefragung 2006 [Teacher opinions on the school-image. Findings from the 3rd IPS teacher survey]. In W. Bos, H. G. Holtappels, H. Pfeiffer, H.-G. Rolff, & R. Schulz-Zander (Eds.), *Jahrbuch der Schulentwicklung. Daten, Beispiele und Perspektiven* (vol. 14, pp. 11–48). Weinheim: Juventa Verlag.

Klug, J., Bruder, S., Keller, S., & Schmitz, B. (2012). Hängen diagnostische Kompetenz und Beratungskompetenz von Lehrkräften zusammen? Eine korrelative Untersuchung [Are teachers'

DEVELOPING TEACHERS' ASSESSMENT CAPACITY

diagnostic competence and counselling competence interrelated? A correlational study]. *Psychologische Rundschau, 63*, 3–10. doi:10.1026/0033-3042/a000104

KMK (Ständige Konferenz der Kultusminister der Länder in der Bundesrepublik Deutschland). (2004/2014). *Standards für die Lehrerbildung: Bildungswissenschaften: Beschluss der Kultusministerkonferenz vom 16.12.2004 i. d. F. vom 12.06.2014* [Standards for teacher training in the educational sciences]. Retrieved from http://www.kmk.org/fileadmin/Dateien/veroeffentlichungen_beschluesse/2004/2004_12_16-Standards-Lehrerbildung-Bildungswissenschaften.pdf

KMK (Ständige Konferenz der Kultusminister der Länder in der Bundesrepublik Deutschland). (2015). *The education system in the Federal Republic of Germany 2013/2014: A description of the responsibilities, structures and developments in education policy for the exchange of information in Europe.* Retrieved from https://www.kmk.org/fileadmin/Dateien/pdf/Eurydice/Bildungswesen-engl-pdfs/dossier_en_ebook.pdf

Leighton, J. P., Gokiert, R. J., Cor, K. M., & Heffernan, C. (2010). Teacher beliefs about the cognitive diagnostic information of classroom- versus large-scale tests: Implications for assessment literacy. *Assessment in Education: Principles, Policy & Practice, 17*, 7–21. doi:10.1080/09695940903565362

Marsh, H. W., Byrne, B. M., & Yeung, A. S. (1999). Causal ordering of academic self-concept and achievement: Reanalysis of a pioneering study and revised recommendations. *Educational Psychologist, 34*, 155–167. doi:10.1207/s15326985ep3403_2

McCrae, R. R., & John, O. P. (1992). An introduction to the five-factor model and its applications. *Journal of Personality, 60*, 175–215. doi:10.1111/j.1467-6494.1992.tb00970.x

Muthén, L., & Muthén, B. O. (2015). *Mplus (Version 7.31)*. Los Angeles, CA: Muthén & Muthén.

OECD (2013). *Education at a glance 2013: OECD indicators.* Paris: OECD Publishing.

Oser, F. (2013). Auf der Suche nach Ausbildungskompetenzen [Searching for vocational competences]. In F. Oser, T. Bauder, P. Salzmann, & S. Heinzer (Eds.), *Ohne Kompetenz keine Qualität. Entwickeln und Einschätzen von Kompetenzprofilen bei Lehrpersonen und Berufsbildungsverantwortlichen* (pp. 7–8). Kempten: Julius Klinkhardt.

Popham, W. J. (2004). All about accountability/why assessment illiteracy is professional suicide. *Educational Leadership: Teaching for Meaning, 62*, 82–83.

Richardson, M., Abraham, C., & Bond, R. (2012). Psychological correlates of university students' academic performance: A systematic review and meta-analysis. *Psychological Bulletin, 138*, 353–387. doi:10.1037/a0026838.

Schermelleh-Engel, K., Moosbrugger, H., & Müller, H. (2003). Evaluating the fit of structural equation models: Tests of significance and descriptive goodness-of-fit measures. *Methods of Psychological Research Online, 8*, 23–74.

Schneider, C., & Bodensohn, R. (2014). Core competences of students in university teacher education and their longitudinal development: First results of the KOSTA study. In K.-H. Arnold, A. Gröschner, & T. Hascher (Eds.), *Pedagogical field experiences in teacher education: Theoretical foundations, programmes, processes, and effects* (pp. 147–163). Münster: Waxmann.

Schneider, C., Bodensohn, R., & Foerster, F. (2014, September). *Does personality predict student teachers' longitudinal competence development? Predicting latent change within the KOSTA project.* Paper presented at the EERA/ECER conference, Porto, Portugal.

Terhart, E. (2002). *Standards für die Lehrerbildung: Eine Expertise für die Kultusministerkonferenz* [Standards for teacher training: An expert's report for the Standing Conference of Cultural Ministers]. Münster: Institut für Schulpädagogik und Allgemeine Didaktik, University of Münster.

Tigelaar, D. E., & Beijaard, D. (2013). Special issue: Formative assessment and teacher professional learning. *Teachers and Teaching: Theory and Practice, 19*, 109–114. doi:10.1080/13540602.2013.741840

Weinert, F. E. (2001). Concept of competence: A conceptual clarification. In D. S. Rychen & L. H. Salganik (Eds.), *Defining and selecting key competencies* (pp. 45–65). Ashland, OH: Hogrefe & Huber Publishers.

Exploring the challenge of developing student teacher data literacy

Bronwen Cowie and Beverley Cooper

ABSTRACT

A number of trends are converging to drive the need for more informed teacher data use. These include advocacy for formative assessment and the need for teachers to account for student learning. In this context, assessment literacy and data literacy have emerged as a focus in research and professional development. Problematically, research signals that developing assessment/data literacy is challenging with evidence that teachers may not have mastered relevant aspects of mathematics and statistics. This paper reports lecturer, student teacher and school leader views of the role and requirements of data literacy using data from a larger study into how to foster student teacher mathematical thinking for the breadth of teacher professional work. Data were generated via interviews, surveys and document analysis. Findings suggest a concern and opportunity to develop assessment/data literacy as this calls on mathematical and statistical understanding.

Introduction

A number of pressures and incentives are converging to drive the need for more informed teacher use of student assessment and achievement data. Advocacy for formative assessment and for assessment for learning (Black & Wiliam, 1998; Stiggins, 2008), and data-driven/evidence-based decision-making (Wayman & Jimerson, 2014) are part of this agenda. Government policies and initiatives that require teachers and schools to account for student learning and to compare their local achievement results with state/national-level data in the expectation they use this to inform practice (Hardy, 2015) are also contributing.

The assumption underlying current interest in the use of data is that it enables teachers to better target their instruction to student needs and strengths, ultimately resulting in higher levels of achievement for *all* students. In this context, assessment literacy and data literacy have emerged as concepts for focus in research and professional development, with both pre and in-service teachers (Council of Chief State School Officers [CCSSO], 2012; DeLuca & Bellara, 2013). Numerous definitions exist for both of these constructs. Their relative positioning is also debated.

DEVELOPING TEACHERS' ASSESSMENT CAPACITY

The imperative for teacher assessment literacy/data literacy is embedded in the graduating and performance standards for teachers in many countries (CCSSO, 2012; New Zealand Teachers Council, 2007). On the whole, these standards encompass the need for teachers to be able to interpret, use and report on data at the local (classroom, school) and national level and to recognise the role assessment can play in supporting and not just measuring learning. The focus on data literacy is linked to the improvements gained when teachers use student achievement and progress data to drive instructional decisions (Mandinach, 2012; Ottmar, Rimm-Kaufman, Larsen, & Berry, 2015; Wayman, Cho, & Johnston, 2007) but also recognises the value of data generated outside the classroom such as data on student absenteeism, health statistics and data from the state, national and international testing regimes (Hardy, 2015; Pierce, Chick, Watson, Les, & Dalton, 2014).

In this paper, drawing on Mandinach and colleagues (Mandinach, Friedman, & Gummer, 2015), we view assessment literacy as a subset of data literacy, which requires knowledge and use of a broader range of data and factors than is typically the focus for assessment. In the paper, we are interested in initial teacher education lecturer, pre-service teacher and school leader understandings of how these two literacies intersect with and are informed by mathematical and statistical literacy. We report on survey and interview data from pre-service teachers from a one-year postgraduate primary initial teacher education programme along with data from their lecturers and the leaders of some of the schools where they undertake practicum. These data are part of a wider study focused on developing pre-service teacher mathematical thinking and reasoning by working across the breadth of their teacher education programme. In the paper, we make a case for a whole programme approach to developing student teacher data and assessment literacy related to the production, analysis, interpretation, presentation and action on quantitative measures.

Data, assessment and mathematical-statistical literacy

Research teams worldwide are vigorously pursuing research and development programmes into student teacher and teacher assessment literacy, data literacy, and mathematical/statistical literacy. On the whole, these programmes are being developed independent of each other although they all have something to say about the needs of and how to support teachers in generating and using data (of various kinds) to make sense of, report on and enhance student learning and school and system effectiveness. The distinction between data and assessment literacy has not been clearly articulated (Coburn & Turner, 2011; DeLuca & Bellara, 2013; Mandinach & Gummer, 2012). In this paper, we use the definition of pedagogical data literacy developed by the expert group convened by Mandinach and colleagues:

> Data literacy for teaching is the ability to transform information into actionable instructional knowledge and practices by collecting, analyzing, and interpreting all types of data (assessment, school climate, behavioral, snapshot, longitudinal, moment-to-moment, etc.) to help determine instructional steps. It combines an understanding of data with standards, disciplinary knowledge and practices, curricular knowledge, pedagogical content knowledge, and an understanding of how children learn. (Mandinach et al., 2015, p. 3)

Data literacy therefore subsumes assessment literacy, which relates to student assessment data specifically. Assessment literacy, broadly defined, encompasses how to construct, administer and score reliable student assessments and communicate valid interpretations about student learning, as well as the capacity to integrate assessment into teaching and learning for formative purposes (DeLuca & Bellara, 2013). Despite the definitions of data and assessment literacy implying the need to understand a range of mathematical and statistical concepts, research on mathematical and statistical literacy is not always taken into account by those investigating teacher assessment and data capacity.

Teacher and student mathematical and statistical literacy is the focus of a substantial body of research. Teacher mathematical knowledge and mathematical knowledge for mathematics teaching have been the focus of numerous research and development programmes (e.g. Hill, Rowan, & Loewenberg Ball, 2015). Relevant to our purposes, Pierce and Chick (2011) have developed a framework for teacher *professional* statistical literacy. This framework incorporates technical and contextual aspects. They propose that teachers working at the lowest level of three nested levels are able to read values and understand features such as keys, scale, and graph type and to interpret specific data points on the graph or table. At the third and highest level, they need to be able to compare, contrast and critique multiple data-sets. Pierce and Chick's framework acknowledges the role of context, specifically the wider policy and professional context and school contextual factors (e.g. student demographics and local events) that give rise to the data. Watson (2006) provides a similar framing, as does Gal (2002). These researchers all emphasise that professional statistical literacy/statistical literacy includes a positive disposition towards the use of data. Gal (2002) sums up this point as follows: 'It is hard to describe a person as fully statistically literate if this person does not show the inclination to activate' and use his/her statistical knowledge (Gal, 2002, p. 17, emphasis in original).

On the whole, research has shown that teachers are underprepared to effectively integrate assessment into their practice, with beginning teachers in particular lacking confidence (DeLuca & Bellara, 2013; Means, Padilla, DeBarger, & Bakia, 2009; Wayman & Jimerson, 2014). Research also suggests that teacher data literacy would benefit from further development (Wayman & Jimerson, 2014). Mandinach et al. (2015), based on their survey of schools of education in the United States, concluded that the difficulties beginning teachers face may be because the content of courses tends to be more to do with assessment literacy than data literacy. Means et al. (2009), found that the USA teachers in their study struggled with examining multiple data points simultaneously (i.e. school and district scores over time), distinguishing absolute values and proportions, and identifying patterns within data. Chick and Pierce (2013), found teachers in Australia appeared to have little difficulty with reading straightforward data and making simple comparisons of single values in clearly presented graphs and tables. However, they often struggled when required to undertake deeper analysis of data-sets and with the technicalities of some of the data presentation format used in reports. Researchers working to meet the challenge of developing student teacher assessment and data literacy have explored the impact of a range of strategies. In the case of assessment education, DeLuca and Klinger (2010) usefully describe these as lying along a continuum from discrete and required assessment courses to embedded assessment topics within general educational studies courses. There is little agreement on whether stand-alone or integrated instruction is most effective (see also Hill, Smith, Cowie, Gilmore, & Gunn, 2013). In addition, questions abound whether and how data use should be integrated into practicum so that students have an opportunity to work with authentic data. Nonetheless, some interesting work is emerging. See, for example, DeLuca and Bellara (2013), Reeves and Honig (2015), Piro and Hutchinson (2014), and Watson (2011). Pierce et al. (2014) findings highlight the impact of and need to pay attention to the statistical context (e.g. key and scales), the professional context, the local context and the need for relevant technical statistical knowledge (e.g. knowledge of particular representations). Given the varied nature of representations used by different agencies, and the varied experiences of teachers, they suggest that targeted professional learning may be necessary to build the fluency necessary to make meaningful interpretations of such data and consequently make appropriate educational decisions in each particular context. In the remainder of this paper, we describe one aspect of a project in the New Zealand context that aimed to enhance student teacher mathematical/statistical thinking by embedding mathematical thinking across courses in a programme.

Explicating the context

The *New Zealand Curriculum* (NZC), (Ministry of Education, 2007) is a framework document that sets out seven learning areas and five key competencies, and describes 'effective pedagogy' as a process of inquiry that is responsive to student needs and interests. Teachers are required to develop their own classroom programmes to address the curriculum requirements. New Zealand has traditionally had a strong emphasis on formative assessment (Crooks, 2011; Ministry of Education, 2011).

The recent introduction of National Standards for Years 1 to 8 in reading, writing and mathematics (Ministry of Education, 2010) and the mandatory reporting requirements associated with these have raised the stakes of teacher assessment in the primary sector. There are no mandated national assessments. Teachers are required to produce an 'Overall Teacher Judgment (OTJ)' of student achievement against the relevant standard using data from a range of qualitative and quantitative sources. The government has provided teachers and schools with a number of assessment tools including the Progressive Achievement Tests (PATs) available in paper and online versions and e-asTTLe (an online assessment tool, developed to assess students' achievement and progress in reading, mathematics, writing). e-asTTLe comes with a range of supports and report formats which set out results in the form of mean scores, mean curriculum level and curriculum expectations. Reports represent results in tables, graphs and use statistical measures such as mean and standard deviation. The Progress and Consistency Tool (PaCT), released in 2015, was developed to support teacher judgement about progress and achievement against National Standards. The PaCT tool enables teachers to generate box and whisker plots, percentages, quartiles and other statistical measures for individuals and groups over time. More generally, school learning management systems in common use support the logging, analysis and representation of data in various forms and formats. There is some evidence that New Zealand schools are generating and interrogating student achievement data for patterns and trends in progress within and across classes, year levels, for different student groups and so on (Cowie, Hipkins, Keown, & Boyd, 2011). In this context, the quantitative aspects of teacher data literacy have come to the fore and assessment and data literacy have come to intersect more strongly with teacher mathematical and statistical literacy.

The *New Zealand Curriculum* 'Mathematics and Statistics' learning area specifies the subcategories of: Number and Algebra, Geometry and Measurement, and Statistics. The more detailed outline of achievement objectives is prefaced with the phrase, 'In a range of meaningful contexts, students will be engaged in thinking mathematically and statistically. They will solve problems and model situations ...' (Ministry of Education, 2007, p. 51).

DEVELOPING TEACHERS' ASSESSMENT CAPACITY

The Education Council Aotearoa New Zealand, requires all initial teacher education providers to assess candidates' numeracy competency prior to entry and to ensure that they meet the Graduating Teaching Standards prior to graduation (New Zealand Teachers New Zealand Teachers Council, 2007). The Council sets University Entrance, which includes Numeracy competency (Level 5 of the New Zealand Curriculum) as a minimum requirement for entry into undergraduate programmes.

The research design

In this paper, we draw on emergent findings from the three-year Mathematical Thinking and Reasoning in Initial Teacher Education study (MARKITE) Teaching and Learning Research Initiative study, funded by the Ministry of Education (http://goo.gl/KJPVks). The MARKITE study is investigating the nature and development of student teacher mathematical thinking and reasoning across the breadth of their initial teacher education programme, not just the mathematics education courses. The study recognises that teachers use mathematical and statistical thinking when teaching in every curriculum learning area, when interpreting and acting on student achievement data and for administrative tasks such as scheduling parent–teacher interviews or field trips. This focus is underpinned by our understanding that people need to experience ideas on a number of occasions and across contexts to develop the robust and flexible understandings needed for proactive use of concepts (Steen, 2001). The study is informed by design-based intervention as detailed by Penuel and Fishman (2012); we are aiming to develop theory and practice concurrently. We are working with lecturers to find out what mathematical thinking is embedded in their courses and to encourage them to make this more explicit. In designing the study, we recognised that lecturers' first responsibility is to ensure student teachers achieve the learning outcomes associated with their particular course in the teacher education programme. On the other hand, we recognised that lecturers may not always be aware of and/or explicitly alert students to the mathematical and statistical foundations ideas and practices in their courses hence our first focus was to assist lecturers to identify and to be more explicit about the mathematical thinking required. This approach is consistent with the notion of teaching mathematical thinking by 'embedding' it within the contexts and activities of a course/programme (DeLuca & Klinger, 2010; Galligan, 2013). At the same time, we are working with student teachers enrolled in the one-year postgraduate primary initial teacher education programme to uncover their existing mathematical/ statistical understandings, to identify any gaps they have and to assist them to address these. Responding to this dual focus, the intervention aspect of the study includes student teacher access to a mathematical thinking mentor who is available to support students and the development of a 'Maths Hub' website to support student teachers' self-directed action to address any gaps they have identified in their mathematical understanding. This paper does not discuss the impact of the intervention.

Data are being generated through surveys of students' mathematical thinking content and attitudes and beliefs at the beginning of the programme, supplemented with interviews to discuss their results and to elicit their ideas about the mathematical thinking involved in teaching before and after their practicum experiences. Curriculum maps have been prepared using document analysis and lecturers have been interviewed about the mathematical thinking in their courses prior to and post teaching. In addition, school leaders have been interviewed to ascertain their ideas about the extent and ways mathematical thinking and reasoning is embedded across the breadth of teachers' work. This paper is restricted to the research question: What mathematical thinking and reasoning do student teachers, lecturers and practicing teachers identify as part of their courses and teacher professional work?

Findings

Here we present an overview of (i) lecturer conceptions of the mathematics/lack of mathematics in their courses (Cooper & Cowie, 2015b), and their reflections on the impact of making this more explicit; (ii) student teacher mathematical understanding and ideas about the mathematical thinking in their courses and practicum (Cooper & Cowie, 2014), and (iii) school leaders' views on the data literacy and mathematical thinking beginning teachers need.

Lecturer views of the nature and role of mathematical thinking and assessment

Fourteen lecturers contributing to the eight non-mathematics education courses in the programme were interviewed – 13 lecturers prior to the teaching and 7 after teaching their course to ascertain their understandings of the mathematical thinking embedded in their courses. Courses include those related to NZC, and professional practice courses looking at the wider issues related to teaching and learning and practicum. Findings from these interviews are reported in full in Cooper and Cowie (in preparation); this paper focuses in on comments linked to data, assessment and or statistical literacy as detailed above. It needs to be noted that at their first interview many lecturers were unsure of the place of mathematical thinking within their courses. As the interview evolved however, they all described and reported a range of ideas and activities which they and we as members of the research team viewed as involving mathematical and statistical thinking. For example the Social Science, Science, and Technology curriculum learning area lecturers identified the need for students to be able to understand, interpret and construct tables and graphs. The science lecturer was particularly interested in students being able to transform data into charts and or tables and then into graphical representations such as bar and or line graphs and or to calculate and use averages and the median. She commented that she did not portray these as mathematics ideas, to her they were 'still science'. Similarly, the technology lecturer advised she used and presented mathematics as a 'tool of our trade'. These lecturers reflected that they made a number of assumptions about their students' mathematics understanding and moved on to wonder if this was appropriate. One of the social science lecturers, when interviewed post teaching his course, reported he had provided his student teachers with tabular data on the number of refugees coming to and being accepted into New Zealand and asked them to draw three conclusions. He had been surprised that most students struggled with this task.

The curriculum lecturers did not raise matters related to student assessment data interpretation in the beginning of the year interview. At their post teaching interview, lecturers commented that in their experience students were not seeing the use of assessment data in schools beyond its use in reporting. They speculated that perhaps this was because a lot of assessment took place early in the school year when it was used for grouping. The literacy lecturer discussed the interpretation of student data with regard to National Standards reporting requirements for writing and reading. She linked her comment to instruction on formal testing requirements as follows:

> I've been thinking about this question and what mathematical sort of knowledge students would need and it really would be when we move in terms of my course, into the assessment of reading. And, in that we look at STAR tests and PAT tests, in particular, where they look at stanines. I define stanines and then we look at examples from the PAT book, and we look at the difference between percentages and percentiles. (Sandra interview 1; all names are pseudonyms)

Sandra explained, 'the notion of embedding, I do try to do that. I don't just toss out the term'. Sandra reported that her course included instruction on the assessment of writing and reading, including the use of progressions and running records. Consistent with the need to attend to context when making sense of data, she reported she shared the following anecdote with her students from when she had been in a classroom and a young girl had told her:

> 'I've got a reading age of 13', something really high. And that might have been her decoding level, but it wasn't her comprehension. And so her teacher had shared that based on her decoding abilities. So she was interpreting that, I don't know if the teacher interpreted it that way or not. So that is another aspect of data in the sense that 'What is this data telling me?'

The three Professional Practice lecturers, whose course content ranges across the New Zealand educational and social context, reflective practice, classroom assessment and issues related to inclusion and diversity, focused mainly on the mathematical and statistical thinking for student achievement data analysis and the social construction of numbers. One of the lecturers in assessment scoped a range of statistical issues including student understanding of mean, standard deviation, percentages and percentiles. The three lecturers touched on the political use and social meaning of numbers in the current context of accountability and competition. Examples included the PISA country rankings that were a focus of media and policy attention at the time of the first round of interviews.

Dawn described a trajectory of course demands for student teacher learning about and using data:

> In Prof. Prac. Two we get into much more in-depth of, you know, PAT tests and drawing on assessment data to make an Overall Teacher Judgment. Prof. Prac One is really, you know, the introduction, talking about why we assess, and what the purpose of it is and different types and forms of assessment data and challenging some of their ideas perhaps. Conceptions about assessment based on their own school, testing, and whatnot. So unpacking some of that and looking at ways teachers gain information about student learning and the purpose of that, to inform student learning and also their own teaching.

Claire, the disability and inclusion lecturer, described in considerable detail why she thought there was a need to help students to interpret and then understand the social and political implications of the numerical categorisation and construction (numbering) of children with different disabilities. She commented that statistical measurements have produced the concept of deviation from the norm, which has negatively influenced her field of special needs and inclusion.

> 'How tall are you? You're under five foot – oh that's a bit dodgy.' You know, so you've got all these things going on. Measuring IQ, measuring appearance, you know, 'Are your eyes a bit close – oh that's a bit dodgy as well.' So it all really comes back to – What is the perfect Leonardo de Vinci? All this sort of thing goes on so the idea of using mathematical ideas, given that we're trying to say this whole thing about appearance and behaviour is a social construction. The idea of using mathematics in that way is very challenging because the fundamentals of it could be so problematic.

I definitely critique anything including figures, there's almost a social responsibility there, but also the social structures behind it. So for example, in 2010 the ERO (Education Review Office, a government department that reports publicly on the quality of education in all New Zealand schools and early childhood centres) reported on how well schools are doing regarding inclusion. Fifty percent of schools are doing well, 30% were doing okay, and 20% are doing badly. Two years later 77% of schools are doing well. What does that mean? What has changed?

Claire commented that a mathematical fact or idea needed to be seen in the social context it was presented because, 'The figure itself doesn't tell you which way it wants to be read'.

And so figures – it is easier to see them as a product of their time, of their origins, and of their efficacy in the social world. The thing about, you know, including people with disabilities in regular classrooms, which is mostly a matter of attitude and values.

Over the course of her first interview, Claire indicated she could definitely see ways that she could embed or use mathematical ideas in her course and made a commitment to attempt to be more overt in the summer school paper she was teaching.

And it's funny, I ask students to write a diary, I could equally well ask students to look at the concept and literally come up with how many times 'ordinary' or 'normal' or something pertaining to the mean. Is it the mean where you're in the middle? And actually note that down, and graph it. And, 'How many times is the word appropriate used?' That is very interesting because that means nothing until you have a social location for it. And if you graphed it, you could see how many times in the document [laughter] … But then you could be saying that the document itself is kinda worthless, and that's not good because its policy.

In her second interview, completed after teaching the course, she reiterated how the use of numbers in the area of special needs and inclusion is fraught because numbers had 'provided the box to put people in the categories they have been put in'. She commented that the 'social implications of numbering' is an important part of her course. When reflecting about the interview process she noted two tensions. Firstly, that the use of numbers has historically been detrimental to social inclusion and secondly that the study focus on mathematics as embedded across the programme had challenged her own conception of mathematics.

My traditional view of maths thinking was of $2 + 2 = 4$. I wasn't thinking of maths conceptually. I wasn't thinking of it as philosophical tool to theorise [people] through number. I now realise I use numbers to interpret the nature of the relationship between stats and policy.

As the conversation unfolded, it was clear that Claire had emphasised the power of numbers within her course and that she provided numerous examples of where the use of mathematics in the inclusion and special education space had influenced policy. Claire explained that she thought students benefited from this approach because it provided them with tools to use to collect data and evidence around a person's well-being which could make them more confident to lobby on the person's behalf. For example, when working with a disabled person, a person might say, 'He's up all the time.' She saw opportunities to use number to define what actually was happening in their environment. Categorising and counting for example could give precise information and these numbers could be used to get things to happen.

It was interesting that most lecturers interviewed did not consider initially that their course included any aspects of mathematical thinking but on reflection most identified aspects such as identification of patterns, organisation of data into tables and graphs, and the use of simple statistics. Their responses are consistent with research that indicates although mathematical thinking underpins many of the decisions people make day-to-day people are largely unaware of its presence or influence (Skovsmose & Greer, 2012). They lend support to Galligan's (2013) findings that this unawareness extends to university lecturers in relation to course demands and suggests that lecturers were unlikely to be actively pursuing and monitoring student understanding of the ideas in their courses that relied on mathematical thinking. Subsequently, as a group and in some cases individually, lecturers scoped ideas associated with all three levels of the hierarchy for professional statistical literacy set out by Pierce and Chick. Hence, findings indicate that all programme lecturers can play a role in providing student teachers with a breadth of contextual mathematical experiences. At the time of writing, eight lecturers had agreed to make more explicit the mathematical ideas embedded within their coursework. The outcomes of this are part of the next stage of the MARKITE study; from preliminary work we are hopeful of the impact of this action on student awareness of the wider role and place of mathematical thinking.

Student teacher mathematical thinking and attunement to mathematics-in-action

The MARKITE project, with consent, used the number questions from the survey developed and used by Young-Loveridge, Bicknell, and Mills (2012) to gauge student teacher understanding of number ideas on entry to their programme. Student response patterns in our study were similar to those established by this group of researchers. Of interest in the context of this paper, the MARKITE assessment task included additional questions that called on student ability to interpret data in graphical and tabular form. These questions were adapted from the UK professional skills test for teachers and required students to make sense of data in the context of making comparative decisions about the outcome of appraisal lesson observations, changes in student performance between two tests, the relationship between children's physical age and reading age, and between school and national progress and achievement profiles. Twenty-seven (80%) of 34 students were able to read a scatter graph to determine how many students had the same reading age as their actual age, whereas 14 (41%) of respondents were able to determine what proportion of the class had the same reading age as their actual age. Twenty-three (68%) of the 34 students were confident or somewhat confident in the first instance, and 12 (86%) of the 14 students in the second case. Interestingly, fewer than half of the 34 the students responded to the proportion question and on the whole these students expressed less confidence in their answer. Approximately 85% of respondents were able to calculate comparative percentages from tabular data and nearly 75% of respondents were able to calculate the percentage of children in a school having extra music lessons from tabular class data. Sixty per cent of respondents were able to answer comparative questions based on a graph that represented school and national achievement over school years 1 to 7. Overall, survey results suggest the students in our study struggle with many of the same aspects of mathematical and statistical thinking identified in the studies reviewed earlier, and they have a similar profile to those of practicing primary teachers in New Zealand. For example Ward and Thomas (2007) found that approximately one-third of practicing teachers displayed a lack of proficiency in the addition and division of fractions and proportional reasoning.

Students also completed a survey on their attitudes towards mathematics based on the Attitudes Toward Mathematics Instrument (Tapia & Marsh, 2004). Students were asked to indicate how strongly they agreed or disagreed with each statement on a five-point Likert scale (from Strongly Disagree to Strongly Agree) on four attitudes scales (self-confidence, value, motivation and enjoyment). Similar to the data reported elsewhere in the literature, on the self-confidence scale, students on average scored 52 out of possible 80 points, on the value scale they scored 40 out of possible 50 points, on the motivation scale they scored 25 out of 35 and on the enjoyment scale they scored 22 out of possible 35 points. While most students could see the value of mathematics, a significant number reported they lacked confidence and motivation and did not enjoy mathematics. This student teacher response is cause for concern given the shifting, and increasing, demands teachers face to make sense of (quantitative) student achievement data.

There were substantial differences between students' attitudes towards number and data. Nineteen students' mathematics assessment results (number of correct answers in the number and data literacy sections) were separately correlated with the four attitudes scales. For the number section all correlations were significant, positive and medium in strength. There was no correlation between the number of correct answers on the data literacy section and any of the attitudes scales.

Students were invited to discuss their assessment results with the study 'mathematical thinking mentors'. Most students were ambiguous about their prior experiences with mathematics and uncertain about its role outside mathematics class. They were not confident with their responses to mathematics content questions in the survey even those who gave correct answers. Data interpretation and their being able to use this information to make decisions about teaching and learning were a major concern for them. Over the course of the interview, and sometimes after it, they began to identify aspects of mathematics within their everyday lives and leisure activities.

Midway through the year, the 12 students who attended the pre-practicum discussion identified that mathematical and statistical thinking had been involved in each of their curriculum learning area courses, other than Mathematics and Statistics (Ministry of Education, 2007). Measurement featured strongly as part of their discussion of the Science and Technology learning areas (in New Zealand Technology is about the design and making of man-made objects); graphs and statistics were mentioned in relation to Science (reporting and understanding data), Social Studies (understanding ideas presented in the media), and Physical Education and Health (understanding sports data, personal progress). The Arts (dance, music, drama, art) were linked to understanding space and spatial awareness. For the English learning area, students spoke of using indexes and being able to critique numerical data in texts. Overall, the mathematical and statistical ideas and activities that the student teachers identified were very similar to those identified by their lecturers (and those specified in their course outlines).

All 6 pre-practicum focus groups (24 students in total) predicted that during practicum they would need to interpret student achievement data along with the use of mathematical thinking for tasks such as managing the classroom budget and lesson scheduling. The students identified the need to understand some of the more technical aspects of data analysis such as percentages, ratio and simple statistics, where these were used to allocate students to groups and or tasks at the appropriate level, and for reporting. They also commented on the need to access and understand class demographic data and census data to answer questions such as 'Who are our students? Where do they come from?' Post practicum the student teachers provided a similar range of examples. They expressed an interest in learning to use software such as Excel for data analysis and presentation. At the end of the year, they again reported on the use of mathematical thinking across a range of contexts and functions. Unsurprisingly, reporting on student achievement featured in their discussion of assessment but they also indicated a strong interest in its formative function. The role of numerical and statistical data was not a feature of these discussions.

Overall student responses indicated a need to consider how to support their confidence and willingness to learn alongside the development of any conceptual understanding. Their growing and positive appreciation of the role mathematical thinking plays outside maths lessons opens up the possibility to develop these attributes in context.

School leaders' views of the nature and place of teacher assessment/data literacy

We held four focus group discussions with school principals and school assessment leaders. In New Zealand, primary schools and teachers develop their own units of work to enact the mandated curriculum. Usually teams identify topics and develop a broad outline of learning objectives and activities. Following this, teachers customise the objectives and activities to meet the needs and strengths of their class. At each focus group, those present commented that they were looking for beginning teachers who had some proficiency in the collection, interpretation and action on data but they were clear that they expected to work with their beginning teachers to further develop these capacities. School Principal J explained:

> I think teams develop collaboratively some of their rich units and things like that but the other parts of the curriculum are very much related to your class and the students in your class and your knowledge of what they already know and what they need to know next and how you will group them. And then, 'How you will garner the information about them and translate that into everyday shifts of practice?' And so what supports are you using for that everyday shift and what are you pulling together for formative assessment and then to summative and then shifting now to OTJs and Standards. … You're the person who's gathered the formative information from those kids, the test information from those tasks and you are the one who has to make the recommendation. You probably will have some mentoring support but you are expected to have your first crack at it yourself and probably most of the advice you would be getting is on the kids on the cusp where you're not sure about your decision.

As we can see in the above quote, consistent with school responsibility for beginning teacher induction and mentoring (Cooper & Cowie, 2015a). Supporting beginning teachers to moderate and understand their data in relation to wider school data was seen as something school mentors could expect to do. The principal from School I explained further:

> Talking about the analysing of data and that sort of stuff, our beginning teachers would sit down with their tutor (mentor) teacher and go through, 'How is my data in relation to the area's data [*the data from teachers teaching at the same year level*] or the school data? Where are the gaps?'

Two focus groups discussed the need for teachers to analyse data in relation to a stated standard or level (a National Standard and or curriculum level) and to compare and contrast individual, group, class and school achievement 'between cohorts both in our school and across schools that are similar to ours in our area' (School assessment leader G). The assessment leader G elaborated as follows:

> National standards data and looking at the school-wide information that is provided at the end of each year and at mid year and setting appropriate targets for their class, year groups, and for the whole school. The teachers have to own the National Standards data of the school and own our annual aims and school wide goals. It would also be beneficial for them to analyse the data in greater detail so they understand the implications of this. They have to have a wider understanding of how the school uses the data and how it fits into the picture on a regional and national basis. So comparing school data with the data from the Waikato and from New Zealand as a whole would be great. And thinking about what the school should do/can do to help improve the data moving forward.

DEVELOPING TEACHERS' ASSESSMENT CAPACITY

They identified a critical stance and positive disposition towards learning and the ability to work in teams as essential attributes if beginning teachers were to develop the literacy to make effective use of data within their classrooms and the school. School principal J explained:

> We expect our beginning teachers to do things like interpret running records, and to do the accuracy levels. There's maths involved in that sort of thing. Some of them expect a recipe given to them rather than actually knowing how things work. One example is how to read school-wide tracking data and what that means for me as teacher in the classroom. There are also implications for understanding that sort of data at the syndicate level, the whole school level. (School principal J)

The leaders we spoke to took a critical approach to data – its source, interpretation and implications. For example,

> The other crucial component is the students understanding the assessment tools that we use and *why* we use them. It is better to use a small number of effective assessment tools that give you lots of information rather than using a wide range of assessments, which takes away from teaching and learning time. (School Principal I)

School principal I provided a detailed explanation of factors that teachers needed to take into account:

> Their portfolio of material (children) now has got data in it which has to be explained to parents, so you're going 'What's the reason my kid's slowed up this year in this?' You've got other data that sits underneath it so you're explaining then that the basic facts on the data can be very low because they only have two test items and that is unfair. Or that, no we don't always expect our Māori children and children with English as a second language to do their best on a PAT test because there's a lot of vocabulary in it, and therefore we might say that we would look more at the child's work in the classroom and their collaborative work and the things they were putting forward, their modeling books. We would say that was more a true reflection of the child than a test that was time-bound or a test that was vocabulary-related so it needs a lot of understanding about assessment, its limitations and its uses and what sits inside and what it actually does tell you or does not tell you, and what you're doing about it.

Another teacher referred to the need for teachers to be 'data detectives'. This teacher spoke of the importance of teacher 'mindset', and orientation that 'we are all learners and everyone has inherent potential'. The group view that more was now being required of teachers in relation to data interpretation and use, with one participant noting:

> Like we always used to use stanines, and now we're not using stanines. We're using those other things … we're printing graphs out that show progress in scatters from years 4 to 5 to 6 as a cohort shifts … (Beginning Teacher Coordinator S)

Within each of the four focus group discussions, principals and assessment leaders identified that teachers needed the technical, contextual, interpretive and critical capacities identified by Pierce and Chick (2011), Watson (2006) and Gal (2002) in order to make effective use of assessment and data. They spoke of the importance of a positive stance towards learning about and using data. They raised the need for common understandings, triangulation across data sources as equity and social justice issues along with time for collaborative data analysis and interpretation, as aspects involved in learning to use data in a manner consistent with the findings from the Wayman and Jimerson (2014) study. Their comments indicated that they understood data use as a situated and social practice, where advice and mentoring from more experienced colleagues is essential (Farley-Ripple & Buttram, 2015).

Concluding comments

Schools are currently subject to increased pressure to report on, account for and demonstrate enhanced student learning through the use of data. Schools of education are facing increased and more explicit demands to develop and report on student teacher assessment, data and mathematical literacy. In this paper, we reflect on one aspect of findings of a project aimed at understanding and developing the mathematical thinking teachers need across the breadth of their professional work through a cross course focus during a one-year postgraduate primary initial teacher education programme. Despite questions about lecturer confidence and/or background to successfully engage with mathematical thinking and data literacy (Dunlap & Piro, 2016), the emergent project findings reported here suggest that lecturers, with prompting, are able to identify the place of mathematical thinking and data literacy in their courses. A number of the lecturers in our study critiqued the role numbers/statistics play in the social construction of people, problems and policies. They discussed the need to consider the context when making sense of and drawing conclusions from data. Student teachers, with prompting, are able to identify aspects of mathematical and statistical thinking across their courses and the breadth of teachers' work post practicum. Both groups addressed the technical, contextual and critical dimensions of data literacy identified as essential in the literature. The principals and school assessment leaders we talked to held expectations that beginning teachers had the disposition and capacity to learn and develop assessment and data capability, and they expected to work with them to extend this capacity. The understandings and expectations of these school-based practitioners also encompassed the breadth of understanding identified in the research. Based on the shifts across time in participant reports, it appears that alerting them to the possibility of mathematical and statistical thinking can sensitise them to the range of contexts where this is used, and also to the possibility that others may not have the requisite expertise or dispositions to make effective use of data to inform teaching and learning. This finding suggests that, to some extent, the research interview process itself can be viewed as an intervention. The interview process served to value and make visible this aspect of coursework/teachers' work in much the same way assessment accords value and visibility to certain aspects of student learning. One limitation of this study to date is that we have limited data on lecture actions to make mathematical thinking more explicit – this is a focus for further development in the study.

Many questions exist about how schools of education and other agencies can best respond to the growing imperative for teachers (student teachers, mentor teachers and initial teacher educators) to be assessment and data literate. The approaches adopted by schools of education range along a continuum of separate to integrated-embedded forms of instruction. Some suggest a 'multi-layered' approach might be of more value for diverse student cohorts (Briguglio & Watson, 2014). In our project, we aimed to work with lecturers to identify the mathematical thinking in their courses and for them to make this more explicit to student teachers. The project plan includes mentoring and a website to support students' self-directed learning. Our approach can be seen as consistent with the systems approach to build data literacy that some scholars are advocating (Mandinach & Gummer, 2013). However, as others have found, each of these aspects has proved more challenging than we had anticipated. We can speculate that this is because some faculty staff lack confidence and or have limited expertise in using data and or may not be aware of their own expertise and the role data already has in their courses. They may not agree that data literacy is important (e.g. Mandinach et al., 2015) or have difficulty prioritising opportunities for this in time-poor courses. Given our initial findings, the implications of raising awareness/embedding would seem to be worthy of further exploration although in suggesting this we note that studies on the development of assessment literacy have not identified a clear advantage to embedded or separate assessment courses.

The lecturers in our study were very clear they did not see it as their role to teach mathematical or statistical thinking outside the context of its use in their courses. The lecturers who spoke to us were confident when talking about its use in their contexts albeit some of them initially responded that they were 'no good at maths'. We can see in their comments echoes of Galligan's (2013) assertion that the thinking required and culture for use is context dependent. As with any initiative, time is required to embed systematically and effectively across a programme and to develop shared goals and vision. Then again, it is possible that this matter can only be, and should only be, progressed with explicit programme wide support from faculty leaders in particular the Dean.

It is possible that data literacy should be progressed at university level through a pan faculty approach as after all, every citizen needs to be data literate in ways appropriate for their professional and personal circumstances and goals. Citizens need to be able to use statistical information to identify and inform them about the issues and opportunities facing their communities and to understand how this information may be being used to influence opinion or even deceive (Watson & Callingham, 2003). As Orrill points out: 'if individuals lack the ability to think numerically, they cannot participate fully in civic life, thereby bringing into question the very basis of government of, by, and for the people' (Orrill, 2001, p. xvi). In the same spirit, there would seem to be merit in researchers and educators interested in teacher assessment literacy, data literacy and statistical/mathematical literacy coming together to share their ideas and expertise. This is a process we hope to build on in future research.

Acknowledgements

We wish to acknowledge other members of our research team: Mira Peter, Jane Furness, Judy Bailey and Merilyn Taylor, and the colleagues and student teachers who have been part of the study. The study is funded by the Teaching and Learning Research Initiative fund, the New Zealand Ministry of Education.

Disclosure statement

No potential conflict of interest was reported by the authors.

Funding

This work was supported by the Teaching and Learning Research Initiative.

References

Black, P., & Wiliam, D. (1998). Assessment and classroom learning. *Assessment in Education: Principles Policy and Practice, 5*, 7–74.

Briguglio, C., & Watson, S. (2014). Embedding English language across the curriculum in higher education: A continuum of development support. *The Australian Journal of Language and Literacy, 37*, 67–74.

Chick, H., & Pierce, R. (2013). The statistical literacy needed to interpret school assessment data. *Mathematics Teacher Education and Development, 15*, 5–26.

Coburn, C., & Turner, E. (2011). Research on data use: A framework and analysis. *Measurement: Interdisciplinary Research & Perspective, 9*, 173–206.

Cooper, B., & Cowie, B. (2014, December). *Student teachers' mathematical thinking*. Paper presented at the meeting of the Australian Association for Research in Education/New Zealand Association for Research in Education, Brisbane.

Cooper, B., & Cowie, B. (2015a). Highlights: Induction. *Secondary math and science teacher preparation: An international study of promising practices in APEC from economies' case studies* (pp. 42–46). APEC and Department of Education. Retrieved from http://publications.apec.org/publication-detail.php?pub_id=1619

Cooper, B., & Cowie, B. (2015b, April). *Lecturer mathematical thinking within a primary initial teacher education programme*. Paper presented at the meeting of the American Education Research Association, Chicago.

Cooper, B., & Cowie, B. (in press). *Scoping teacher educators' views of the opportunities for mathematical thinking in an ITE programme*.

Council of Chief State School Officers (CCSSO). (2012). Our responsibility, our promise: Transforming educator preparation and entry into the profession. Retrieved from http://ccsso.org/Documents/2012/Our%20Responsibility%20Our%20Promise_2012.pdf

Cowie, B., Hipkins, R., Keown, P., & Boyd, S. (2011). *The shape of curriculum change: A short discussion of key findings from the Curriculum Implementation Studies (CIES) project* (pp. 1–15). Wellington: Ministry of Education.

Crooks, T. (2011). Assessment for learning in the accountability era: New Zealand. *Studies in Educational Evaluation, 37*, 71–77.

DeLuca, C., & Bellara, A. (2013). The current state of assessment education: Aligning policy, standards, and teacher education curriculum. *Journal of Teacher Education, 64*, 356–372.

DeLuca, C., & Klinger, D. A. (2010). Assessment literacy development: Identifying gaps in teacher candidates' learning. *Assessment in Education: Principles, Policy & Practice, 17*, 419–438.

Dunlap, K., & Piro, J. (2016). Diving into data: Developing the capacity for data literacy in teacher education. *Cogent Education, 3*, 1–13: 1132526.

Farley-Ripple, E., & Buttram, J. (2015). The development of capacity for data use: The role of teacher networks in an elementary school. *Teachers College Record, 117*, 1–34.

Gal, I. (2002). Adults' statistical literacy: meanings, components, responsibilities. *International Statistical Review, 70*, 1–25.

Galligan, L. (2013). A systematic approach to embedding academic numeracy at university. *Higher Education Research & Development, 32*, 734–747.

Hardy, I. (2015). Data, numbers and accountability: The complexity, nature and effects of data use in schools, *British Journal of Educational Studies, 63*, 467–486.

Hill, H., Rowan, B., & Loewenberg Ball, D. (2015). Effects of teachers' mathematical knowledge for teaching on student achievement. *American Educational Research Journal, 42*, 371–406.

DEVELOPING TEACHERS' ASSESSMENT CAPACITY

Hill, M., Smith, L., Cowie, B., Gilmore, A., & Gunn, A. (2013). *Preparing initial primary and early childhood teacher education students to use assessment.* Wellington, New Zealand: TLRI.

Mandinach, E. B. (2012). A perfect time for data use: using data-driven decision making to inform practice. *Educational Psychologist, 47,* 71–85.

Mandinach, E., Friedman, J., & Gummer, E. (2015). How can schools of education help to build educators' capacity to use data? A systemic view of the issue. *Teachers College Record, 117,* 1–50.

Mandinach, E. B., & Gummer, E. S. (2012). *Navigating the landscape of data literacy: It IS complex.* Washington, DC, and Portland, OR: WestEd and Education Northwest.

Mandinach, E. B., & Gummer, E. S. (2013). A systemic view of implementing data literacy in educator preparation. *Educational Researcher, 42,* 30–37.

Means, B., Padilla, C., DeBarger, A., & Bakia, M. (2009). *Implementing data-informed decision making in schools: Teacher access, supports and use.* Washington, DC: U.S. Department of Education.

Ministry of Education. (2007). *The New Zealand curriculum.* Wellington: Learning Media.

Ministry of Education. (2010). *National standards.* Wellington: Learning Media.

Ministry of Education. (2011). *Position paper: Assessment (schooling sector).* Wellington: Learning Media.

New Zealand Teachers Council. (2007). *Graduating teacher standards: Aotearoa New Zealand.* Wellington: New Zealand Government.

Orrill, R. (2001). Mathematics, numeracy, and democracy xiii. In A. Steen (Ed.), *Mathematics and democracy: The case for quantitative literacy* (pp. xiii–xx). Princeton NJ: National Council on Education and the Disciplines and The Woodrow Wilson National Fellowship Foundation.

Ottmar, E., Rimm-Kaufman, S., Larsen, R., & Berry, R. (2015). Mathematical knowledge for teaching, standards-based mathematics teaching practices, and student achievement in the context of the responsive classroom approach. *American Educational Research Journal, 52,* 787–821.

Penuel, W., & Fishman, B. (2012). Large-scale science education intervention research we can use. *Journal of Research in Science Teaching, 49,* 281–304.

Pierce, R., & Chick, H. (2011). Reacting to quantitative data: Teachers' perceptions of student achievement reports. In J. Clark, B. Kissane, J. Mousley, T. Spencer, & S. Thornton (Eds.), *Mathematics: Traditions and [new] practices.* Proceedings of the 34th Annual Conference of the Mathematics Education Research Group of Australasia, Alice Springs (pp. 631–639). Adelaide: AAMT/MERGA.

Pierce, R., Chick, H., Watson, J., Les, M., & Dalton, M. (2014). A statistical literacy hierarchy for interpreting educational system data. *Australian Journal of Education, 58,* 195–217.

Piro, J. S., & Hutchinson, C. J. (2014). Using a data chat to teach instructional interventions: Student perceptions of data literacy in an assessment course. *The New Educator, 10,* 95–111.

Reeves, T., & Honig, S. (2015). A classroom data literacy intervention for pre-service teachers. *Teaching and Teacher Education, 50,* 90–101.

Skovsmose, O., & Greer, B. (2012). Seeing the cage?: The emergence of critical mathematics education. In O. Skovsmose, & B. Greer (Eds.), *Opening the cage: Critique and politics of mathematics education.* (pp. 1–20). Chapter 1. Rotterdam: Sense Publishers.

Steen, L. (2001). The case for quantitative literacy. In L. Steen (Ed.), *Mathematics and democracy: The case for quantitative literacy* (pp. 1–22). Princeton: National Council on Education and the Disciplines.

Stiggins, R., (2008). *Assessment manifesto: A call for the development of balanced assessment systems.* Portland, OR: ETS Assessment Training Institute.

Tapia, M., & Marsh, G. E. (2004). An instrument to measure mathematics attitudes. *Academic Exchange Quarterly, 8,* 16–21.

Ward, J., & Thomas, G. (2007). What do teachers know about fractions? *Findings from the New Zealand numeracy development projects 2006* (pp. 128–138). Wellington: Learning Media.

Watson, J. (2006). *Statistical literacy at school: Growth and goals.* Mahwah NJ: Lawrence Erlbaum.

Watson, J. (2011). Personal and professional numeracy: A unit for pre-service teachers at the University of Tasmania. *Numeracy, 4,* Article 2. doi:10.5038/1936-4660.4.1.2. Retrieved from http://scholarcommons.usf.edu/numeracy/vol4/iss1/art2

Watson, J., & Callingham, R. (2003). Statistical literacy: A complex hierarchical construct. *Statistics Education Research Journal, 2*, 3–46.

Wayman, J., Cho, V., & Johnston, M. (2007). *The data-informed district: A district-wide evaluation of data use in the Natrona County school district.* Austin: The University of Texas.

Wayman, J., & Jimerson, J. (2014). Teacher needs for data-related professional learning. *Studies in Educational Evaluation, 42*, 25–34.

Young-Loveridge, J., Bicknell, B., & Mills, J. (2012). The mathematical content knowledge and attitudes of New Zealand pre-service primary teachers. *Mathematics Teacher Education and Development, 14*, 28–49.

Integrating assessment for learning in the teacher education programme at the University of Oslo

Lisbeth M. Brevik, Marte Blikstad-Balas and Kirsti Lyngvær Engelien

ABSTRACT
This article provides an analysis of the integration of assessment for learning principles in the newly revised five-year Master of Education programme at the University of Oslo, Norway, across didactic subjects, pedagogy and school practice. The analysis draws on lecture notes, student videos and student exam papers among 143 student teachers, aiming to identify (a) the operationalisation of the assessment curriculum at the university campus, and in school practice, (b) how the student teachers use assessment principles as tools in their instructional designs and (c) how they self-assess their teaching practice. Our main finding is that student teachers seem to be more concerned with assessing their students than using self-assessment to improve their instruction. Based on the findings, we argue the importance of relating the teaching and learning activities with the assessment situations used in the teacher education programme.

Introduction

Newly educated teachers often struggle with using the knowledge from research-based teacher education programmes when facing challenges in the classroom (Cochran-Smith & Fries, 2005). Cochran-Smith (2003) argued that the knowledge acquired during teacher education only to a small extent influences teachers' instructional practices. Teacher education must enable student teachers to use knowledge and skills in their practices to enhance the link between theory and practice (Darling-Hammond, 2006; Hammerness, 2006, 2013; Hatlevik & Smeby, 2015). The use of assessment principles is no exception (e.g. Newton, 2007; Stobart, 2006), and can be subsumed under a sociocultural perspective. This perspective will serve as a theoretical and methodological lens in this article.

In line with Black and Wiliam's (1998b) definition, we use

the general term *assessment* to refer to all those activities undertaken by teachers – and their students in assessing themselves – that provide information to be used as feedback to modify the teaching and learning activities. Such assessment becomes *formative assessment* when the evidence is actually used to adapt the teaching to meet student needs. (p. 140)

Several assessment researchers (e.g. Black, Harrison, Lee, Marshall, & Wiliam, 2004; Wiliam, 2011a) have discussed the distinctions between assessment for learning (AfL) and assessment of learning (AoL) on the one hand, and between formative and summative assessment on the other. Although Wiliam (2011a) stated that these distinctions are different in kind, he argued that it might be more helpful to acknowledge that AfL and formative assessment are conducted to improve learning, whether or not one term or the other is used.

In this article, we use the term AfL, mainly because in the Norwegian context of this study, AfL is the preferred term in the educational context and policy documents, and is used synonymously with formative assessment (Norwegian Directorate for Education and Training [UDIR], 2011, p. 2). In the article, we elaborate on how AfL is integrated in the teacher education programme at the University of Oslo, an issue which arguably is relevant not only for Norwegian education, but concerns teacher education in general.

A crucial issue concerns how to develop assessment capacity in teachers through teacher education, as teacher education has historically neglected assessment. The question of how to educate future teachers in effectively using assessments to promote, monitor and report on student learning is timelier than ever; in an increasingly accountability-oriented educational context, teachers are expected to provide dependable assessment. As a result, teacher education programmes across the world are expected to enable their student teachers to use assessment in ways that increase and reflect student performance (DeLuca & Klinger, 2010).

This article responds to the call for increased research in assessment education by examining a newly revised five-year, integrated Master of Education (ME) programme at the University of Oslo, Norway (UiO). The UiO and the Norwegian Centre for Professional Learning in Teacher Education (ProTed) have collaborated to develop a future-oriented, knowledge-based programme that involves activating the innovative, future- and internationally oriented teacher.

This article addresses key topics in assessment education, as it investigates how assessment principles and practices are integrated in the ME programme, how the student teachers use assessment principles in planning their own teaching at UiO's partner schools and to what extent they use self-assessment (SA) principles to develop their practices. Such a perspective is in line with constructive alignment (CA), in which Biggs (1996) argued the importance of relating the teaching and learning activities with the assessment situations used in teacher education, (Lund & Engelien, 2015). We will argue the importance of enabling student teachers to use assessment principles as mediating tools in the design of their teaching, while at the same time using the principles to self-assess their teaching practices.

We investigate the following overarching research question: *How and to what extent does the ME programme at UiO develop assessment capacity in student teachers?* We use qualitative and quantitative data to investigate: first, how teacher educators at UiO teach principles of assessment; second, how student teachers use assessment principles as tools in their instructional designs at partner schools; and third, how they use assessment principles in their own assessment situations at UiO. In the following, we describe the structure of the ME programme in general. We also discuss implications for the student teachers' professional development. In order to contextualise this study, we first review key features that characterise this programme and the literature related to educational assessment.

University of Oslo: ME programme

In Norway, as in many other countries, there has been an increased focus on educational assessment over the past decade (Norwegian Directorate for Education and Training [UDIR], 2010; Tveit, 2014). Given this emphasis, the Norwegian Ministry of Education and Research (KD) requires teacher education to address assessment as a topic of study. The National Curriculum for Teacher Education (2013) states that student teachers should have knowledge about assessment and testing, and methods to enable assessment practice aligned to the core curriculum. The review by Tveit (2014) in this journal suggests that Norwegian teachers have found it challenging to implement the new assessment principles, making it all the more important to prepare new teachers for the new assessment demands in contemporary education.

The ME programme at UiO qualifies teachers to teach in Years 8–13 (13- to 18-year-old students)[1] and is structured in a two-term model, with a normal progression rate of 30 credits each term.[2] The first term comprises the two components 'instruction and learning' and 'classroom management', while the second term comprises the components 'differentiation' and 'assessment'. The assessment component is the focus for analysis in this article. In this course, the students learn assessment practices in their pedagogy seminars and in their subject didactics seminars, as wells as during their supervised training at partner schools. This course design involves three formal assessment situations: (a) a practice exam, (b) a research and development (R&D) report and (c) an exam essay where the student is required to deliberate a topic from the field of assessment and/or differentiated instruction. In following the principles of CA (Biggs, 1996), these exams are integrated, the student needs to build upon pedagogy and subject didactics theory, as well as experiences from their teaching practice. Together, the three formal assessment situations have a licensing purpose (Newton, 2007).

The content of the assessment component is in adherence with the requirements in the Norwegian Education Act (KD, 2006/2013), which regulates assessment for students in primary and secondary schools. Specifically, the assessment component aims to provide student teachers with (a) *knowledge* about assessment theory, assessment practices and challenges in the disciplines and the links between feedback, assessment and learning; (b) *skills* that enable them to assess and document their students' learning and development, and provide feedback that promotes learning in the disciplines; and (c) *competence* to develop and discuss their professionalism. Based on these aims, the assessment component comprises open lectures across scientific subjects, workshops in subject domains, as well as didactics and pedagogy and seminars. As discussed in the next section, little is known about the kind of content and structure that are useful in developing assessment capacity in student teachers.

What we know about assessment education

As several researchers have pointed out, assessment is integral to effective instruction (e.g. Black & Wiliam, 1998a, 1998b, 2009; Wiliam, 2010; Wiliam, 2011b), and teachers are increasingly expected to use assessments to form valid judgements about student learning and for the improvement of instruction (Brevik, 2015; Brevik & Blikstad-Balas, 2014;

DeLuca, Chavez, & Cao, 2013; DeLuca & Klinger, 2010; Mausethagen & Mølstad, 2015; Stobart, 2006; Tiknaz & Sutton, 2006; Tveit, 2014).

This emphasis on formative assessment raises the question of what role teacher education plays in preparing teachers to meet such demands. Due to the limited number of studies investigating how assessment is taught in teacher education, the review is not extensive. While the general interest in assessment is high, not many teacher education programmes offer formalised assessment education (DeLuca & Klinger, 2010; Dempster, 1992; Stiggins, 2004).

There seems to be consensus that explicit assessment courses have the potential to positively impact student teachers' understandings of assessment (DeLuca & Klinger, 2010; DeLuca et al., 2013; Graham, 2005). In a study about assessment development in a teacher education programme in Canada, DeLuca and Klinger (2010) identified the participating student teachers' perceived confidence levels in assessment practice, theory and philosophy. The results of this research demonstrate a serious challenge related to the lack of mandatory assessment courses in teacher education. In the absence of such courses, the student teachers in this study by DeLuca and Klinger (2010) obtained their confidence in assessment through practicum experience – provided by teachers who most likely also lacked assessment education. This study also identified positive effects of providing student teachers with explicit assessment instruction, and 'a real benefit of direct assessment instruction in preservice, on-campus, teacher education programmes' (DeLuca & Klinger, 2010, p. 434).

It has been problematised that assessment is too often summative, implying that assessment tends to report back and summarise what has been learned, rather than being formative and in support and guidance of ongoing learning and development (e.g. Stobart, 2006; Tiknaz & Sutton, 2006), which makes it important to investigate student teachers' use of assessment principles in their instructional designs and to identify the assessment practices they meet in their teacher education. For example, Volante and Fazio (2007) found that the student teachers in their study were primarily concerned with summative assessment such as tests and final grades. In a later study, DeLuca and colleagues (2013) likewise found that student teachers' conception of assessment was based solely on summative testing. They discovered, however, that these student teachers expanded their conception of assessment to one that recognised multiple forms of assessment, after taking only a one-term measurement course.

The studies by Volante and Fazio (2007) and DeLuca and colleagues (2013) both suggest that teacher education may have a critical role to play in providing student teachers with deep understandings of assessment. Nicol, Thomson and Breslin (2014, p. 102) conclude their study about assessment and student peer review in higher education by highlighting how 'the capacity to produce quality feedback is a fundamental graduate skill, and, as such, it should receive much greater attention in higher education curricula'. As argued by DeLuca and Klinger (2010), 'emphasis needs to be placed on enabling teachers to maximise the learning potential of assessment while also monitoring student progress' (p. 420). The estimate that teachers spend between 30 and 50% of their professional time engaged in assessment activities (Stiggins, 2004) further underscores the need to practise formative assessment. In order for students to be able to perform formative assessment and develop their repertoire of formative assessment practices, we believe it to be crucial for student teachers to provide feedback to their students in a way that not only evaluates finished activities, but also monitors, guides and motivates student work while the students consider the process to be ongoing. The reviewed literature suggests that training teachers in assessment is crucial. In line with this suggested need for more assessment training and more focus on the formative aspects of assessment, the present study explores how student teachers are trained in assessment. Further, we will analyse and discuss the implementation of assessment education in the ME programme at UiO. In the following, we discuss how our study is framed by a Vygotskian approach.

A Vygotskian approach to assessment education

This study is based on the view that the use of AfL principles takes place within a sociocultural environment at the university and at the practice schools. This framing contributes to seeing assessment as a tool which is also a social construction (Afflerbach & Cho, 2011). In line with Edwards' (in press), we argue that conceptualising learning for student teachers as the increasingly informed use of assessment as a tool has implications for their development:

> Vygotsky explained the process by explaining learning as both internalisation and externalisation: we take in new ideas and use them as tools as we take forward our intentions. Internalisation and externalisation are key to the dialectic, our minds and behaviours are shaped as we take part in practices, but we can also shape the practices through our actions, through externalising. While Vygotsky developed these ideas to explain how children learn, they apply equally well to adults as learners and appear particularly relevant to the challenge of learning to teach while teaching, where we would expect to find evidence of student teachers' learning in their actions in the activity of teaching.

Thus, using a Vygotskian framing in this study, we argue that there is an ongoing relationship between the student teachers and the affordances and demands they encounter at the university and in school settings. We therefore employ a Vygotskian framing (Vygotsky, 1986) to examine how assessment principles are employed as tools, first by the teacher educators in teacher education at the university, and second by the student teachers at their practice schools in order to support the students as learners. Because of the particular emphasis on assessment as a pedagogic tool, we also draw on the arguments of later interpreters of Vygotsky such as Daniels (2008) and Edwards (2015, in press).

Since the sociocultural contexts of the school and classrooms are different from the educational context of the university, the assessment principles will inevitably be transformed, adapted and marked by the school context. In the present study, we therefore argue the importance of relating the assessment training situations used in the ME programme with the teaching and learning activities the student teachers design and experience at the practice schools (Lund & Engelien, 2015). The Vygotskian framing therefore provides a perspective on the student teachers' use of assessment principles to develop their practices.

Assessment as a pedagogic tool

In a sociocultural approach to teaching and learning, assessment principles are tools which should mediate school assessment practices. The argument is that used as a pedagogic tool, AfL or formative assessment has the potential to expand student teachers' knowledge of their students while seeing them as active in their own development as learners, thereby resulting in the affordance of a pedagogy that meets the needs of students. In addition, one aspect of their active learning is that students can learn how to use SA as a tool, creating demands on themselves which help them move forward as learners, by helping them monitor and control their own progress as students (Black, 2015; Gipps, 1999).

The notion of assessment as a tool finds support in the assessment literature where, for example, Newton (2007) observed that much depends on how and why a type of assessment is used and that the same assessment technique may be used for a variety of purposes. He noted, for example, that the purpose of formative assessment is to use individual (or aggregated) results to identify student (or group) learning needs to direct subsequent teaching and learning (p. 163). He explained that there is no summative purpose, only summative judgement, although we 'routinely characterise formative assessment by contrasting it with summative assessment and 'summative' clearly does refer to a type of assessment judgement, one which involves 'summing up' (the cue's in the name)' (p. 160). Along this line of argument, a summative assessment can be used for formative purposes, e.g. using test results to identify learning needs and design instruction accordingly.

It is worth noting that assessment traditionally has focused on the effect of various teaching activities *after* these are over (Wiliam, 2011a), indicating a need to develop student teachers' ability to perform AfL, providing feedback to promote student learning (Black & Wiliam, 1998a; Brevik & Blikstad-Balas, 2014; Hattie & Timperley, 2007; Wiliam, 2011a). A useful perspective on feedback is described in the Protocol for Language Arts Teaching Observation (PLATO),[3] a research-based instrument used to observe the effectiveness of teachers, including feedback practices:

> Feedback includes comments on the quality or nature of student work as well as suggestions for how students can improve the quality of their work. At the high end, feedback is specific and targets the skills at the heart of the activity. The feedback helps students understand the quality of their work and helps students better perform the task at hand by addressing substantive elements of the task. At the low end, feedback consists of vague comments that are not clearly anchored in student work and suggestions for improvement tend to be procedural (i.e. focused on the instructions for the activity rather than the skills or knowledge that students are applying). These comments do not help students gauge their progress and do not provide a means for students to improve. At the low end, feedback may also be confusing or misleading.

The quadrant model as a tool in assessment education

The Vygotskian approach to pedagogy requires us to recognise how teacher educators use assessment principles as tools to engage student teachers with powerful cultural meanings and ways of working. This way of teaching to promote learning is emphasised in the Vygotsky-based *Quadrant model* of a pedagogic sequence (Edwards, 2015). The model emphasises how learners are first introduced to new concepts, or ways of working, and participate in learning situations through guided instruction (quadrant 1). Then, they move towards independent use, first through tightly structured tasks (quadrant 2) and later through more open tasks (quadrant 3). Finally, they display their knowledge in some form of summative assessment (quadrant 4).

Edwards (2015) explained that the sequence is frequently disrupted with recursive loops occurring. The sequence is meant to be a flexible framework, for example, learners may take time in quadrants 2 and 3 to actively engage with the task demands, to both acquire and use AfL as tools, to make mistakes, get stuck and attempt an effort after meaning and to move from quadrant 3 to 2 or 1 if additional help is needed. It is primarily in quadrants

2 and 3 that students' use of AfL as a pedagogic tool can inform the guidance the teacher educators give. There, the student teachers are able to go back and forth flexibly between the quadrants in their learning process, to use AfL as a pedagogic tool and monitor their own progress or to be assessed formatively by the teacher educator – with these activities informing the support they need as they take themselves forward as learners. According to this analysis, student teachers do not easily move from hearing about AfL and then using them to design their assessment practices; rather, the potential and relevance of AfL need to be explored. Edwards (2015) emphasised that formative assessment occurs throughout the process. Building on her argument, we suggest a need to include attention to the purposes of using AfL as a tool in the ME programme at UiO. In this manner, a sociocultural framing includes social, material and contextual resources.

Methods

This study used a multiple methods design (Bazeley & Kemp, 2012; Creswell, 2013) involving qualitative and quantitative data to identify how assessment principles are taught and assessed in the assessment component, and how student teachers use assessment principles as tools to design their teaching practices. We ask: *How and to what extent does the ME programme at UiO develop assessment capacity in student teachers?* In order to answer this main research question, we have specified three research questions (RQs):

- RQ1: How are assessment principles taught across lectures, workshops and seminars?
- RQ2: How and to what extent do student teachers use assessment principles in designing their school practices?
- RQ3: How and to what extent do student teachers use SA principles to reflect on their practices?

Participants, data collection and data analysis

The participants in this study were student teachers in the ME programme at UiO, who were in their seventh term in the autumn of 2015, and thus participated in the assessment component ($N = 143$).

We collected data from the assessment education at the university (lecture notes); assessment situations the student teachers participated in (films; praxis cards) and designed for their students at the partner schools (lesson plans; R&D reports); and assessment situations for the student teachers (praxis cards; R&D reports). The data analysis included five steps (Table 1).

Validity, reliability and ethics

We took a number of steps to assure data validity and reliability (Creswell, 2013). First, we combined data from teacher educators and student teachers, as well as data from the university and the partner schools, seeking thematic convergence through triangulation (Creswell & Miller, 2000; Patton, 1999). Thus, we aimed to counter some of the challenges concerning self-reported data and the collection of texts, namely that self-reported data might reflect intentions rather than actual practice, and that texts per se provide no information on how

DEVELOPING TEACHERS' ASSESSMENT CAPACITY

Table 1. Steps of analysis.

Readings	Aim	Tools of analysis	Research question
1st step (lecture notes)	To identify assessment principles referred to in the notes	First, we identified the following concepts in the data: assessment for learning (AfL), assessment of learning (AoL), formative and/or summative assessment, aims, criteria, feedback, feed forward, SA, exams and tests	**RQ1**: How are assessment principles taught across lectures, workshops and seminars?
2nd step (film)	To identify teacher educators' and student teachers' perception of video-based AfL		
3rd step (praxis card)	To identify student teachers' participation in assessment practices at the practice schools	Second, we analysed the lectures using the four quadrants in Edwards's Quadrant model (2015)	
4th step (lesson plans)	To identify how student teachers designed assessment situations for their students, and their SA of their own instructional designs	We identified the same concepts in these data: assessment for learning (AfL), assessment of learning (AoL), formative and/or summative assessment, aims, criteria, feedback, feed forward, SA, exams and tests	**RQ2**: How and to what extend do student teachers use assessment principles as tools in designing their school practices?
5th step (R&D reports)	To identify how student teachers designed research on their assessment practices		**RQ3**: How and to what extent do student teachers use SA principles to reflect on their practices?

they have been used. It should be noted that the goal of triangulation is not to 'demonstrate that different data sources or inquiry approaches yield essentially the same result' (Patton, 1999, p. 1193), but to test for such consistency. In this study, we have used sources that could not by themselves provide the 'same results' but, taken together, the lecture notes, the film, the praxis cards, the lesson plans and the R&D reports all contribute with different nuances to the same phenomenon, namely: how assessment capacity is being developed in the ME programme at UiO. We could have wished for a higher response rate than 56% to our survey asking for lesson plans, with 70% of the respondents giving their consent to our use of their documents. However, two student teachers gave answers that indicated a lack of time and plans as the reason, rather than a lack of willingness to share the content. Specifically, they stated 'I cannot find my lesson plan anymore; otherwise, you could have used it', and '[I] have no time or energy to find it. Otherwise, I would have bothered'.

As all three authors are employed at the department responsible for the ME programme, we took measures to increase the credibility of the study. First of all, one or more of the authors were present during several of the lectures in the assessment component in order to validate whether what was emphasised in the lectures aligned with the documents (lecture notes) we use as data. The consistency observed gave us confidence that the lecture notes represent reliable data. Another validation of the lecture notes is that the teacher educators make their notes available online for the students immediately after the lectures, and it is customary to confer that the notes are consistent with the lesson. Second, we attempted to validate our analysis by member-checking (Creswell, 2013), asking the teacher educators to comment on our analysis of their lecture notes. Third, we used peer debriefing as recommended by Creswell (2013). These were qualified peers who not only provided support, but also challenged our assumptions methodologically and theoretically. The teacher educators and student teachers gave their voluntary consent to the use of all documents (Busher & James, 2012; Ryen, 2011), and the data collection adheres to the ethical requirements of the Norwegian Social Science Data Services.

51

Limitations

A limitation of this study is that we have not analysed the actual lectures, workshops or seminars where assessment was taught, nor the student teachers' teaching at the schools. Although these are important limitations, document analysis provides information about assessment principles expressed in these texts, and as described above, we validated the lecture notes by observing several of the lectures. Further, these documents provide insight into how the student teachers were enculturated into assessment practice that values formative purposes of assessment and AfI practices. Moreover, although we did not observe how the student teachers conducted their lessons at the practice schools, they report extensively from these lessons themselves in their R&D reports, and use detailed examples from their classroom instructions when discussing their assessment practices. Thus, we argue that our reliance on documentary analysis does take praxis into account, as several of the documents (R&D reports and praxis cards) draw heavily on what happened in these lessons.

The potential for generalising the findings in our study is also limited. Still, we consider the study to be important due to its innovative and empirically substantiated approaches to – and the discussion of – challenges and dilemmas in assessment education.

Findings

In the data analysed, we found that both the teacher educators and the student teachers included assessment in their instructional designs, indicating that assessment principles taught at the university enabled the student teachers to use such principles as tools in their teaching designs. Three strands emerged in relation to how the ME programme at UiO developed assessment capacity in the student teachers. First, the majority of the lectures, workshops and seminars concerned AfL, and included AfL practice. Second, the AfL practices the student teachers used in their teaching designs mainly concerned feedback practices during classroom teaching. Third, a clear difference existed between how the teacher educators taught SA principles, and how the student teachers used SA in and of their teaching. We discovered that this distinction can be explained by a lack of SA practice at the university. In the following sections, we will present the findings according to the three research questions, before discussing implications for assessment education.

RQ1: How are assessment principles taught across lectures, workshops and seminars?

The lecture notes suggested that a variety of assessment principles and practices were taught in the assessment component. The notes clearly showed integration across the lectures, workshops and seminars, with a gradual release of assessment responsibility from the teacher educators to the student teachers.[4] This integration initially occurred as a set of terms presented in the lectures, which were subsequently made deference to in the workshops and seminars, where they were repeated and elaborated. The notes further indicated integration between assessment theory and practice, and provided definitions of and references to national guidelines and research; international large-scale tests, assessment theory and research; and research and theory in the subject domains.

DEVELOPING TEACHERS' ASSESSMENT CAPACITY

The integration was further developed by the gradual release of assessment responsibility in four sequences, in line with Edwards's (2015) *Quadrant model* presented in the theory section. First, the teacher educators introduced key principles and terms as well as ways of working with assessment (quadrant 1). Second, they provided tightly structured tasks, in which the student teachers discussed and performed assessment collaboratively based on video-taped classroom situations and student work (quadrant 2). Third, they provided open tasks in which the student teachers independently assessed student work and gave feedback based on aims and criteria (quadrant 3). Finally, the teacher educators assessed the student teachers' use of assessment principles in their teaching designs and in exam tasks (quadrant 4). Below, we will present how the teacher educators orchestrated these learning sequences.

Quadrant 1: introduction of key principles and terms, and ways of working with assessment

Assessment terms were initially introduced in the lectures, in line with Edwards's (2015) quadrant 1: (i) introduction to AfL, (ii) assessment of and for learning based on test use, (iii–iv) provision of feedback that promotes learning, (v) AfL: examples from school practice and (vi) AoL. The first two covered the terms *assessment, AfL, AoL, formative* and *summative assessment, aims, criteria, feedback, SA, exams* and *tests*, with references to assessment literature and examples from school practice. The next two elaborated on feedback using the PLATO criteria, including references to aims and SA. The last two lectures elaborated on all these terms and were directly linked to national guidelines: one from an AfL perspective, and the other from an AoL perspective. Still, while the terms were compared and contrasted, two pairs seemed to be presented as synonyms: AfL and formative assessment, and AoL and summative assessment. In the lectures, the student teachers were asked to reflect on assessment practices:

Lecture i: Which assessment situations will you design in your own teaching?

Lecture ii: Why is there a need for tests – or do we need them? Who needs them – the students, the teachers, the school, the parents, the politicians…? Have you experienced good AfL yourself? What characterised it?

Lecture iv: What kind of feedback promotes learning?

Lecture v: What are some challenges with providing feedback?

Asking the student teachers to discuss these questions seemed to require active participation in pairs and collectively. In the workshops and seminars, the teacher educators adapted the assessment terms and principles to subject-specific characteristics. Two examples illustrate this adaptation:

Foreign languages: In foreign languages, we assess communicative competence, facts and reflections about culture and society, written production, and oral interaction.

Religion and ethics: We recommend that the students' development of attitudes is not assessed summatively, but considered an aspect of competences assessed formatively. We do this so there is no doubt that the students' beliefs are exempt from assessment.

Notably, by adapting assessment principles to the subjects, the lecture notes indicated that while some of the didactics seminars covered most of the terms, others focused on a few

53

terms in depth. In this manner, the introduction of principles and terms occurred across the various contexts created for the assessment component. However, it is important to note that these practices are not quite the same, even if they are classified in the same quadrant. The findings might give the impression that all the teacher educators shared the same principles of AfL, which needs to be nuanced. On the one hand, the assessment component is rather new and the teacher education programme has strived to implement a shared view on AfL, which is suggested in the notes for lectures i–v. On the other hand, since the majority of the lecturers focused on AfL activities, while a minority focused on summative assessment principles in the workshops and seminars, different views on the matter are clearly suggested.

Quadrant 2: tightly structured assessment tasks

The teacher educators created tightly structured assessment tasks, in line with Edwards's (2015) quadrant 2, in which the student teachers collaboratively practised formative assessment of video-based classroom observations and student work. The student teachers were guided by the teacher educators, who presented the aims and criteria, and modelled assessment practice by showing the student teachers what to look for in videos and texts. These tightly structured tasks were provided in two lectures (iii–iv), and in two didactics seminars (mathematics and social studies) to achieve agreement among the student teachers in terms of identifying the quality of the teachers' feedback (in the two lectures), and strengths in the student work, suggesting what to improve and how to get there (in the two seminars). In the lectures, a teacher educator trained them in how to use criteria to identify high- and low-quality feedback, and to use the PLATO criteria as tools in writing high-quality feedback to a student's video-based presentation:

Lecture iii: Do you think this film illustrates low- or high-quality feedback?

Lecture iv: Search for evidence of feedback in these films. In groups of four, agree on a final assessment of the observed teachers' feedback practices.

Lecture iv: Watch this oral student presentation. Use the criteria to write high-quality feedback to the student to promote learning and development.

Tightly structured tasks were also presented in two seminars, although instead of the PLATO criteria, the student teachers were given criteria from national exams alongside student answers that had already been assessed by examiners appointed by UDIR:

Mathematics: We assess written exam tasks in mathematics, years 10 and 11. While assessing student answers, we discuss the assessment principles throughout, aiming to understand the grades/marks given by the examiners.

In these tightly structured tasks, the student teachers had opportunities to practise formative or summative assessment, as opposed to sequence 3, which focused on formative feedback practices.

Quadrant 3: open assessment tasks of student work

The teacher educators gradually released the assessment responsibility to the student teachers in the workshops and seminars, in line with Edwards's (2015) quadrant 3. In the workshops, they assessed a written student text, and/or a video-taped student presentation. The assessment process seemed to be modelled on the tightly structured tasks in quadrant 2, but more openly acknowledging the student teachers' views. The following tasks illustrate how this sequence moves back and forth between the collective and the individual, requiring active participation:

Workshop I (languages, humanities): In groups of four, draw up criteria for assessing oral skills. Then watch the video and use the criteria to give oral feedback on the students' presentations. Individually, write feedback to one of them.

Workshop II (languages, humanities): Individually, use the criteria to give feedback on the student text. Discuss these in groups of four. What can you learn from each other's assessments?

In the following seminars, these practices were integrated in the disciplines, requiring the student teachers to assess oral student work (English; religion), written student work (history; Norwegian) or to discuss how to design an assessment situation to get evidence of a student's oral skills based on a case description (foreign languages). In the seminars, they were asked either to create criteria based on competence aims in their school subject UDIR, (2006, 2013), or to use standardised criteria from exam tasks. These open tasks emphasised formative assessment practices, aiming to give quality feedback to develop student learning. Paradoxically, this emphasis on formative assessment was not reflected in the assessment of the student teachers' own work and performances at UiO.

Quadrant 4: assessing the student teachers

The teacher educators assessed the student teachers' use of assessment principles in designing their teaching and in exam tasks, in line with Edwards's (2015) quadrant 4. Four situations were directly linked to the assessment component (Figure 1); one voluntary assessment (video-based AfL), and three mandatory (praxis cards, lesson plans and R&D reports).

The video-based AfL integrated feedback from teacher educators at UiO and school supervisors during their practice:

Teacher educator: We want to do this project because the national guidelines require all teaching practice to be supervised, assessed, and varied. We […] watch the videos and comment on them, bearing in mind the theory we have gone through on campus and, at the same time, commenting on things that happen in the classroom.

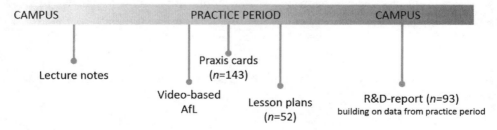

Figure 1. Lecture notes and formal assessments for the student teachers at UiO, linked to the assessment component (seventh term). n = distinct student teachers. Each of the 143 student teachers handed in their praxis card (mandatory). 52 of these student teachers submitted one lesson plan each for this study (voluntary). One R&D report was handed in by each of the student teachers who chose assessment as their topic (mandatory).

The assessment purpose was to develop the student teachers' ability to self-assess their teaching, and to receive feedback to improve their practices. This is an ongoing pilot project where only a group of student teachers was invited to participate ($n = 35$). The participants seemed positive towards this assessment practice, as expressed in these two quotes:

> *Student teacher 1*: The video clips increase my professional understanding because I can go back and observe myself. [...] I submit a video, for example, to the university and receive concrete feedback. Then I can read the feedback and go back to the video. To have this combination of concrete feedback and watching the video develops my learning.

> *Student teacher 2*: I think the videos could be useful in increasing my professional understanding, because I get to see my teaching from the students' perspective. [...] You can watch it and sort of assess your own performance. We get a lot of supervision both from supervisors and peers, but I feel it's useful to see it for myself as well, because then I may have a better understanding of the feedback I get.

These quotes not only underline the formative purpose of the assessment, but also indicate that it was used to improve their practice. The formative nature of the video-based AfL was not mirrored in the mandatory assessments, although we found some aspects of formative purposes. For example, the *praxis cards* documented the student teachers' participation in assessment situations at the schools, although the content of these situations was not documented. The card was signed by their supervisor, and was then part of their summative assessment at the university. Our analysis showed that all the student teachers ($N = 143$) had participated in such assessment, potentially using the experience in their assessment designs in the lesson plans and the R&D reports.

While the *lesson plans* showed the student teachers' design for their practice exams (45–90 min), the *R&D reports* were written over 14 weeks to develop teacher professionalism through research-based practices, choosing whether to study assessment or differentiation. Categorising the reports, we found that 68% ($n = 93$) concerned assessment, indicating a willingness to develop their assessment capacity. In these documents, the student teachers were required to integrate pedagogy and didactics theory with school practice. Teacher educators offered feedback on the research questions for the R&D reports, and while the supervisors assessed the lesson plans formatively before the exam, teacher educators assessed the plan and the exam summatively *in situ*.

In sum, the assessment principles and practices found in these sequences suggest that, although the main part of the assessment component concerned formative assessment, the majority of such assessments happened at the schools. At the university, they were mainly summatively judged to determine whether they should become licensed teachers. This apparent paradox will be addressed in the discussion section.

RQ2: How and to what extent do student teachers use assessment principles as tools in their teaching designs?

We have analysed two formal assessment situations directly linked to the assessment component: the student teachers' lesson plans and R&D reports (Figure 2).

Figure 2 shows that only some lesson plans included summative assessment (24%) or AoL (6%), while more included formative assessment (46%) and AfL (30%), with similar patterns revealed in the R&D reports. For the lesson plans, 44% ($n = 23$) included at least two of the formative assessment terms: AfL, formative assessment, feedback or SA.

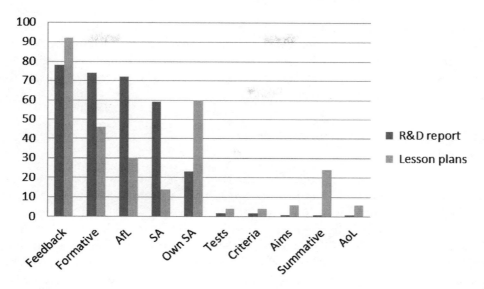

Figure 2. Assessment principles applied to the R&D reports and the lesson plans. The percentages indicate the amount of R&D assessment reports ($n = 93$) and lesson plans ($n = 50$) that included each of the assessment principles in the figure. R&D = research and development. AfL = assessment for learning. SA = self-assessment. AoL = assessment of learning.

Specifically, 10% of these plans ($n = 5$) included references to all four terms, another 19% ($n = 10$) included three of these, with an additional 15% ($n = 8$) including two of them. In comparison, 60% ($n = 30$) included SA of their own teaching practices, which all of the student teachers were expected to do.

These findings show that the majority of these documents indicated that the student teachers planned to give their students feedback during teaching, as illustrated here:

Foreign languages: Feedback will be given to each student individually, depending on which task they work with and what I know about their mastery from previous lessons. I will give feedback when students ask for help to solve a task, or when I approach a student. I do this to offer help based on their individual needs.

English: Feedback on pronunciation in line with the principles of flow and communication, rather than strict correctness in pronunciation and intonation.

Social studies: The students will get feedback from a peer when working together. […] The students will get feedback from me while working individually.

The first example indicates a formative assessment purpose, while the latter two are formulated in general terms and have the potential to satisfy both summative and formative assessment: summative because they indicate intentions to provide judgements of the students' mastery at a particular point in time, and formative because the feedback might relate to their students' learning and performance to help them improve.

In a similar vein, 89% ($n = 83$) of the R&D reports included at least two of the formative assessment terms: AfL, formative assessment, feedback or SA. Specifically, 33% of these reports ($n = 31$) included references to all four terms, another 32% ($n = 30$) included three of these, with an additional 24% ($n = 22$) including two of them. In comparison, only

25% ($n = 23$) included SA of their own teaching practices, and only one report referred to AoL and summative assessment. Although our analyses indicate a willingness in pursuing assessment principles, we revealed a tendency to describe *what* they intended to do, without explaining *how* or *why*. This is also suggested by the low percentage linking these assessments to aims (6%) or criteria (4%).

RQ3: How and to what extent do student teachers use SA to reflect on their practices?

Our findings suggest that the relevance and potential of SA might be under-communicated at the university. The lecture notes suggest that practising SA was not a priority, although SA was mentioned in most of the lectures and workshops, and in half the seminars. This finding aligns with the student teachers' lack of SA inclusion in their lesson plans (14%) (Figure 2), although the lesson plan template includes two rubrics explicitly requiring the student teachers' to elaborate on SA. However, in the R&D reports, 59% included student SA in their research questions, and 23% concerned how their own SA can influence their future instruction and professionalism. This is indeed a positive finding, as it was not an explicit objective of learning to integrate SA in their reports. Two examples illustrate this matter:

> *History*: How can I improve my assessment practice so that the students understand what they need to work with to develop their historical consciousness?

> *Sociology and social anthropology*: How do the students experience my formative feedback in the subject sociology and social anthropology, and how can I use their feedback to improve my future practice?

Notably, while the first example illustrates SA to develop the student teacher's instructional practice, the second expresses a double SA focus: the students' SA of how they perceived the feedback on their work, and the student teacher's SA to develop future practices. Figure 2 further shows that 60% of the student teachers also included own SA in their lesson plans, a typical example being: 'I find it difficult to assess what my students have learned: I wish to develop my ability to ask relevant questions. I also wish to improve my ability to give oral feedback that improves learning'. Given that the plans explicitly require student teachers to fill in a rubric for SA of their teaching, we find it concerning that only 60% did so, particularly since their supervisor offers feedback. The remaining 40% all had content in this rubric, but it is not actual assessment of how to improve their practice; rather, such content serves as descriptive justification for their instructional designs.

Taken together, these findings highlight both the student teachers' willingness to conduct SA practices, and an indication that SA is under-communicated and seems not to be practised at the university.

Discussion

The question guiding this article is: *How and to what extent does the ME programme at UiO develop assessment capacity in student teachers through the assessment component?* As the article has illustrated, the assessment component comprises education across open lectures, workshops in subject domains and didactics seminars. Based on our findings, we here discuss three topics we consider essential in developing assessment capacity in student teachers: the questions of assessment integration, assessment of finished products and the apparent lack of consistency between formative and summative assessment situations.

First, the student teachers are expected to perform assessment and be assessed at the university and during their school practice. This way of integrating assessment practices at the university and at the practice schools is an attempt to make a more coherent ME programme, providing opportunities to develop their assessment competence across a range of situations. Using assessment principles as tools in school subjects in order to increase learning is a challenge for teacher education in general, with student teachers reporting that the link between theory and practice is too vague (Darling-Hammond, Hammerness, Grossman, Frances, & Shulman, 2005). Thus, we believe the crucial element of success in a model such as the one employed at UiO is the move from teaching assessment principles in the lectures to the use of these principles in the student teachers' school subjects, in the workshops and seminars and in schools. We argue that the value of teaching isolated assessment principles is limited at best, and that the success criteria for assessment education are whether student teachers actually *choose* to use the principles as tools in their own teaching and research. For this to happen, it is essential for teacher education to focus on assessment not only as a theoretical principle, but as a tool for learning in the disciplines, in line with the sociocultural view of learning (Daniels, 2008; Edwards, 2015; Vygotsky, 1986). In this regard, the findings in the present study are uplifting, as a majority of the student teachers chose to actively integrate assessment in their teaching designs, using theoretical and research-based assessment knowledge (e.g. Black & Wiliam, 1998b, 2009; Brevik & Blikstad-Balas, 2014; Hattie & Timperley, 2007; Stobart, 2008; Wiliam, 2010).

However, our findings also indicate that student teachers are more concerned with assessing their students, than using SA to improve their instruction. Black and Wiliam's (1998a, 1998b) definition of formative assessment underscores the use of feedback to modify teaching and learning activities. In order to use evidence from assessment activities to adapt their teaching to student needs, it is crucial that student teachers also use the opportunities provided for SA, particularly to use students' feedback. Our analyses of the lesson plans suggested that only 60% of the student teachers successfully identified aspects of their practices that they wanted to improve, although all of them were expected to do so. We identify this as a missed opportunity, and suggest that SA should be a key area of improvement of the current model, not least as the ability to improve one's own practice is a crucial part of being a professional teacher. Thus, while we have found that the emphasis on formative assessment at the university is used as a tool to design their R&D reports, the lack of SA practices might be manifesting itself in the student teachers' lacking SA of their own teaching in the lesson plans.

Another issue worth discussing is the nature of the assessment the student teachers participate in at the university and in schools. While they appear to have many opportunities to assess authentic written and oral student work, our findings suggest that at the university, the student teachers are mainly asked to assess finished student work, in line with Wiliam's (2011b) emphasis that assessment has traditionally focused on the effect of various teaching activities after these are over. Our findings indicate that the assessment component at UiO reinforces such practices by overemphasising student teachers' assessment of finished products such as exams, texts and oral presentations. These assessments may have a formative nature, encouraging the student teachers to find ways of improving the student work, and discuss how feedback should be given to the students, but in order to become teachers who practise dependable AfL, they should also be provided with opportunities to provide assessment *before* the students consider their own work finished.

Student teachers should practise how to give feedback to students in different stages of their work, such as during planning and drafting, or in the middle of an activity. Needless to say, a student struggling with deciding how to write, for instance, a science report requires a different kind of feedback than a student who is finishing the report. If student teachers are expected to provide quality feedback at an early stage of students' work and during classroom activities, it is crucial that they encounter such opportunities in their teacher education as well. While our analyses indicate that the student teachers are indeed concerned with providing spontaneous quality feedback at the partner schools (Grossman, Loeb, Cohen, & Wyckoff, 2013), they need to encounter more such situations at the university as well.

Our final topic of discussion concerns the division of responsibility in providing the student teachers with formative assessment on their own work. This is a matter of 'walking the walk' instead of 'talking the talk'; while the student teachers are repeatedly taught the importance of formative assessment and encouraged to assess their students formatively, they experience several summative judgements at the university, but only the voluntary video-based AfL offers formative assessment from the teacher educators. As our findings illustrate, those who participated in this project valued the experience not only as a way to enhance their own learning during practice, but also as a way to experience first-hand the value of formative assessment. We suggest that this video project be made mandatory to integrate formative assessment also at the university. A potential problem in placing the majority of the student teachers' experience in receiving formative assessment at the schools is the very same issue discussed by DeLuca and Klinger (2010), namely that they end up obtaining their confidence in assessment from supervisors who most likely lack explicit assessment education. The recommended increased focus on SA could also be a way to meet this challenge, as SA at UiO could provide important formative assessment experiences.

Conclusion

This study highlights the importance of including assessment training in teacher education programmes using assessment principles as tools in situations where the student teachers are assessed themselves. Introducing, modelling and ensuring assessment principles are used by the student teachers is the teacher educators' responsibility, just as introducing, modelling and ensuring assessment principles are used by their students is a teacher's responsibility. Focusing on the design of assessment situations in which student teachers can transfer, use and perform assessment based on their competence leads to a focus on mastery instead of lack of mastery. This in turn measures more than knowledge and skills, and the assessment principles will ideally be transferable from the university to school practice.

We therefore argue that competence in using assessment principles is an important aspect of teacher education. The idea is that if we can learn more about how assessment education contributes to this relationship, we can help student teachers develop and practise more dependable assessment to respond to their learning needs. It also seems that enabling student teachers to practise formal assessment at the university before designing, participating in and conducting AfL could help develop their assessment capacity, in terms

DEVELOPING TEACHERS' ASSESSMENT CAPACITY

of experiencing assessment on their own performances and exams during as part of their teacher education. It will be interesting to follow future research in this area, and we hope to contribute to this avenue of research.

Notes

1. In Norway, students are obliged to attend primary and lower secondary education (Years 1–10), with a subsequent right to three years' upper secondary education and training (Years 11–13). The national curriculum introduced in 2006 and revised in 2013, *The Knowledge Promotion* (UDIR, 2006), defines students' learning outcome in the school subjects for the Years 1–13.
2. The ME programme at UiO offers 48 different courses of study. The students can choose two school subjects (180 + 60 credits), specialising in one by writing a master thesis. In addition, they take a total of 60 credits of professional teaching courses.
3. http://platorubric.stanford.edu/.
4. This description is inspired by Pearson and Gallagher's (1983) *Gradual Release of Responsibility Model*, which describes a process of how the responsibility for reading comprehension strategy use ideally transfers from the teacher to the student.

Acknowledgements

The authors would like to thank the editors of this special issue of *Assessment in Education: principles, policy & practice*, and the two anonymous reviewers for their invaluable comments on an earlier draft of this article. We would also like to thank The Centre for Professional Learning in Teacher Education (ProTed) at the University of Oslo, for supporting this study.

Disclosure statement

No potential conflict of interest was reported by the authors.

References

Afflerbach, P., & Cho, B. Y. (2011). The classroom assessment of reading. In M. L. Kamil, P. D. Pearson, E. B. Moje, & P. Afflerbach (Eds.), *Handbook of reading research* (Vol. IV, pp. 487–518). London: Routledge.

DEVELOPING TEACHERS' ASSESSMENT CAPACITY

Bazeley, P., & Kemp, L. (2012). Mosaics, triangles, and DNA metaphors for integrated analysis in mixed methods research. *Journal of Mixed Methods Research, 6*, 55–72.

Biggs, J. (1996). Enhancing teaching through constructive alignment. *Higher Education, 32*, 347–364.

Black, P. (2015). Formative assessment – An optimistic but incomplete vision. *Assessment in Education: Principles, Policy & Practice, 22*, 161–177. doi:10.1080/0969594X.2014.999643

Black, P., Harrison, C., Lee, C., Marshall, B., & Wiliam, D. (2004). Working inside the black box: Assessment for learning in the classroom. *Phi Delta Kappan, 86*, 8–21.

Black, P., & Wiliam, D. (1998a). Assessment and classroom learning. *Assessment in Education: Principles, Policy & Practice, 5*, 7–74.

Black, P., & Wiliam, D. (1998b). Inside the black box: Raising the standards through classroom assessment. *Phi Delta Kappan, 80*, 139–148.

Black, P., & Wiliam, D. (2009). Developing the theory of formative assessment. *Educational Assessment, Evaluation and Accountability, 21*, 5–31.

Brevik, L. M. (2015). Strategies and shoes: Can we ever have enough? Teaching and using reading comprehension strategies in general and vocational programmes. *Scandinavian Journal of Educational Research.* doi:10.1080/00313831.2015.1075310

Brevik, L. M., & Blikstad-Balas, M. (2014). 'Blir dette vurdert, laerer?' Om vurdering for læring i klasserommet [Will this be assessed, teacher? On assessment for learning in the classroom]. In E. Elstad & K. Helstad (Eds.), *Profesjonsutvikling i skolen* (pp. 191–206). Oslo: Universitetsforlaget.

Busher, H., & James, N. (2012). The ethical framework of research practice. In A. Briggs, M. Coleman, & M. Morrison (Eds.), *Research methods in educational leadership & management* (3rd ed.). London: SAGE Publications.

Cochran-Smith, M. (2003). Assessing assessment in teacher education. *Journal of Teacher Education, 54*, 187–191.

Cochran-Smith, M., & Fries, K. (2005). Researching teacher education in changing times: Politics and paradigms. In M. Cochran-Smith & K. M. Zeichner (Eds.), *Studying teacher education: The report of the AERA Panel on research and teacher education* (pp. 69–110). Mahwah, NJ: Lawrence Erlbaum Associates Inc.

Creswell, J. W. (2013). *Qualitative inquiry & research design. Choosing among five approaches* (3rd ed.). Los Angeles, CA: Sage.

Creswell, J. W., & Miller, D. L. (2000). Determining validity in qualitative inquiry. *Theory into Practice, 39*, 124–130.

Daniels, H. (2008). *Vygotsky and research.* London: Routledge.

Darling-Hammond, L. (2006). Assessing teacher education: The usefulness of multiple measures for assessing program outcomes. *Journal of Teacher Education, 57*, 120–138.

Darling-Hammond, L., Hammerness, K., Grossman, P., Frances, R., & Shulman, L. (2005). The design of teacher education programs. In Darling-Hammond, L., Bransford, J., LePage, P., Hammerness, K., & Duffy, H. (Eds.), *Preparing teachers for a changing world. What teachers should learn and be able to do* (pp. 390–441). San Francisco: Jossey-Bass.

DeLuca, C., Chavez, T., & Cao, C. (2013). Pedagogies for preservice assessment education: Supporting teacher candidates' assessment literacy development. *The Teacher Educator, 48*, 128–142.

DeLuca, C., & Klinger, D. A. (2010). Assessment literacy development: Identifying gaps in teacher candidates' learning. *Assessment in Education: Principles, Policy & Practice, 17*, 419–438.

Dempster, F. N. (1992). Using tests to promote learning: A neglected classroom resource. *Journal of Research and Development in Education, 25*, 213–217.

Edwards, A. (2015). Designing tasks which engage learners with knowledge. In I. Thompson (Ed.), *Designing tasks in secondary education. Enhancing subject understanding and student engagement* (pp. 13–27). Abingdon: Routledge.

Edwards, A. (in press). The dialectic of person and practice: How cultural-historical accounts of agency can inform teacher education. In J. Clandinin & J. Husu (Eds.) *International Handbook on Research on Teacher Education,* Thousand Oaks, CA: Sage.

Gipps, C. (1999). Socio-cultural aspects of assessment. *Review of Research in Education, 24*, 355–392.

Graham, P. (2005). Classroom-based assessment: Changing knowledge and practice through preservice teacher education. *Teaching and Teacher Education, 21*, 607–621.

Grossman, P., Loeb, S., Cohen, J., & Wyckoff, J. (2013). Measure for measure: The relationship between measures of instructional practice in middle school English language arts and teachers' value-added scores. *American Journal of Education, 119*, 445–470.

Hammerness, K. (2006). From coherence in theory to coherence in practice. *Teachers College Record, 108*, 1241–1265.

Hammerness, K. (2013). Examining features of teacher education in Norway. *Scandinavian Journal of Educational Research, 57*, 400–419.

Hatlevik, I. K. R., & Smeby, J. C. (2015). Programme coherence and epistemological beliefs. *Nordic Psychology, 67*, 136–153.

Hattie, J., & Timperley, H. (2007). The power of feedback. *Review of Educational Research, 77*, 81–112.

Lund, A., & Engelien, K. L. (2015). Oppgaver og vurdering i digitale omgivelser [Tasks and assessment in digital environments]. In U. E. Rindal, A. Lund, & R. E. Jakhelln (Eds.), *Veier til fremragende lærerutdanning* (pp. 136–148). Oslo: Universitetsforlaget.

Mausethagen, S., & Mølstad, C. E. (2015). Shifts in curriculum control: Contesting ideas of teacher autonomy. *Nordic Journal of Studies in Educational Policy, 1*, 30–41.

Newton, P. E. (2007). Clarifying the purposes of educational assessment. *Assessment in Education: Principles, Policy & Practice, 14*, 149–170.

Nicol, D., Thomson, A., & Breslin, C. (2014). Rethinking feedback practices in higher education: a peer review perspective. *Assessment & Evaluation in Higher Education, 39*, 102–122.

Norwegian Directorate for Education and Training [UDIR]. (2006/2013). *Laereplan for grunnskolen og videregående skole* [Curriculum for elementary and secondary school]. Oslo: Author.

Norwegian Directorate for Education and Training [UDIR]. (2010). *Underveisvurdering i fag. Lære mer og bedre – hvilken betydning har læreres vurderingspraksis?* [Assessment for learning in the disciplines. Learning more and better – What is the effects of teachers' assessment practice?]. Oslo: Author.

Norwegian Directorate for Education and Training [UDIR]. (2011). *Grunnlagsdokument. Satsingen Vurdering for Laering 2010–2014* [Main document. Programme Assessment for Learning 2010–2014]. Oslo: Author.

Norwegian Ministry of Education and Research [KD]. (2013). *Forskrift om rammeplan for lektorutdanning for trinn 8–13* [National curriculum for five-year teacher education programmes]. Oslo: Author.

Patton, M. Q. (1999). Enhancing the quality and credibility of qualitative analysis. *Health Services Research, 34*, 1189–1208.

Pearson, P. D., & Gallagher, M. C. (1983). The instruction of reading comprehension. *Contemporary Educational Psychology, 8*, 317–344.

Ryen, A. (2011). Ethics and qualitative research. In D. Silverman (Ed.), *Qualitative research* (3rd ed., pp. 416–438). London: Sage.

Stiggins, R. J. (2004). *Classroom assessment for student learning: Doing it right – using it well.* Portland, OR: Assessment Training Institute.

Stobart, G. (2006). Influencing classroom assessment. *Assessment in Education Principles, Policy, & Practice, 13*, 235–238.

Stobart, G. (2008). Introduction. In G. Stobart (Ed.), *Testing times. The uses and abuses of assessment* (pp. 1–11). Oxon: Routledge.

Tiknaz, Y., & Sutton, A. (2006). Exploring the role of assessment tasks to promote formative assessment in Key Stage 3 geography: Evidence from twelve teachers. *Assessment in Education: Principles, Policy, & Practice, 13*, 327–343.

Tveit, S. (2014). Educational assessment in Norway. *Assessment in Education: Principles, Policy & Practice, 21*, 221–237.

Volante, L., & Fazio, X. (2007). Exploring teacher candidates' assessment literacy: Implications for teacher education reform and professional development. *Canadian Journal of Education, 30*, 749–770.

Vygotsky, L. S. (1986). *Thought and language.* A. Kozulin (Ed.). London: MIT Press.

Wiliam, D. (2010). The role of formative assessment in effective learning environments. In H. Dumont, D. Istance, & F. Benavides (Eds.), *The nature of learning: Using research to inspire practice* (pp. 135–159). Paris: OECD Publishing.

Wiliam, D. (2011a). *Embedded formative assessment*. Bloomington, IN: Solution Tree Press.

Wiliam, D. (2011b). What is assessment for learning? *Studies in Educational Evaluation, 37*, 3–14.

Assessment for equity: learning how to use evidence to scaffold learning and improve teaching

Mary F. Hill ⓘ, Fiona Ell, Lexie Grudnoff, Mavis Haigh, Marilyn Cochran-Smith, Wen-Chia Chang and Larry Ludlow

ABSTRACT

This article examines evidence regarding the assessment learning of preservice teachers (PTs) in a new Master of Teaching designed to prepare teachers to address the less than equitable outcomes of certain groups of students in New Zealand. The assessment curriculum was integrated across all of the courses and the in-school experiences as one of six interconnected facets of practice for equity. Evidence about the assessment learning of 27 preservice teachers was collected using a survey, interpretive analysis of three assignments and a focus group interview. The findings demonstrated that preservice teachers combined theory and practice encountered in many contexts to build the assessment understanding and competence needed to address equity issues. We argue that this was facilitated by incorporating the assessment curriculum within each course, intertwining university and school experiences, and the specific focus on addressing equity throughout the programme.

Introduction

In 2013, the New Zealand Ministry of Education called for proposals from teacher preparation providers to offer programmes that intentionally prepared teachers who can achieve positive and equitable outcomes for priority learners. In New Zealand, priority learners are groups of students who have been identified as historically not experiencing success in the schooling system (Ministry of Education, 2014), including many Māori and Pacific learners, those from low socio-economic backgrounds and students with special education needs. The Master of teaching (M Tchg) degree, a one-year postgraduate programme, was designed and implemented in response to this call with six facets of practice for equity, explained below, at its core. This article explores preservice teachers' learning regarding one of those facets: facet 4, using evidence to scaffold learning and improve teaching, a set of principles for practice aligned with the formative use of assessment. We argue that preparing preservice teachers (PTs) for their assessment role is challenging and that incorporating assessment learning within all courses, and interweaving it through coursework, observations of classroom teaching and learning, and teaching practice, builds the foundations for using assessment formatively as one approach to increasing educational equity.

Using evidence to scaffold learning and inform teaching, and assessment for learning

In order to understand what it would take to put equity at the centre in initial teacher education (Cochran-Smith et al., 2016), the authors of this article have been working together for some years on Project Rethinking Initial Teacher Education for Equity (RITE). An aspect of this work has been to describe the concept of 'patterns of practice for equity' (Grudnoff et al., 2015), which the Project RITE team developed based on an analysis of selected international research syntheses and programmes of research. We intentionally selected and considered five very different syntheses/frameworks, undertaken in a range of countries and different from one another in purpose, scope and format in order to see whether, despite such differences, we could find similarities that could inform our work as researchers and teacher educators who were concerned about equity-centred teacher education. As described in more detail elsewhere (Grudnoff et al., 2015), we reasoned that similar findings about successful practice for equitable outcomes for marginalised students across such diverse contexts would yield principles that might justifiably form the foundation of an initial teacher education programme with equity at the centre.

Using directed qualitative content analysis procedures (Hsieh & Shannon, 2005), six interconnected principles or facets of practice for equity emerged. These are: (1) selecting worthwhile content and designing and implementing learning opportunities aligned to valued learning outcomes; (2) connecting to students as learners, and their lives and experiences; (3) creating learning-focused, respectful and supportive learning environments; (4) using evidence to scaffold learning and improve teaching; (5) adopting an inquiry stance and taking responsibility for professional engagement and learning; and, (6) recognising and challenging classroom, school and societal practices that reproduce inequity. A careful process of validation followed using both team members and external academics (Grudnoff et al., 2015).

Our iterative process of research evidence comparison indicated that, while distinguishable, the six facets of practice for equity are highly contextualised as well as interconnected and, because each pattern is in relationship with other patterns, it would be difficult to enact one of these practices without enacting many of the others. A further analysis of the five programmes of research evidence identified teaching actions associated with each facet (Chang & Ludlow, 2016). For facet 4, using evidence to scaffold learning and improve teaching to bring about more equitable outcomes, these practices are:

- Designs classroom assessment that is well integrated into instructional activities.
- Circulates and interacts with students, using a variety of approaches (e.g. questions, prompts and traditional tests) to elicit evidence of diverse students' learning.
- Provides timely, substantive, constructive and highly responsive feedback.
- Is flexible and responsive in adjusting instruction and using alternative approaches to help all students to learn based on the results of diagnostic assessment.
- Proactively involves students in the process of setting specific learning goals, and students are fully aware of the assessment criteria.

DEVELOPING TEACHERS' ASSESSMENT CAPACITY

- Provides an evaluative climate that is positive, and all students are motivated to learn and engage in self-monitoring their own progress.

These indicators are similar to the guiding principles of assessment for learning (AfL) (Assessment Reform Group, 1999) and demonstrate that using evidence to scaffold learning and improve teaching is intimately related to the formative purpose of assessment. Formative assessment uses information gathered from both formal instruments such as tests and diagnostic tools, and from day to day, minute by minute observations, to gain insight into students' learning, and then uses this information to adapt teaching and assist students to better learn whatever is the goal of the learning process (Bennett, 2011; Black & Wiliam, 1998a). Black and Wiliam describe formative assessment in this way:

> Practice in a classroom is formative to the extent that evidence about student achievement is elicited, interpreted, and used by teachers, learners, or their peers, to make decisions about the next steps in instruction that are likely to be better, or better founded, than the decisions they would have taken in the absence of the evidence that was elicited. (2009, p. 9)

Though subject to appropriate critique (for example, Bennett, 2011; Shute, 2008), there is a large body of evidence that indicates that formative assessment using valid evidence to make informed inferences about student understanding, providing appropriate feedback and scaffolding, and involving the learner in the process, can improve student outcomes (Bennett, 2011; Black & Wiliam, 1998a, 1998b). Providing formative evaluation was ranked third in effect size of 138 influences related to student achievement in a meta-analysis by Hattie (2008), with feedback as one of the most powerful ways to raise student achievement.

There is also evidence that the effective use of formative assessment can promote more equitable outcomes for students most at risk of underachievement. Several OECD case study schools, where students had moved from 'failing' to 'exemplary', featured a shift to formative practices (OECD, 2005). Studies have also demonstrated that where teachers adjust their teaching to work consistently with formative assessment principles to recognise cultural, linguistic and individual differences, more equitable outcomes can be achieved (Bishop, Berryman, Cavanagh, & Teddy, 2009; Bishop & Glynn, 1999; Shepard, 2001). An important aspect of teacher preparation, therefore, is to ensure that new teachers understand and can implement such formative practices.

Despite the promise of formative assessment for improving learning and addressing equity issues, assessment experts caution that formative assessment is 'a formidable undertaking' (Black & Wiliam, 1998a, p. 63) as rather than providing a framework or model for teachers to follow, the research evidence provides a set of guiding principles that each teacher in his or her own way needs to incorporate in daily classroom practice (Bennett, 2011; Hill, 2000). Bennett summarises these guiding principles as a big idea of 'students and teachers using evidence to adapt teaching and learning to meet immediate learning needs minute by minute and day by day' (ETS, 2010 cited in Bennett, 2011, p. 8). Five principles (Black & Wiliam, 2009) follow from this idea: clarifying learning goals and intentions; facilitating classroom activities such that evidence of learning is elicited; providing differential and plentiful feedback; engaging students as owners of their own learning; and, involving peers as critical friends in the assessment and feedback process. These principles guide 'assessment for learning'. Fuller explanations of, and discussions about, AfL can be found in a publication of the same name (Assessment Reform Group, 1999) and more recently in Klenowski (2009), Swaffield (2011) and Smith (2016). Internationally, efforts are underway to understand how teachers learn to implement these principles in practice (for example, Kanjee & Mthembu, 2015; O'Leary, Lysaught, & Ludlow, 2013; Poskitt, 2014) and perhaps even more challenging, how PTs come to understand and use this guidance (DeLuca, Chavez, Bellara, & Cao, 2013; DeLuca & Klinger, 2010; Eyers, 2014; Hill, Smith, Cowie, Gilmore, & Gunn, 2013).

Preparing preservice teachers for their assessment role

Existing reviews of the assessment learning of PTs (Brookhart, 2001; Campbell, 2013; Hill & Eyers, 2016) demonstrate that the complexity of teaching and assessment, and the diversity of contexts in which PTs experience teaching and assessment practices, present challenges in changing preservice teacher assessment attitudes, conceptions and practices. Just as studies of classroom teachers have consistently reported less than optimal assessment skills and knowledge (Campbell, 2013; Dixon, 2011; Hill, 2000; McMillan, Myran, & Workman, 2002), studies of PTs entering teacher education show that they have low levels of confidence and negative views about assessment (Smith, Hill, Cowie, & Gilmore, 2014; Volante & Fazio, 2007; Wang, Kao, & Lin, 2010), value the formative worth of assessment but feel unable to implement it (Winterbottom et al., 2008), and have conceptions of assessment that differ from those of practising teachers (Brown, 2011; Brown & Remesal, 2012). Research attention has recently turned to finding ways to prepare PTs for their complex assessment role including, but not limited to, formative assessment (DeLuca & Klinger, 2010). Changing such conceptions and emotions can be challenging (Richardson & Placier, 2001), and studies have raised questions about the effectiveness of assessment coursework (Alkharusi, Kazem, & Al-Musawai, 2011; Chen, 2005; DeLuca & Klinger, 2010; Smith et al., 2014). Changes are often partial, may not affect all PTs within a programme (Buck, Trauth-Nare, & Kaftan, 2010; Smith et al., 2014) and studies have suggested that 'one dedicated assessment course is not enough, on its own, to bring about the substantial changes required to prepare assessment literate teachers' (Hill, Ell, Grudnoff, & Limbrick, 2014, p. 107).

Variable outcomes in assessment preparation also appear to relate to the extent to which assessment preparation is embedded within authentic teaching practice in school classrooms (DeLuca & Klinger, 2010; Jiang, 2015). In the absence of specific teaching, practicum becomes the primary site for assessment learning, posing both benefits and risks, depending on what the PTs experience (DeLuca & Klinger, 2010). Due to mentor teachers' powerful influence, PTs can learn by simply copying the practices they see, rather than building their own conceptual base or having a critically reflective approach. Thus, finding ways to intertwine course work and practice-based learning is an important goal for teacher preparation. Furthermore, preservice teachers' status within the profession means that teaching practices associated with assessment are not simply something that PTs have more or less facility with, or accept or reject. Rather, the use of such practices 'require(s) constant situational negotiation' (Nolen, Horn, Ward, & Childers, 2011, p. 90) with those who might have different status, such as mentor teachers, course lecturers, learners in schools and their parents. Building upon small case studies of up to eight PTs (for example, Eyers, 2014; Nolen et al., 2011) and surveys (for example, DeLuca & Klinger, 2010) that have suggested the importance of aligning coursework with practice in assessment learning, we explored the assessment learning of an entire primary PT cohort within an innovative programme in the New Zealand assessment context.

The New Zealand context

New Zealand is diverse in terms of its ethnic, religious, and linguistic makeup. While Māori (the country's indigenous population) comprise about 15% of the population, 25% of New Zealand's population was born overseas, mainly in Europe and the Pacific Islands (the Cook Islands, Niue, Samoa and Tonga), and in Asia, particularly China, India and Korea (NZ Census, 2013). The university at which the M Tchg is taught is located in a large, ethnically and culturally diverse city. While differential achievement by groups of students is an international problem, New Zealand has been identified as a 'high achievement, low equity' country (OECD, 2011) because on international tests such as TIMSS and PISA, students who are Māori and Pacific Islanders are over-represented in the low achieving group, while European New Zealanders and Asian students are over-represented in the high achieving group (Snook & O'Neill, 2014).

The New Zealand government's aim is to reduce the achievement gap to become a high achievement and high equity nation. Improving the quality of teacher preparation is viewed as being a key to achieving this aim (New Zealand Government, 2010). Hence, in 2013, the Ministry of Education introduced a competitive tendering process for 'exemplary post-graduate initial teacher education programmes' to 'improve the expertise of graduating teachers and to strengthen their practice' (New Zealand Ministry of Education, 2013, p. 2). The programme had to be more intellectually demanding (i.e. tougher entrance criteria and located at postgraduate level) and more practice-focused (i.e. greater time on practicum in schools in partnership with universities) than traditional preparation programmes. The aim was to lift the quality of graduating teachers' practice in order to raise student achievement, particularly those who are at most risk of under achievement. The university's proposal for a M Tchg was one of two programmes contracted in the first round of the highly competitive tendering process. The process provided the university with an opportunity to design an innovative programme that put equity at the centre of teacher education, and gave Project RITE the chance to investigate how these PTs learn to use evidence to scaffold learning and improve their teaching as defined earlier in this paper and use assessment to recognise and challenge inequity.

The focus of this article is on the first cohort of the M Tchg, and specifically on how PTs learnt to use evidence to improve their teaching and scaffold learning with their students (facet 4). In 2014–2015 the M Tchg was taught in 1 year across three semesters in partnership with 13 local primary schools with very diverse student populations. In the first week of the programme, PTs were immersed in a cultural programme that connected them to the language and world-views of Māori. For the majority of the rest of the programme, the PTs spent two days each week in two different partner schools and three days on campus. They also had a full-time teaching practicum in each semester: a three-week practicum in November in the same school as their two days a week in the first semester; and, in the final semester, an eight week practicum comprising two weeks in February at the start of the school year and six weeks in May–June at the end of the semester at the school in a low socio-economic area they had been working in. Over the summer semester, PTs undertook two campus-based summer school courses, one focused on social justice and the other on accelerating the learning of priority students through the use of assessment data in mathematics and literacy.

The M Tchg team worked collaboratively to construct every course around the six facets of practice for equity, and to embody the facets in the content, teaching and assessment of each course. In contrast with traditional approaches to structuring teacher education programmes around primary school curriculum areas, this programme placed different curriculum areas in juxtaposition to each other as a way of making the facets of practice for equity obvious and more relevant to the PTs. For example, mathematics and literacy were intentionally integrated and taught by cross-disciplinary teams in three courses across the programme. The courses focused on teaching to promote equity, including a focus on how assessment evidence might be used formatively to increase achievement, especially for priority learners.

Embedded within all courses, and within work in schools, were multiple opportunities to consider, use and critique how each of the indicators of facet 4 could address the needs of priority learners. In the study reported in this article, PTs' responses to the three mathematics and literacy courses were examined. These courses wove the use of assessment data through their content and in school teaching activities. Furthermore, in each, course assignments were designed to have the PTs critically examine and explain how they had engaged with facet 4 during their coursework, professional reading and practicum experiences. Towards the end of the first semester, PTs were asked to write a series of extended paragraphs critically examining their in-class tasks in relation to the facets of practice for equity. In the second semester, following practical involvement in using assessment data from observations and diagnostic tests in school classrooms, PTs were asked to summarise the assessment data, note the specific strengths and needs of particular learners, make judgements about these learners against the national standards, describe the possible next steps for learning, the strategies they might use for these and alternative approaches they might use if those didn't work. Following this, they wrote critical reflections with reference to the assessment literature in the course readings about wider issues arising from their decisions in this assignment.

In the third semester of the programme, the PTs were required to draw on observations, reflections on their own teaching and evidence of student learning, to identify an inquiry focus that they then investigated during their final practicum. In this assignment, they justified their focus in terms of their students' learning needs, their own strengths and needs as teachers, relevant research literature, and in relation to the facets of practice for equity. The inquiry served to further integrate their on-campus and in-school experiences and provided another opportunity to consider how they might use evidence to inform their teaching and address equitable outcomes for their students. These assignments exemplify how facet 4 was woven throughout the programme, in courses, in the PTs' work in schools and through their assessment requirements and how the infusion of indicators for using evidence to scaffold learning and inform teaching was deliberate and sustained. The purpose of our study, therefore, was to investigate what assessment understandings PTs developed in a programme designed to prepare teachers to teach for equity. Specifically, the research questions were: What assessment understandings do PTs develop in a programme designed to prepare teachers to teach for equity? And, in what programme contexts do these understandings develop?

Method

The first iteration of the M Tchg took place between July 2014 and June 2015. Following ethical approval, all PTs in the programme were invited, and 27 consented, to participate in research and evaluation designed to understand how the programme influenced their learning and implementation of practice for equity.

Data sources

Four data sources provided the evidence for the findings in this article. The PTs completed an electronic questionnaire at entry and exit comprising demographic questions and 126 Likert-type items. The survey (Grudnoff, Ward, Ritchie, Brooker, & Simpson, 2013) relates to perceptions of preparedness to teach, and use of a range of practices known to positively influence diverse students' learning (Grudnoff et al., 2015). The tool was developed and trialled by a team of researchers and expert teacher educators from three universities and was pilot tested twice with PTs in two universities. Data were analysed to determine the performance and robustness of the tool. Redundant items identified due to high correlation with other items were removed following expert agreement to ensure the items that were retained had the strongest face validity. Feedback was sought and received from experienced teacher educators from three universities to ensure the survey responses related to learning to teach consistent with the intent of the National Curriculum (Ministry of Education, 2007) and the NZ Graduating Teacher Standards (Education Council, n.d.) and iterative changes have been made to improve the survey. The items were designed generically to apply across programmes, that is, the survey items are not programme specific and the survey is now used frequently to track preparedness to teach across NZ teacher education institutions. Five of the Likert-type items focused on their confidence in aspects of assessment (see Table 1 below).

The second data source comprised the responses to open-ended questions drawn from an earlier study of the assessment learning of New Zealand PTs (Hill et al., 2013). These were also administered before and after the programme to access participants' understandings regarding assessment practices and purposes:

- Imagine you were in a classroom where assessment is taking place. What would you see the teacher doing? What would you see the students doing?
- In your teacher education programme you will (have been) learning about assessment. Why do you think assessment is important?

Table 1. Confidence to incorporate identified assessment practices by respondent group.

| | Entry ($n = 27$) | | Matched sample | | | | | |
| | | | Entry $n = 12$ | | Exit $n = 12$ | | | |
	$\bar{X}$	SD	$\bar{X}$	SD	$\bar{X}$	SD	t	p-value
Communicating with parents and caregivers about their children's learning	3.29	.897	3.33	.779	4.42	.669	−4.73	.001
Establishing and articulating goals with individual learners	3.11	.875	3.25	.754	4.17	.718	−3.53	.005
Supporting individual learners to reflect on and assess their own learning	3.04	.793	3.17	.577	4.25	.622	−4.73	.001
Collecting multiple sources of information to assess learning	2.86	1.113	2.83	.937	4.83	.937	−4.90	<.001
Using multiple sources of information to assess learning	2.86	1.079	2.83	.835	4.83	.937	−5.42	<.001
Using assessment practices and other evidence to inform your teaching	2.82	.905	2.92	.900	4.33	.492	−4.21	.001

A third data source comprised a content analysis of the three mathematics and literacy course assignments, described above, submitted during the programme. These assignments were selected because they sampled the PTs' understandings about facet 4 across the three semesters of the programme.

Lastly, a focus group interview with nine of the PTs was held at the conclusion of the programme. The interview was not focused on their assessment learning but asked five general questions:

(1) Why do you think some practices are more effective than others?
(2) How can you use student assessment information to reflect on teaching?
(3) How will you know if your practice is culturally and linguistically responsive?
(4) How do the assumptions you bring to teaching influence your practice?
(5) How might you inquire with others about how effective you are being for your students?

Participants

Twenty-seven PTs participated. Data from Likert-type items regarding confidence in assessment in the entry and exit surveys are reported for a matched sample of respondents ($n = 12$) who completed both the entry and exit survey. In both groups (the full cohort and the matched sample), the majority of respondents were female (85%, 91%), the most common age group was 21–25 (39, 42%), the largest group identified as New Zealanders (36, 50%) with English as their first language (86, 92%). The respondents were more likely than not to come from families where someone else had been to university (86, 75%).

Analysis

The open-ended survey responses, assignments and the interviews were transcribed and the qualitative data assembled as numbered texts. Each individual participant was assigned a code number and the texts were analysed qualitatively against the indicators of facet 4 and then open coded for other information about assessment learning. Specifically, the first author and a research assistant conversant with qualitative content analysis each independently read the students' responses/assignments and labelled all relevant statements according to the theoretical facet 4 indicators. Any assessment ideas or practices that did not fit these predetermined categories, or provided information about assessment learning, were also noted and open coded. Coding decisions were then compared and discrepancies were discussed and any inconsistencies were addressed.

Findings

Analysis of the Likert-type items in the surveys indicated that on a six point positively packed confidence scale (1 = not confident at all, 2 = slightly confident, 3 = moderately confident, 4 = highly confident, 5 = very highly confident, 6 = extremely confident) this cohort had felt slightly confident to collect and use multiple sources of information to assess learning at entry to the programme, but at exit, most reported feeling highly/very highly

DEVELOPING TEACHERS' ASSESSMENT CAPACITY

Table 2. Frequency with which indicators were included in responses to the entry and exit open-ended item responses.

Indicators of using assessment to scaffold learning and improve teaching	Percentage of PTs including indicator at entry ($n = 27$)	Percentage of PTs including indicator at exit ($n = 14$)
1. Teacher designs classroom assessment well integrated into instructional activities	–	50%
2. Teacher circulates and interacts with students, uses various approaches to elicit evidence of diverse students' learning	36%	57%
3. Teacher provides timely, substantive, constructive and responsive feedback	–	7%
4. Teacher is flexible and responsive in adjusting instruction and uses alternative approaches to help all students to learn based on diagnostic assessment	25%	36%
5. Teacher involves students in the process of setting specific learning goals, students fully aware of the assessment criteria	–	14%
6. Evaluative climate is positive, students are motivated to learn and engage in self-monitoring their own progress	4%	–

confident. Significance testing (using paired-sample t-tests) was undertaken for the matched sample. Correlations between entry and exit were also tested for the matched sample and for most items the correlation was weak (less than .4), suggesting very little relationship between responses to the two surveys. As one would normally expect correlations of at least .7 when retesting using the same tool (with no other intervening variable), it appears that there was a great deal more movement in how people responded in this group than would normally be expected. The conclusion to be drawn is that there was a lot more movement in how people responded than would normally be expected. There were also high standard deviations in most instances.

Confidence had also increased from moderately confident to highly confident by exit for: communicating with parents about children's learning; establishing and articulating their learning goals with individual learners; supporting learners to reflect upon and assess their own learning; and, using assessment practices and other evidence to inform teaching (see Table 1). Thus, while the number of respondents to the exit survey was disappointing, indications are that the cohort left the programme more confident about their ability to use evidence from assessment to support learners and inform their teaching.

The qualitative analysis of the open-ended items from the entry and exit surveys also showed clear evidence that participants' ideas about, and understanding of, aspects of assessment changed during the programme. Using the indicators of facet 4 as a frame, analysis revealed that there was an increase in the times indicators 1–6 were mentioned in the exit survey (see Table 2).

By the end of the programme more PTs were aware of a range of strategies for using evidence for improving teaching and assisting learners. The PTs also provided responses relating to giving and taking tests (82% entry, 64% exit), giving/listening to instructions (18% entry), being anxious (10% entry), comparing outcomes with a standard or other students' results (28% exit), or undertaking collegial analysis (7% exit). Thus, the surveys indicated that over the course of the programme, PTs expanded their ideas about the use and importance of assessment, and the use of the information gained from it.

DEVELOPING TEACHERS' ASSESSMENT CAPACITY

Table 3. Number of PT assignments demonstrating evidence of understanding indicators of facet 4 in four different contexts.

Contexts of learning	Indicators of facet 4			
	Participating in university courses, activities, assignments, readings	Observing teachers during 2 days a week in a classroom	Reflecting on own teaching during practicum and during 2 days per week in a classroom	Experiencing assessment of their own learning in the programme
1. Teacher designs classroom assessment well integrated into instructional activities	9	9	16	–
2. Teacher circulates and interacts with students, uses various approaches to elicit evidence of diverse students' learning	16	10	14	–
3. Teacher provides timely, substantive, constructive and responsive feedback	14	1	6	3
4. Teacher is flexible and responsive in adjusting instruction and uses alternative approaches to help all students to learn based on diagnostic assessment	19	14	14	–
5. Teacher involves students in the process of setting specific learning goals, students fully aware of the assessment criteria	15	6	3	3
6. Evaluative climate is positive, students are motivated to learn and engage in self-monitoring their own progress	18	5	6	–

Most PTs (23/27) demonstrated very different ideas about assessment between their entry and exit responses. Indicative of this, PT 26 stated on entry that during assessment in a classroom, the teacher would be 'supervising the students … or sitting at the teachers' desk reading or marking assignments'. But at exit, PT 26 stated that 'it depends on the type of assessment. For summative, you might see the teacher testing or doing running records (of reading). For formative … just see the teacher talking with the students or observing them/listening to them while they are working'. Four PTs though did not appear to have moved beyond viewing assessment as a summative practice. For example, responding to the same question, PT 3 at entry stated '(t)he teacher would have prepared the assessment ahead of time. This could be an online assessment or on paper', and at exit wrote 'Setting the children up on their chrome books, guiding them to open Google drive and find the (test) document prepared, then starting the assessment…'.

The entry survey suggests most arrived with summative views, with 19/27 responding to questions about what the teachers and students would be doing during some assessment by describing a formal test situation. Some, however, began the programme already conversant with different purposes for assessment. For example, PT 07, who had had some prior teaching experiences, wrote at entry about the formative and summative purposes of assessment. While this response was different from most, it demonstrates that the PTs entered the programme with varied experiences and knowledge about this facet of practice.

Seventy-two assignments were available for analysis; 22 from the first semester, 25 from the second and 25 from the third. As the assignments served different purposes, it was not possible to trace individual PT progress across each of the assignments. However, the assignments provided a great deal of information about the PTs developing knowledge and understanding of assessment and the influence of the programme across contexts in which they were learning about it.

As Table 3 demonstrates, the PTs wrote about each of the six indicators of using evidence for improving teaching and scaffolding learning. In particular, the PTs in this cohort focused upon ways the teacher circulates and interacts to elicit evidence of learning (Indicator 2) and adjusts teaching based on the use of diagnostic assessments (indicator 4). Sixteen (of the 25) drew on readings and class activities to describe how teachers circulate to collect such evidence, 14 indicated how they reflected on their own practice of doing so and 10 described observing how their mentor teachers approached this. Five PTs wove their learning from all three contexts together. For example, demonstrating how important informal observations were, one PT stated, 'On a day-to-day basis the teachers at the school where I have been working collect regular information on how the students are progressing, and what they do and do not understand' (PT 20). Then went on:

> I used a range of information sources to base my lessons on from observations, running record data, samples from their workbooks, and conversations with the children. In this way teachers learn 'what is working and what is not, and are able to make informed teaching and learning decisions'. (Anthony and Walshaw, 2007, p. 17)

Twenty PTs provided 90 statements about teachers using the results of diagnostic tools to adjust teaching. More than half (14), provided examples from observing such practice and from their own teaching experiences. Indicative of these was PT 10:

> I have discovered my observations and reflections heavily influence my method of teaching. I found my knowledge of students and a wide range of GloSS[1] and asTTle[2] testing helped me to determine what they need next for further learning. I was able to offer different approaches to the same problem as I recognised the ways certain students 'viewed' the equation.

Confirming the findings of smaller case study research (e.g. Eyers, 2014) and surveys (e.g. DeLuca & Klinger, 2010), these PTs clearly understood the need to gather evidence in both formal and informal settings to find out what students are learning and make judgements about progress and achievement.

Indicators 1, 3, 5 and 6 received less attention. Assessment integrated into instructional activities appeared to be less obvious to the PTs than ways to elicit evidence or use diagnostic tools although 16 of the PTs did include ways they had achieved this in their own teaching. Perhaps surprising, given the importance of feedback to formative assessment, was the lower number of inclusions for indicator 3, providing timely, substantive, constructive and responsive feedback. Although just over half (14) noted this in reference to their reading, only six gave examples of giving feedback themselves and only one reported observing teachers doing this. Three mentioned that receiving such feedback from lecturers and mentor teachers was helpful for their own learning.

Involving students in the assessment process and motivating them to engage in self-assessment and monitoring were also included less often within these assignments. This finding is aligned with a previous New Zealand study (Smith et al., 2014). While the PTs cited readings to support their statements about these two indicators, few reported observing teachers using such strategies or trying them out themselves.

From this analysis, it appears that the course activities, readings and assignments are central to stimulating thinking about this facet. This is borne out by the number of times the

DEVELOPING TEACHERS' ASSESSMENT CAPACITY

PTs drew on their course activities, and readings. Given that these data were in assignments, this is perhaps an obvious finding. However, in most (though not all) cases, the PTs built on that coursework and related it to their observations of teachers using evidence. They often commented upon what they had observed more experienced teachers doing during their two-day in school component and during the practicum blocks. PTs also reflected on their own teaching when considering how facet 4 could be enacted and discussed this in relation to their reading about assessment.

Those demonstrating a richer understanding of facet 4 tended to integrate their reading with what they had witnessed and how this might impact their own future practice. Hence, the course work was used to bind the information together. For example, from the course activities PT 6 noted in the assignment ,'the running record is a valid assessment tool as it has been designed to assess the strategies Tom uses and also those he needs to develop … thus it provides the teacher with a course of action'. This PT described ways in which s/he had observed a teacher using evidence to adjust teaching, '(w)hen the teacher observed the students were able to individually complete the questions she moved the instruction into the ZPD by setting a more challenging task of finding fractions in kilograms, litres, dollars'. And then went further to reflect on his/her own use of evidence to adjust teaching. 'A more appropriate approach would be (for me) to model the process, scaffold the appropriate vocabulary and to break the process of peer feedback into manageable chunks for learners and follow this up with feedback and the opportunity to practice'.

This intertwining of information from several learning contexts provides evidence that the structure of the programme, combining university coursework with regular time in schools, as well as embedding assessment learning within a combined math and literacy context, enabled most PTs in this cohort to build conceptions of how assessment supports learning.

In addition to demonstrating understanding related to the different aspects of facet 4, several other important assessment concepts appeared regularly within the PTs' assignments. In one assignment, the PTs were asked to discuss the process of making overall teacher judgements, an essential component of comparing student achievement against national standards in New Zealand. Through this assignment, in particular, most (23/25) demonstrated a developing understanding of validity and reliability in the use of assessments. Ten of the 25 PTs elaborated upon the use of moderation processes where teachers collaborate and discuss assessment; for example, what it means to 'meet the standard' in making overall teacher judgements. And, crucially, over half (17/25) examined the equity and fairness issues that teachers must consider in order to address inequalities. Assessment purposes and the need to use 'fit for purpose' assessment in order to support and improve learning were included by nine PTs and two noted possible negative effects of assessment. In summary, these assignments provided a great deal of evidence about the PTs' assessment learning and suggested that the way the programme was designed and structured had supported this development.

Interviews with nine volunteer PTs at exit from the programme provided an opportunity to delve further into how they had come to understand and make sense of the facets of practice for equity, particularly facet 4. The PTs confirmed the importance of the integration of coursework and time in schools. '(B)ecause we were actually teaching so I had to reflect on what I was actually doing and I think it was the first time I really thought about it, quite critically about my practice' (PT 3). And PT 10 concurred: 'I think being in a more culturally diverse school for the second practicum really changed things up because you were seeing how to be really culturally responsive; I didn't get that in my first practicum school'.

The PTs also credited involvement in courses as instrumental in assisting them to use evidence in their teaching. For example, PT 10 stated that 'using the assessment information really clicked for me in the first semester of this year (summer school), particularly with the teaching for social justice and the [maths/literacy] courses'. When asked why, PT 10 said 'I guess the assignments and asking us to provide the next steps, reflecting on our teaching, looking at the outcomes of the students, designing proper assessment for them to assist their learning'.

Confirming the evidence from the assignment analysis, another indicated that it was towards the end of the programme, in the last practicum, that they gained confidence understanding and implementing assessment. PT 11 explained how the interweaving of the ideas about assessment in courses with the opportunity to use these in the last six-week practicum in semester 3 had been critical.

> Like we learnt about these things all the way through … but … I didn't really understand them or use them until the six weeks when I was just doing that on a day-to-day basis. Like … assessment for learning, I understood what it was but I didn't really use that, or really feel comfortable or confident with that until the six weeks and I think what really helped me with the assessment one was (the) Maths and Literacy papers. I thought they were really, really helpful for gaining knowledge and how to use assessment.

PT 11 then referred specifically to assessment for learning, explaining how theoretical ideas really began to make sense when used in practice.

> Like … assessment for learning, I understood what it was but I didn't really use that, or really feel comfortable or confident with that until the six weeks (practicum). (M)y AT (mentor teacher) on my first practicum showed me all of her assessment and why she was planning lessons a certain way, but that was only superficial understanding for me until … actually using that in the six week practicum.

These extracts demonstrate how even though the programme was short in duration in comparison with three-year undergraduate programmes, the focus on this facet throughout the programme, the interweaving of theory and practice across the programme in innovative courses and alignment between what was included in the courses and how assessment was practised in the partner schools all appeared to assist the PTs to learn to use assessment evidence for multiple purposes.

Discussion

By the end of their programme, most of this cohort had engaged with and learnt much about using evidence to scaffold learning and improve teaching and about other aspects of assessment literacy including reliability, validity and fairness and moderation, all necessary to assist them in recognising and challenging inequities that can arise through assessment processes. Like PTs in other similar studies (Brown, 2011; DeLuca et al., 2012; Hill et al., 2014), most had entered teacher preparation with mainly summative views regarding assessment. Analysis of responses to open-ended questions suggested that, at entry, they mainly understood assessment as testing in formal exam-like conditions. In comparison with the entry data, at exit, most of these PTs were more positive and confident about assessment, and had expanded their ideas about the use of assessment information. In contrast with Campbell (2013) who argued that teacher preparation in assessment has been less than adequate and that formal instruction in assessment may be overridden by either teaching practice experiences and/or certain personal characteristics of the PTs themselves, this study suggests that a programme with an interwoven focus on curriculum and assessment can change ideas and understanding and, hopefully, practice.

In contrast with previous studies where either no assessment courses were included in the programme (Jiang, 2015) or a separate assessment course was included (DeLuca et al., 2010; Eyers, 2014), the PTs in this programme encountered assessment as a facet of practice for equity within most of their courses and these experiences were purposefully linked with observing and using assessment in classrooms on a weekly basis. While this configuration appears to have had an impact upon their assessment learning, it was surprising that there were not more references to the importance and use of feedback and involving learners in goal setting and their own assessment as these aspects of assessment for learning are also important for using evidence for scaffolding learning and improving teaching.

The PTs in this study are not alone in finding these aspects of facet 4 challenging to develop, however. Findings from studies regarding teachers' (Kanjee & Mthembu, 2015; O'Leary et al., 2013) and preservice teachers' (DeLuca & Klinger, 2010; Hill et al., 2013) assessment practices and learning confirm that these aspects develop slowly for many. This finding is important for assessment course instructors. We speculate that although each of these aspects was taught within the programme, they may not have had as much attention drawn to them as to the other indicators and speculate that these practices might have been less visible in classrooms also. Studies of teachers within the same city (Dixon et al., 2011; Hawe et al., 2008) have reported that despite a national assessment strategy emphasising the need for teachers to provide constructive feedback and foster partnerships with learners focused on co-constructing goals and involving students in their own assessment, when observed, not all teachers use such practices. Furthermore, when they do, feedback can often be restricted to whether or not learners have met the set success criteria (Hawe et al., 2008), limiting feedback to a summative purpose. Coupled with the findings from another study (Dixon et al., 2011), where teachers who believed in involving learners through self and peer assessment only provided fleeting opportunities for their students to actually be involved in the assessment process, this suggests that the students in our cohort may not have had as many instances of these practices to observe as we assumed they would have. Because it is critical that PTs have mentor teachers who model the aspects of formative assessment we are attempting to teach, it may also be necessary to include clinical sessions in which such skills are introduced and practised in both university and school settings. Moreover, monitoring PTs as they learn challenging aspects of assessment, such as giving constructive, responsive feedback, as well as proactively involving PTs in the process of setting specific learning goals, and ensuring they are fully aware of how to co-construct assessment criteria, seems advisable in order to model these practices.

Unlike conventional teacher education programmes that (sometimes) include assessment modules or courses (Hill & Eyers, 2016), the M Tchg deliberately integrates assessment pedagogy throughout the programme, weaving it within every course and between the university-based teaching and the school-based aspects. The evidence from the interviews suggests that it was not until the end of the programme, in the last six-week practicum, that many PTs gained confidence in understanding and implementing formative assessment strategies. This finding confirms and extends evidence from surveys and small case studies that indicate that combining assessment learning with experiencing the use of assessment in real classrooms is critical in developing assessment capability (DeLuca & Klinger, 2010; Eyers, 2014; Jiang, 2015). This study also adds weight to studies that suggest expert mentorship in practical settings is necessary to assist in the development of a more comprehensive and dynamic understanding of assessment practices (Eyers, 2014; Graham, 2005). Unfortunately, not all mentor teachers provide rich conditions for this type of assessment learning (DeLuca & Klinger, 2010; Eyers, 2014) and this might be one of the contributing factors for differences in PT outcomes noted in our findings.

Even though the PTs had experienced the same programme, not all left the programme with the same ideas and understandings about using assessment evidence to support learning and teaching. Because only 12 PTs completed the exit questionnaire, our data are incomplete. However, the data from the survey and the 72 assignments indicate many completed the programme with a rich understanding of this facet along with critical understandings about technical assessment issues such as reliability and validity, moderation, fairness and making overall teacher judgements against standards from evidence. We argue that such understanding is vital in order for teachers to recognise and challenge inequity and to understand the role of assessment in this.

While most PTs in this cohort graduated confident and ready to use assessment to inform teaching and learning and address equity issues, four appeared to have retained a summative focus and provided sparse evidence of assessment learning in the analysed assignments. Unfortunately, none of the PTs who retained summative views of assessment volunteered to participate in the focus group so we were unable to delve further into what the reasons for retaining such views might have been. Along with variations in the quality of mentoring in school settings (DeLuca & Klinger, 2010; Hill et al., 2014; Jiang, 2015), other factors relating to the PTs themselves, could account for these variable outcomes. For example, some entered the programme having had previous teaching experiences. Nine indicated that they had been working full or part time in a teaching-related job prior to entering the programme. Chen (2005) found that those PTs who had had prior teaching experiences before entering teacher education scored better across the seven standards she used to measure teacher competence in the educational assessment of students than those who had not. Other factors such as being parents, serving on school boards, and having well-developed metacognitive and critical thinking skills have also been shown to affect the development of knowledge and confidence in assessment learning (DeLuca et al., 2013; Eyers, 2014; Hill & Eyers, 2016). No doubt such complex factors were also at play within this cohort.

Despite our best efforts as teacher educators, the complex nature of the overlapping systems of the university and schools in which teacher preparation takes place, and the PTs as systems themselves, may lead to less than even outcomes (Hill et al., 2014). Overall, the evidence indicates most PTs in this programme did increase their understanding of using assessment evidence to achieve more equitable outcomes, and the assignments and interview transcripts suggest that the multiple interwoven opportunities provided within the courses, assignments and in-school teaching experiences enabled time for the PTs to practise and critically reflect upon these aspects. But consistent with other studies (Smith et al., 2014, for example) some PTs, even with these multiple and overlapping opportunities, did not appear to develop these ideas in the same way. It is therefore important for teacher educators, concerned to graduate teachers capable of using assessment for learning to improve educational outcomes for all learners, to find better ways to track learning in this facet of practice in order to use such evidence to work with those PTs who seem to have more difficulty with this aspect of teaching.

Conclusion

This study reaffirms that preparing preservice teachers to use evidence from classroom assessment to inform teaching and scaffold learning is both possible and desirable, but indicates that such learning is complex. Teacher educators need to know more about individual preservice teachers' progress in understanding and use principles of assessment for equitable outcomes themselves. Knowing that giving constructive feedback and involving learners in their own assessment appear less frequently in PTs' explanations about this facet indicates that more focus on these aspects, both in courses and particularly in teaching experiences, would be beneficial. Clearly, the intertwined university/school nature of the programme and the way facet 4 was embedded within the curricula contexts of mathematics and literacy, and in every course, facilitated understanding. While the positive outcomes for most of the PTs in this study were undoubtedly linked to some other factors such as personal experiences and dispositions, intentionally integrating the assessment curriculum, in the way described facilitated professional learning. It would be helpful, however, to know much more about why some PTs did not appear to move beyond a summative view of assessment even with these supports in place. As this finding is consistent with other studies, further investigation is required to understand the barriers for some in developing formative views and practices.

Furthermore, this study does not tell us how the graduates of this programme used evidence for improving learning in their own teaching while in the programme or upon graduation. These issues require further examination and are part of our research agenda. As the participants in this study were in the first cohort in the M Tchg, the findings will inform how assessment teaching within the programme is shaped and modified for future cohorts. For instance, it appears important to retain the interwoven coursework and school experiences of assessment embedded within curriculum contexts but seems essential to include more ways to help PTs learn to give constructive feedback maybe through clinical sessions where they learn to do this with small groups of children or with peers during university classes. Actually practising, and then critiquing, this skill and others, such as individual goal setting and self assessment, as set tasks or assignments may well help to strengthen these aspects of pedagogy. It also seems advisable to know more about the mentor teachers and their assessment beliefs and practices when forming teacher education partnerships with schools. As prior studies have shown, the influence of mentor teachers is strong and thus having teachers who model excellent assessment practices is advisable.

While learning to teach for equity is a complex process, learning to use assessment evidence that improves outcomes for priority learners is an important outcome of teacher preparation. Although we have separated this facet from the other five identified from our synthesis of the international evidence in this article, using evidence in this way cannot, in practice, be disentangled from other facets of practice for equity such as challenging inequities, connecting learning with students' lives, selecting worthwhile learning intentions or engaging students.

Notes

1. GLoSS is a diagnostic test comprised of individually-administered, standardised interview protocols that yield information about a child's number sense and approaches to arithmetic problems.
2. AsTTLe – assessment for teaching and learning, is a set of diagnostic tests for mathematics and literacy available free to all NZ schools.

Acknowledgements

We wish to acknowledge the preservice teachers who were part of this study as well as Susan Ng and Kane Meissel for their assistance.

Disclosure statement

No potential conflict of interest was reported by the authors.

ORCID

Mary F. Hill 🆔 http://orcid.org/0000-0001-9552-8112

References

Alkharusi, H., Kazem, A. M., & Al-Musawai, A. (2011). Knowledge, skills, and attitudes of preservice and inservice teachers in educational measurement. *Asia-Pacific Journal of Teacher Education, 39*, 113–123. doi:10.1080/1359866X.2011.560649

Anthony, G., & Walshaw, M. (2007). *Effective pedagogy in mathematics/pangarau*. Wellington: Ministry of Education.

Assessment Reform Group. (1999). *Assessment for learning: Beyond the black box*. Cambridge: University of Cambridge School of Education.

Bennett, R. E. (2011). Formative assessment: A critical review. *Assessment in Education: Principles, Policy & Practice, 18*, 5–25.

Bishop, R., Berryman, M., Cavanagh, T., & Teddy, L. (2009). Te Kotahitanga: Addressing educational disparities facing Māori students in New Zealand. *Teaching and Teacher Education, 25*, 734–742.

Bishop, R., & Glynn, T. (1999). *Culture counts: Changing power relations in education*. Palmerston North: Dunmore Press.

Black, P., & Wiliam, D. (1998a). Assessment and classroom learning. *Assessment in Education: Principles, Policy & Practice, 5*, 7–74.

Black, P., & Wiliam, D. (1998b). *Inside the black box: Raising standards through classroom assessment*. London: Kings College, London School of Education.

Black, P., & Wiliam, D. (2009). Developing the theory of formative assessment. *Educational Assessment, Evaluation and Accountability, 21*, 5–31.

Brookhart, S. M. (2001). *The 'standards' and classroom assessment research*. Paper presented at the annual meeting of the American Association of Colleges for Teacher Education, Dallas, TX. (ERIC Document Reproduction Service No. ED451189).

Brown, G. T. L. (2011). New Zealand prospective teacher conceptions of assessment and academic performance: Neither student nor practising teacher. In R. Kahn, J. C. McDermott, & A. Akimjak (Eds.), *Democratic access to education* (pp. 119–132). Los Angeles, CA: Department of Education, Antioch University Los Angeles.

Brown, G. T. L., & Remesal, A. (2012). Prospective teachers' conceptions of assessment: A cross-cultural comparison. *The Spanish journal of psychology, 15*, 75–89.

DEVELOPING TEACHERS' ASSESSMENT CAPACITY

Buck, G. A., Trauth-Nare, A., & Kaftan, J. (2010). Making formative assessment discernable to preservice teachers of science. *Journal of Research in Science Education, 47*, 402–421.

Campbell, C. (2013). Research on teacher competency in classroom assessment. In J. H. McMillan (Ed.), *Sage handbook of research on classroom assessment* (pp. 71–84). Thousand Oaks, CA: Sage.

Chang, W-C., & Ludlow, L. (2016, April 9). *Teaching for equity: How do we measure it?* Paper presented at the American Educational Research Association annual meeting, Washington, DC.

Chen, P. P. (2005). Teacher candidates' literacy in assessment. *Academic Exchange Quarterly, 62*, 62–66.

Cochran-Smith, M., Ell, F., Grudnoff, L., Haigh, M., Hill, M. F., & Ludlow, L. (2016). Initial teacher education: What does it take to put equity at the centre? *Teaching and Teacher Education, 57*, 67–78. doi:10.1016/j.tate.2016.03.006

DeLuca, C., Chavez, T., Bellara, A., & Cao, C. (2013). Pedagogies for preservice assessment education: Supporting teacher candidates' assessment literacy development. *The Teacher Educator, 48*, 128–142.

DeLuca, C., Chavez, T., & Cao, C. (2012). Establishing a foundation for valid teacher judgement on student learning: The role of pre-service assessment education. *Assessment in Education: Principles, Policy & Practice, 20*, 107–126.

DeLuca, C., & Klinger, D. A. (2010). Assessment literacy development: Identifying gaps in teacher candidates' learning. *Assessment in Education: Principles, Policy & Practice, 17*, 419–438.

DeLuca, C., Klinger, D. A., Searle, M., & Shulha, L. (2010). Developing a curriculum for assessment education. *Assessment Matters, 2*, 20–42.

Dixon, H. (2011). The problem of enactment: The influence of teachers' self-efficacy beliefs on their uptake and implementation of feedback-related ideas and practices. *Assessment Matters, 3*, 71–92.

Dixon, H., Hawe, E., & Parr, J. (2011). Enacting assessment for learning: The beliefs practice nexus. *Assessment in Education: Principles, Policy and Practice, 18*, 365–379.

Education Council New Zealand. (n.d.). *Graduating teacher standards: Aotearoa New Zealand.* Retrieved from https://educationcouncil.org.nz/content/graduating-teacher-standards

Eyers, G. (2014). *Preservice teachers' assessment learning: Change, development and growth* (Unpublished doctoral thesis). Auckland: The University of Auckland.

Graham, P. (2005). Classroom-based assessment: Changing knowledge and practice through preservice teacher education. *Teaching and Teacher Education, 21*, 607–621.

Grudnoff, L., Hill, M.F., Haigh, M., Cochran-Smith, M. Ell, F., & Ludlow, L. (2015, April 16–20). *Teaching for equity: Insights from international evidence.* Presented at American Education Research Association, Chicago, IL.

Grudnoff, L., Ward, L., Ritchie, J., Brooker, B., & Simpson, M. (2013, September 10–13). *A collaborative multi institutional approach to evidence gathering: Graduating student teachers' perceptions of their teacher preparation programmes.* Paper presented at the European Educational Research Association Conference, Istanbul.

Hattie, J. (2008). *Visible learning: A synthesis of over 800 meta-analyses relating to achievement.* London: Routledge.

Hawe, E., Dixon, H., & Watson, E. (2008). Oral feedback in the context of written language. *Australian Journal of Language and Literacy, 31*, 43–58.

Hill, M. F. (2000). *Remapping the assessment landscape: Primary teachers reconstructing assessment in self-managing schools* (Unpublished doctoral thesis). Waikato University, Hamilton.

Hill, M. F., Ell, F., Grudnoff, L., & Limbrick, L. (2014). Practice what you preach: Initial teacher education students learning about assessment. *Assessment Matters, 7*, 90–112.

Hill, M. F., & Eyers, G. (2016). Moving from student to teacher: Changing perspectives about assessment through teacher education. In G. T. L. Brown & L. Harris (Eds.), *Handbook of the human and social factors of assessment* (pp. 57–76). New York, NY: Routledge.

Hill, M. F., Smith, L. F., Cowie, B., Gilmore, A., & Gunn, A. (2013). *Preparing initial primary and early childhood teachers to use assessment.* Final Report for the Teaching and Learning Research Initiative. Retrieved from http://www.tlri.org.nz/sites/default/files/projects/Hill_Final%20Summary%20Report_signed%20off.pdf

Hsieh, H.-F., & Shannon, S. (2005). Three approaches to qualitative content analysis. *Qualitative Health Research, 15*, 1277–1288.

DEVELOPING TEACHERS' ASSESSMENT CAPACITY

Jiang, H. (2015). *Learning to teach with assessment: A student teaching experience in China.* Singapore: Springer.

Kanjee, A., & Mthembu, J. (2015). Assessment literacy of foundation phase teachers: An exploratory study. *South African Journal of Childhood Education, 5,* 142–168.

Klenowski, V. (2009). Assessment for learning revisited: An Asia-Pacific perspective. *Assessment in Education: Principles, Policy and Practice, 16,* 263–268.

McMillan, J. H., Myran, S., & Workman, D. (2002). Elementary teachers' classroom assessment and grading practices. *The Journal of Educational Research, 95,* 203–213.

Ministry of Education. (2007). *The New Zealand curriculum.* Retrieved from www.nzcurriculum.tki. org.nz/The-New-Zealand-Curriculum

Ministry of Education. (2013). *Exemplary postgraduate initial teacher education programmes.* Retrieved from www.education.govt.nz/.../ExemplaryPostgradEducation-ECACsep2013

Ministry of Education. (2014). *The New Zealand curriculum: Priority learners.* Retrieved from http:// nzcurriculum.tki.org.nz/Priority-learners

New Zealand Census. (2013). Retrieved from http://www.stats.govt.nz/Census/2013-census.aspx

New Zealand Government. (2010). *A vision for the teaching profession: Education workforce advisory group report to the Minister of Education.* Wellington: Ministry of Education. Retrieved from http:// www.beehive.govt.nz

Nolen, S. B., Horn, I. S., Ward, C. J., & Childers, S. A. (2011). Novice teacher learning and motivation across contexts: Assessment tools as boundary objects. *Cognition and Instruction, 29,* 88–122. do i:10.1080/07370008.2010.533221

OECD. (2005). *Formative assessment improving learning in secondary classrooms.* Paris: OECD.

OECD. (2011). *Society at a glance: Key findings New Zealand.* Retrieved from http://www.oecd.org/ dataoecd/38/35/47573309.pdf

O'Leary, M., Lysaught, Z., & Ludlow, L. H. (2013). A measurement instrument to evaluate teachers' assessment for learning classroom practices. *International Journal of Educational and Psychological Assessment, 14,* 40–62.

Poskitt, J. (2014). Transforming professional learning and practice in assessment for learning. *The Curriculum Journal, 25,* 542–566.

Richardson, V., & Placier, P. (2001). Teacher change. In V. Richardson (Ed.), *Handbook of research on teaching* (4th ed., pp. 905–947). Washington, DC: American Educational Research Association.

Shepard, L. A. (2001). *The role of classroom assessment in teaching and learning* (Technical Report 517). Los Angeles, CA: National Center for Research on Evaluation, Standards, and Student Testing (CRESST).

Shute, V. J. (2008). Focus on formative feedback. *Review of Educational Research, 78,* 153–189.

Smith, K. (2016). Assessment for learning: A pedagogical tool. In D. Wyse, L. Hayward, & J. Pandya (Eds.), *The Sage handbook of curriculum, pedagogy and assessment* (Vol. 2, pp. 740–755). London: Sage.

Smith, L. F., Hill, M. F., Cowie, B., & Gilmore, A. (2014). Preparing teachers to use the enabling power of assessment. In C. Wyatt-Smith, V. Klenowski, & P. Colbert (Eds.), *Designing assessment for quality learning* (Vol. 1, pp. 303–323). Dordrecht: Springer.

Snook, I., & O'Neill, J. (2014). Poverty and inequality of educational achievement. In V. Carpenter & S. Osborne (Eds.), *Twelve thousand hours: Education and poverty in Aotearoa New Zealand* (pp. 19–43). Auckland: Dunmore Publishing.

Swaffield, S. (2011). Getting to the heart of authentic assessment for learning. *Assessment in Education: Principles, Policy and Practice, 18,* 433–449.

Volante, L., & Fazio, X. (2007). Exploring teacher candidates' assessment literacy: Implications for teacher education reform and professional development [abstract]. *Canadian Journal of Education, 30,* 749–770.

Wang, J.-R., Kao, H.-L., & Lin, S.-W. (2010). Preservice teachers' initial conceptions about assessment of science learning: The coherence with their views of learning science. *Teaching and Teacher Education, 26,* 522–529. doi:10.1016/j.tate.2009.06.014

Winterbottom, M., Brindley, S., Taber, K. S., Fisher, L. G., Finney, J., & Riga, F. (2008). Conceptions of assessment: Trainee teachers' practices and values. *Curriculum Journal, 19,* 193–213.

A rubric to track the development of secondary pre-service and novice teachers' summative assessment literacy

Frances Edwards

ABSTRACT

Teachers require specialised assessment knowledge and skills in order to effectively assess student learning. These knowledge and skills develop over time through ongoing teacher learning and experiences. The first part of this paper presents a Summative Assessment Literacy Rubric (SALRubric) constructed to track the development of secondary science teachers' summative assessment literacy. The analytic rubric consists of 10 dimensions spread across three categories drawn from the literature and context-specific empirical evidence: knowledge of assessment, understanding the context for assessment, and recognising the impact of assessment. The second part of this paper applies the SALRubric in a case study to explore the development of summative assessment literacy of New Zealand secondary science pre-service and novice teachers. An increasing sophistication in these teachers' summative assessment literacy was evident over 20 months albeit in a nuanced manner for individual teachers. The rubric was a very useful tool for evaluating and documenting shifts in teachers' summative assessment literacy over time. Implications of the use of SALRubric are discussed in terms of summative assessment literacy practice and development.

Introduction

Teachers need to be assessment literate in order to meet the complex demands of using assessment as a means to affirm, extend and account for student learning. Assessment literacy has been defined as 'an individual's understandings of the fundamental assessment concepts and procedures deemed likely to influence educational decisions' (Popham, 2011, p. 267). Teacher assessment literacy develops over time and is influenced by initial teacher education (ITE), in-service teacher education, and ongoing teaching experience.

A number of studies have reported that ITE has had limited effectiveness in developing teacher confidence and competence in classroom assessment (DeLuca & Klinger, 2010; Popham, 2009). Most of the literature has focussed either on a description of teacher assessment literacy (as a one-off snapshot or as it applies in ITE) or on how assessment literacy can be measured through the use of tools, such as, Mertler and Campbell's *Assessment*

DEVELOPING TEACHERS' ASSESSMENT CAPACITY

Literacy Inventory (Bakx, Baartman, & van Schilt-Mol, 2014; Chen, 2005; Christoforidou, Kyriakides, Antoniou, & Creemers, 2014; McGee & Colby, 2014; Mertler & Campbell, 2005; Schneider & Plasman, 2011). Although, some research (e.g. Eyers, 2014; Hill, Smith, Cowie, Gilmore, & Gunn, 2013) has monitored the development of pre-service teachers' assessment capability and beliefs about assessment over three-year undergraduate ITE programmes, no research has monitored multiple dimensions of assessment literacy, particularly through ITE and into early career roles.

The purpose of this research was twofold: to develop an analytical rubric of Summative Assessment Literacy, *SALRubric,* and to use the rubric to track the development of summative assessment literacy for a cohort of postgraduate secondary teachers during their one-year ITE and the first six months of teaching in a school. The use of the SALRubric with the pre-service to novice teachers over a 20-month period provided information to simultaneously further develop, refine and validate the rubric, and then apply the final version of the rubric retrospectively to report how the development of assessment literacy tracked for these participants.

Assessment literacy for pre-service and novice teachers

Teachers need to be able to apply assessment knowledge and skills in a wide range of classroom settings as part of their teaching practice (Harlen & Gardner, 2010). Teacher education programmes for both pre-service and in-service teachers include elements which aim to help teachers learn to do this as they develop a capacity to work more effectively within their educational contexts. Much current scholarship points to the effects of ITE programmes in developing teacher confidence and assessment literacy (DeLuca & Klinger, 2010; Eyers, 2014; McGee & Colby, 2014). However, some studies indicate inconsistent or weak assessment literacy development in ITE programmes (Maclellan, 2004; Volante & Fazio, 2007). Many novice teachers report being inadequately prepared and feeling challenged by aspects of assessment, such as, assessment task design, the need to ensure equity for all learners, and to mark fairly and to communicate assessment results (Koh, 2014; Lyon, 2013a; Smith, Corkery, Buckley, & Calvert, 2013). Unfortunately, the constraints within ITE programmes mean that only a rudimentary level of assessment literacy can be expected of pre-service and novice teachers. In light of this, researchers internationally argue for a closer scrutiny of what and how ITE can best be delivered to enhance in-service teacher education and support ongoing teacher assessment literacy development (Black, Harrison, Hodgen, Marshall, & Serret, 2010; Hill, Cowie, Gilmore, & Smith, 2010; Struyven, Dochy, & Janssens, 2008).

While there are elements of assessment literacy that are common for all teachers, some elements of assessment literacy are context dependent. Indeed, every education jurisdiction has a particular combination of assessment history, policies and practices that make it unique and therefore requires distinctive assessment literacy understanding and practice. There is some consensus that assessment is a cultural activity incorporating dynamic social practices occurring within specific contexts (Gipps, 1999; Pryor & Crossouard, 2008; Willis, Adie, & Klenowski, 2013). Consequently, published lists of teacher competencies in educational assessment (e.g. Brookhart, 2011) will be of most use for teacher education when employed using the lens(es) of the contexts in which assessment will be used (Shepard, 2000; Spillane & Miele, 2007). This paper reports on the context for secondary science teachers in New Zealand.

The New Zealand context

New Zealand's education policy is distinctive in that it operates within one of the most devolved school systems in the world, where self-managing schools work with considerable freedom and flexibility to develop teaching programmes that best suit their students within the broad framework of the New Zealand Curriculum. National assessment policy has placed substantial significance on teachers' use of formative assessment over a number of years (Crooks, 2011; Nusche, Laveault, MacBeath, & Santiago, 2012). This means that all teachers are expected to use formative assessment practices. In senior secondary schools though, formative assessment is somewhat shaped by the needs for summative assessment where students and teachers work towards the qualification, National Certificate of Educational Achievement (NCEA). NCEA is gained through standards-based summative assessment and is the main secondary school leavers' qualification. NCEA requires secondary teachers to have a high level of assessment literacy as NCEA is achieved through the accumulation of credits gained by success in standards that are externally examined and marked, and standards that are internally assessed. Individual schools and classroom teachers decide on the range and proportion of internally assessed versus externally assessed standards offered to their students. The national pattern is that a higher proportion of NCEA credits are gained through internally assessed standards than those that are externally assessed (New Zealand Qualifications Authority, 2015). Consequently, almost all senior secondary school teachers are involved in designing, administering and marking a wide range of internal summative assessments. Teachers make decisions about student readiness, choose what standards are assessed, design or modify the assessment tasks, decide when the assessments will take place and mark and grade assessment tasks. Quality assurance for this process is ensured through a sample of all teacher assessments being externally moderated by the New Zealand Qualifications Authority (NZQA). NZQA provides feedback to teachers on assessment tasks and graded work that has been selected for moderation, as well as other standard-specific tasks that teachers voluntarily submit for critique. Therefore, in New Zealand, teachers play a central role in decision-making with respect to summative assessment processes in ways not commonly seen elsewhere in the world (Crooks, 2011). New Zealand's assessment approach has been characterised by a high level of trust in schools and teachers' professionalism (Nusche et al., 2012). This means that summative assessment literacy is particularly important for New Zealand secondary teachers.

Tracking complex teacher learning and development over time

Researchers in other professional fields have found that rubrics can be used as a professional practice tool to track developmental trajectories (e.g. Cendan, Hernandez, & Castiglioni, 2015; Keister, Larson, Dostal, & Baglia, 2012; Lasater, 2007). Lasater (2007), for example, described how a rubric could be used in ways to support learning in nursing education, where a list of competencies was clearly defined. The rubric she developed was found to help students understand dimensions of clinical judgement, and more accurately track their progress.

Unlike a list of competencies to be achieved, analytic rubrics set out expectations for a set of key skills and understandings, with detailed descriptions of increasingly sophisticated levels of performance or understanding. Such rubrics provide a robust means to determine a person's performance or level of understanding (Brookhart, 1999; Luft, 1999; Stevens & Levi, 2005). A rubric can be used repeatedly and therefore is able to assess changes in understanding, knowledge or performance over time. When used with a careful selection of evidence, a rubric can lead to inferences with high levels of validity and reliability (Harris, Grandgenett, & Hofer, 2012). For these reasons, rubrics have been suggested as useful tools in a range of professional fields, including teacher education, where expertise in decision-making and performance are important (Lyon, 2013a, 2013b; Windschitl, Thompson, Braaten, & Stroupe, 2012). However, rubrics have not often been used to track teacher development in education.

Over time, as teachers become more adept and skilful in their practice, there is generally a shift from limited, relatively inflexible thinking and practice to more elaborate, responsive, flexible and adaptive situative practice (Bransford, Brown, & Cocking, 2000; Dreyfus & Dreyfus, 1986). Teacher education has a very important role to play in this shift from novice to adaptive expertise (Aitken, Sinnema, & Meyer, 2012; Hill et al., 2013; Timperley, 2013). The analytic SALRubric discussed in this paper was developed by the author as a tool to assist pre-service teachers and teacher-educators to jointly track development across a number of dimensions. An analytic rubric was chosen because of its advantage in identifying and describing separate components of the process, rather than a holistic rubric which would only describe the process as a whole without looking at components separately (Mertler, 2001; Moskal, 2000).

Like other learners, pre-service and novice teachers learn and develop over time by building on their prior knowledge and experiences to gain fuller knowledge and deeper understandings of concepts, and develop capabilities and an awareness of the scope of their teaching contexts. Attempts have been made to describe the progression of skill acquisition or development in a range of professions by describing levels of expertise from novice to mastery (Dreyfus & Dreyfus, 1986). Progressions in teacher development have also been described, as seen, for example, in the progressions for science teachers in school science content (Martín del Pozo, Porlán, & Rivero, 2011), in pedagogical content knowledge (Schneider & Plasman, 2011) and in assessment expertise (Lyon, 2013a). These descriptions usefully inform the developmental trajectories of specific knowledge and skills that teachers gain within the broader context of teacher learning.

Lyon (2013a, 2013b) investigated the development of assessment expertise in science teachers in USA over time with a particular interest in how teachers responded to the needs of students with English as a second language. He used the developmental framework of Dreyfus & Dreyfus (1986); Dreyfus (2004) to conceptualise the development of assessment expertise over time. He focused on the importance of the shift from 'knowing that', which is based on adhering to generally accepted rules and principles, to 'knowing how', which calls on the more 'flexible application of principles in practice to adapt to constantly changing situations' (Lyon, 2013a, p. 1210). This led to a conceptualisation of assessment expertise in which three dimensions were identified: designing aligned and theoretically cohesive assessment ('Design'), using assessment to support students' science learning ('Use'), and equitably assessing students with English as a second language ('Equity'). The theoretical progression of expertise was validated by comparing it with actual data from pre-service teachers. Lyon's four-level *Assessment Expertise Rubric* was found to be useful for tracking pre-service teachers' development in the context of a small study of an ITE programme vested in language and equity issues. This sort of example is rare, and there are very few other descriptions of the use of rubrics in teacher education to assess assessment literacy, and none for assessing summative assessment literacy development of secondary school teachers in New Zealand.

Summative Assessment Literacy Rubric (SALRubric) development and refinement

The SALRubric was developed using a combination of deductive observations from the literature and inductive observations from a 20-month qualitative study that investigated the nature and development of a group of secondary science teachers' assessment literacy through their one-year postgraduate ITE programme and into the first six months of working as teachers in New Zealand (see Edwards, 2014, 2016; Edwards & Edwards, 2016).

Deductive development

The author consulted the literature to develop the initial SALRubric by identifying (i) relevant dimensions of skills and knowledge of assessment literacy, (ii) articulating levels of expertise from novice to expert, (iii) developing a framework of descriptors, and (iv) considering the New Zealand context in which the SALRubric would be used. Each step is discussed in turn.

Dimensions of assessment literacy

Abell and Siegel's (2011) developmental model for science teachers' assessment literacy (MSTAL) was based on conceptions of pedagogical content knowledge and the assessment triangle. Incorporating findings from their own work, the MSTAL has, at its core, teachers' assessment values and principles that are grounded in teachers' views of learning. Abell and Siegel argue that these aspects influence teachers' use of knowledge in decision-making. Their model provided an initial framework for the SALRubric across multiple dimensions comprised of: knowledge of four aspects of assessment, values in assessment and teacher orientation. (Abell & Siegel, 2011; Lyon, 2013a, 2013b; Schneider & Plasman, 2011; Siegel, 2014).

Levels of expertise

Dreyfus and Dreyfus (1986) model described levels of expertise existing in skill acquisition development that mapped routines and decision-making from novice to expert levels. As discussed earlier, a key element of teacher development illustrated in this model was the shift in teachers' thinking by adhering to rules or 'knowing that', to being able to flexibly adapt or apply principles in practice or 'knowing how' (Dreyfus, 2004; Dreyfus & Dreyfus, 1986; Eyers, 2014; Schneider & Plasman, 2011).

Descriptors of levels

Lyon (2013a) developed a framework and set of descriptors for developing assessment expertise in pre-service teachers working in linguistically diverse classrooms. His work informed the development of descriptors for the SALRubric.

The New Zealand context

Finally, elements of policies and practices related to summative assessment in the New Zealand context, in particular the requirements with respect to secondary school qualifications (NCEA) and the strong policy focus on formative assessment, were considered to ensure the SALRubric was appropriate for teachers working in the New Zealand context.

Inductive observations based on findings from a case study

The SALRubric was used in a study of an ITE programme in a New Zealand university where eight pre-service secondary science teachers were tracked from the beginning of their initial one-year ITE programme until six months into their first teaching job (see Edwards, 2014, 2016; Edwards & Edwards, 2016 for more details on this study). Over the 20-month period, data was gathered at five time points using a series of interviews, a questionnaire (*Beliefs about Assessment* (Smith, Hill, Cowie, & Gilmore, 2014)), the collection of artefacts that the teachers felt represented their summative assessment practice and observations during university lectures/classes. The author was involved in all aspects of the data collection.

The interviews were semi-structured and the same questions were used at each time point, to allow development be more easily mapped (see Appendix). The questions focussed on what the teachers' understood and were learning about assessment, how they were using assessment, and a self-assessment of their assessment capability. For each time point, teachers were asked to bring any artefacts that they felt displayed their assessment literacy. These artefacts included assessment tasks that the teachers had written and marked, unit plans, examples of students' portfolios, school-developed tasks they wanted to discuss, NCEA tasks and schemes of work. At each interview, the teachers were asked what they felt these artefacts represented with respect to their developing understandings and use of assessment. Observations in university classes were completed by the author as non-participation observer. Notes were made of any content deemed as relevant to assessment that occurred in the class; for example, lectures which focussed on assessment, activities the teachers completed, class discussions and individual work. During data analysis all of the data collected for each teacher was considered as a whole. The timeline for data gathering is summarised in Table 1.

An iterative process of refinement has been found to be useful in constructing learning progressions (Furtak, Morrison, & Kroog, 2014) and rubrics (Lyon, 2013a). Draft dimensions for the SALRubric were reconsidered in response to the analysis of the data generated by the participants in the study mentioned above, particularly after later data collection points. This allowed other important dimensions to be added and descriptors to be more finely tuned. Decisions about which dimensions would be included were influenced by their importance in the assessment literature, their importance in the New Zealand context, and their relevance and importance for teachers as evidenced in data gathered from participants. As a result of this refinement, dimensions that focussed on using summative assessment for formative purposes, and on assessment consequences and fairness were added. Further refinements were made to the wording of criteria in the SALRubric based on expert advice from within New Zealand and overseas when the work was presented, and from the *Practising Teacher Criteria* (Education Council, 2015).

The final version of the SALRubric includes 10 dimensions spread across three categories: Knowledge of assessment, Understanding the context for assessment, and Recognising

Table 1. Timeline for data gathering.

	Teacher activity	Data gathering	
Phase 1 – Teacher education 2013			
February – April	University courses	February (beginning of ITE programme):• Interview 1 • Artefact collection 1 • Questionnaire 1	University classes• Observations over 8 weeks
April – May	Practicum 1		
June – August	University courses	June (post-practicum 1):• Interview 2 • Artefact collection 2 August (pre-practicum 2):• Interview 3 • Artefact collection 3	University classes• Observations over 6 weeks
August – September	Practicum 2		
October – November	University courses	October/November (post practicum 2)• Interview 4 • Artefact collection 4 • Questionnaire 2	University classes• Observations over 2 weeks
Phase 2 – Working as teacher 2014			
February – July	Working in schools	June/July• Interview 5 • Artefact collection 5 • Questionnaire 3	

DEVELOPING TEACHERS' ASSESSMENT CAPACITY

Table 2. Levels of competence used in SALRubric.

Level	Definition
Novice	Limited competence in dimensions of assessment literacy, where a teacher either does not consider the relevance of the dimension, or shows limited understanding, and follows basic assessment tasks provided by others
Advanced beginner	A general understanding of most of the dimension at a basic level, taking notice of the context but still detached from the learning situation
Competent	An overall understanding or competency in the dimension, becoming more emotionally invested in the context, but yet to demonstrate the nuanced detail inherent in the dimension
Proficient	A clear understanding of the complexities of the dimension within the contextual framework, approaching decision-making from the perspective of deciding between options, applying analytic reasoning
Expert	A thorough understanding of the detail of the dimension within its context, applying intuitive decision-making, and having the capability to contribute understandings to the wider teaching community

the impact of assessment. Each dimension described five levels of competency: 'novice', 'advanced beginner', 'competent', 'proficient' and 'expert'. These were anchored at the novice level with what was observed as the lowest level of summative assessment literacy on student teachers' entry to ITE, combined with the pattern seen in other rubrics. The expert level was anchored by the New Zealand Education Council's criteria for practising teachers (Education Council, 2015), and the expectations of teachers reaching Advanced Classroom Expertise Teacher Recognition (TeachNZ, 2006).

Table 2 summarises the broad definitions of the five levels of competence from novice to expert.

The full SALRubric is presented in Table 3.

Quality and the SALRubric

Moskal and Leydens (2000) raise the challenges of ensuring validity and reliability in scoring rubric development, and these were considered in the development and use of the SALRubric. With respect to validation of the SALRubric, it was important to consider the accumulated evidence that supported the descriptions of teachers' assessment literacy. The inductive element of the SALRubric's development used assessment-related evidence from the participating teachers in the study including: questionnaire and interview data, documented summative assessment planning linked to unit planning, assessment tasks, marking schedules, judgement statements produced by the teachers and student work marked by the teachers, alongside discussions with the teachers about the artefacts of their summative assessment practice. This array of content-related evidence reflected the teachers' knowledge of the content area being assessed. Care was taken to ensure that the evaluation criteria within the rubric measured factors related to the construct of interest, that is, assessment literacy, establishing construct validity. The adjustment of criteria made later in the development of the rubric meant better alignment between the descriptors and the construct of assessment literacy. Much of the evidence used when developing the SALRubric's dimensions and descriptors was generated while the teachers were in ITE programmes which modelled pedagogies seen in schools, or while they were working in schools, so it is likely that the SALRubric scores reflect practices in the field, that is, high scores using the SALRubric should suggest high scores when teachers are working in their own classrooms as teachers.

Table 3. Summative Assessment Literacy Rubric (SALRubric) indicating levels of expertise for dimensions of summative assessment literacy.

Novice	Advanced beginner	Competent	Proficient	Expert
I. Knowledge of assessment				
1. Ability to describe assessment				
Can describe assessment in very broad terms based on own experience	Can describe summative assessment, formative assessment, diagnostic assessment and their purposes using simple descriptions	Can describe assessment purposes and their effects and uses in a more integrated way, understanding that teachers' ethical decision-making is required	Can describe assessment in detail and considers its forms and functions and its effects within the class. Aware of complexities involved in assessment decision-making including fairness and ethics, and issues of authenticity	Can describe assessment in detail and demonstrates critical engagement with assessment dimensions, focussing on awareness, impact, and challenging the naturalness of assessment practices within assessment community
2. Knowledge of purposes of summative assessment				
Considers summative assessment purposes in vague terms, without using any specific terminology or without identifying specific purposes	Considers specific purpose/s for summative assessment such as accountability, qualifications, schools uses or formative functions	Considers a range of specific purposes for summative assessment including reporting progress, formative uses, qualifications, school uses. Understands that the same assessment task can serve a range of purposes	Considers accountability, reporting, qualifications and formative use of summative assessment as valuable purposes of summative assessment as it links to teaching and to the New Zealand Curriculum (NZC)	Considers a wide range of specific purposes for summative assessment including reporting progress, formative use, qualifications, school wide/national uses. Makes contributions of the creative use of summative assessment for a range of purposes to the wider teaching community
3. Knowledge of what to assess				
Considers assessment as a generic activity and does not yet link assessment to the specifics of what has been taught	Considers that some subject knowledge is important to assess or that what is taught needs to be assessed. Understands that NZC provides levels that must be assessed against, and that NCEA standards provide specific assessment criteria	Considers specific subject knowledge and skills that are important to assess, and is comfortable in critiquing assessments for this content. Links assessment to what has been taught. Considers the importance of linking assessment to standards criteria	Considers the need to identify specific subject-specific skills and knowledge that are important to assess. Can see need for alignment between NZC, teaching and assessment. Considers validity. Can accurately critique for content within assessment tasks, including NCEA tasks	Considers their use of an in-depth knowledge of subject-specific content and NZC, and learning progressions when assessing the subject. Can identify critical content to assess for a range of topics, and can critique assessment tasks for this content. Considers their contribution of this knowledge to the wider teaching community

(Continued)

Table 3. (*Continued*)

Novice	Advanced beginner	Competent	Proficient	Expert
4. Knowledge of assessment strategies and design				
Describes generic forms of assessment	Considers assessment types and uses prepared materials to assess students. Considers the need to use own ideas and a range of task types But is not yet confident designing own tasks	Considers the need for assessment tasks to match specific learning objectives (SLOs), and considers the need to adjust/adapt materials to suit context and students. Considers reliability and validity in task construction	Considers the design of assessment tasks that best match SLOs/ standards and students that use authentic subject-specific practices. Understands the need for assessment tasks to be critiqued for validity and reliability	Considers the design of assessment tasks that best match SLOs/ standards and the need to create a range of assessment tasks that engage students in authentic subject-specific practices. Understands the need for assessment tasks to be critiqued for validity and reliability. Willing to share these with the teaching community
5. Knowledge of assessment interpretation				
Considers the use of a marking scheme directly to give a grade	Considers importance of using marking scheme accurately and making judgements based on this	Considers importance of using marking scheme accurately and making judgements based on interpretation of evidence	Considers importance of using marking scheme accurately and making judgements based on evidence. Considers individual students' contexts when interpreting assessment data	Considers clear accurate judgements about students based on summative assessment evidence, using marking scheme. Thinks critically about what assessment results mean – in terms of child, school, community
II. Understanding the context for assessment				
6. NCEA assessment				
Understands basics of NCEA without knowledge of particular standards, or teachers' specific roles in NCEA assessment	Considers and uses pre-written assessments tasks for NCEA internal standards but not comfortable in writing own tasks. Has some confidence in marking and moderation, but still needs guidance	Considers the need for alignment between teaching, NCEA standards and assessment tasks, and understands the marking and moderation of NCEA tasks. Adjusts/adapts assessment tasks to suit class/students	Considers all aspects of NCEA assessment with confidence, with ability to set and critique NCEA assessment materials that meet standards, and consider and adapt tasks to match students' needs. Understands and uses moderation processes	Understands and can critically engage with all aspects of the NCEA system and can communicate recognised best practice in NCEA with teachers in wider teaching community
7. Preparing students for standards-based assessment				
Does not consider the teachers' role in developing students' assessment literacy or preparing students for assessment tasks	Considers the needs students have to understand assessment processes and procedures. Considers sharing assessment criteria with students	Considers the teacher's role in preparing students for assessment. Considers sharing assessment criteria with students, using practice tasks, marking these and providing feedback	Considers the teachers' role in preparing students for assessments including developing formative/ practice tasks and providing feedback and feedforward to students on their performance. Helps students develop deeper understanding of successful engagement with assessment	Considers it part of the teachers' role to prepare students for assessment tasks by ensuring they understand the expectations around criteria and marking/ feedback, use of exemplars. Considers the development of student assessment literacy. Contributing this practice to the wider teaching community

8. Using summative assessment formatively

Taking action as a result of summative assessment is not considered	Considers teachers can learn from NCEA summative assessment in general terms, and that action may result	Considers NCEA summative assessment evidence as an important source of information for teachers, for feedback on their teaching, for feedforward for further teaching, planning	Considers NCEA summative assessment results and the appropriate analysis of these as important data on which to act with their class and with individuals	Considers all summative assessment to be useful data from which to learn and can analyse individual and class data. Can articulate findings and actions from their analysis of summative assessment data and considers using this for future planning in class, school, community

III. Recognising the impact of assessment

9. Understanding assessment consequences

Does not consider that assessment really affects people or has consequences for them	Considers the effects of assessment on students (e.g. emotional, motivational), or that assessment has effects for teachers	Considers effects of assessment on students and uses them to students' advantage /mitigates harm, and considers the effects of summative assessment results on teachers/schools	Considers the effects of assessment on students and teachers – uses this knowledge to mitigate negative effects and to benefit student learning	Considers the consequences of assessment on teachers and students, and uses this knowledge for students' benefits. Considers wider impacts of assessment and assessment policy and communicates these to wider community

10. Fairness

Considers that fairness means treating all students identically	Considers fairness as an important issue in assessment (or the assessment system), but does not feel able to adapt assessment materials for individuals. Considers it is more important that all students are treated the same or did not mention need for differentiation in assessment	Considers fairness when assessing students. Considers the need to identify ways that would enable students to provide evidence of their learning. Willing to investigate different modes to assess students against the same SLO/ standards, but with a limited range of skills	Considers the complexity of fairness issues in assessment and the need to design /adapt assessments to allow access for all students. Considers 'giving opportunity to meet the criteria' more important than having the same tasks (for students). Considers the adaptation of assessment tasks to give students access/equity	Explicitly considers fairness and access for all students. Tailors assessment in order to give all students the best opportunity to demonstrate their learning. Contributes these understanding to others in the teaching community

DEVELOPING TEACHERS' ASSESSMENT CAPACITY

Reliability of the SALRubric was also a focus in its development. Well defined and clear descriptors assist with consistency in a rubric's use. In the case of the SALRubric, a number of colleagues and assessment experts were asked to review the level descriptors for dimensions, and their advice aided the clarification of the descriptors. Because of the size of the study used in the validation and exemplars given later in this paper, the researcher alone used the SALRubric to evaluate teachers' levels of assessment literacy. In order to ensure reliability in judgements, two independent senior academics with expertise in assessment from a University were asked to independently score a sample of data using this SALRubric. Their judgements did align with those of the researcher.

Scoring with the rubric

This rubric allows teacher growth and development in summative assessment literacy to be documented and visually represented using the scores it generates. For example, when the SALRubric was used to generate scores for the case study described above, all data were aggregated for each data collection point. The largest data source was interview transcripts, and some teachers contributed many more artefacts than others. Teachers were scored 1–5 at each of five data collection points with 1 being 'novice' and 5 being 'expert' based on consideration of all the data gathered from each teacher at each data collection point. Where no evidence was available, a score of 0 was recorded, and data was treated as missing, as the data collection methods might not allow an opportunity for the teacher to demonstrate a particular competency.

To illustrate scoring, the following are examples from three teachers, Jane, Elizabeth and Ryan, being scored for dimensions of summative assessment literacy using the SALRubric.

Jane: The issues of fairness were raised in each interview with Jane. At the beginning of the study, Jane talked only in terms of all students being treated the same, and this was evident in the artefacts she contributed, therefore for the dimension of *Dimension 10: Fairness* she was scored as a 1 (novice). For the next data collection time point Jane did acknowledge that fairness was an issue in assessment, and should be considered by teachers, including herself. However, she said that she ended up assessing all students in the same way, as she wasn't sure how to adapt materials to suit students with, for example, literacy challenges. The artefacts she provided confirmed this. This meant that she was scored as 2 (advanced beginner) for *Fairness*. The evidence she provided during later time points showed that she did not change from this stance, so the score remained at 2.

Elizabeth: At the beginning of her ITE programme, Elizabeth spoke of assessment in broad terms in her first interview saying 'well I just see it as being able to understand what a student understands … understands of what you're teaching', her questionnaire revealed that she knew of a number of assessment types: essays, examinations, tests, but had no confidence in her ability to generate assessment tasks, and she had no artefacts to present that reflected her understanding or ability to assess students. This meant she was scored as a 1 (novice) for *Dimension 4: Knowledge of strategies and design*. However, near the end of her ITE year, she was able to explain and show evidence of how she designed and used an assessment task that aligned with an NCEA achievement standard and the NZC. She had designed, critiqued, used and had moderated an assessment task designed around Edible Vaccines. This task was of good quality and incorporated the investigation and research skills required of a senior class in a Biotechnology unit. She was able to explain her assessment decision-making in the construction and use of the task. She was scored at 4 (proficient) for *Dimension 4* at this stage, as the task design was appropriate and matched the Achievement Standard, and she had followed the protocols required for the NCEA assessment.

Ryan: When Ryan was assessed against *Dimension 2: Knowledge of purposes of summative assessment* he was scored at 1 (novice) on entry to his ITE programme. In his interview, he spoke about assessment vaguely and only from his experience as a student saying 'So you got your marks, and you passed, and whatever you had to do, and then you just forgot about it …. From my own personal experiences, mainly exams, and as I say I hated them'. However, by the end of his first six months of employment as a teacher Ryan was able to explain a range of specific purposes for which he used summative assessment tasks, including NCEA assessment, reporting, formative use and data analysis for school-wide programme appraisal. He provided samples of assessment tasks he had developed and marked, and he described how some of these were used formatively. However, he was not yet able to articulate how this assessment related to the New Zealand curriculum, nor did he talk show an awareness of the accountability aspect of summative assessment. He was scored at 3 (competent).

The application of the SALRubric

The final SALRubric was applied to tracking the development of summative assessment literacy of eight pre-service to novice teachers in New Zealand. In order to document the development of assessment literacy in these participant teachers, data was collected over time, as shown in Table 1. Data gathered at each time point in the study was carefully analysed and considered as a whole, and a judgement about each teacher's level of competency was made for each of the 10 dimensions in the SALRubric. The combination of interview transcripts, artefacts and questionnaire responses were analysed thematically and allowed triangulation and enabled the researcher to make holistic judgements regarding which level in the rubric best matched each teacher's assessment literacy development for each dimension at each time point.

In this study, a summary of each teacher's scores for all dimensions was tabulated. Radar charts were created that visually represented this data. The radar charts enabled teacher-educators to retrospectively view the development of assessment literacy for individuals and for the group as a whole.

Patterns of teachers' development

For each individual pre-service/novice teacher in the case study, a distinct pattern of development was observed and individuals developed at varying rates across a number of dimensions. SALRubric scores from this study indicated that all eight teachers in the full study had demonstrated increased assessment literacy competence over time on each dimension. Six teachers showed increasing competency in all 10 dimensions, one teacher showed an increased competency in 9 dimensions, and one teacher showed an increased competency in 8 dimensions.

All eight teachers in this study scored 1 (novice) for the majority of dimensions at the first data gathering point. For the majority of teachers an increased competency in most dimensions was particularly noticed between the first and second data gathering points. This coincided with teachers having a period of time on practicum. A further significant

DEVELOPING TEACHERS' ASSESSMENT CAPACITY

Table 4. Teachers' scores using SALRubric for each of five data collection time points.

	Int 1	Int 2	Int 3	Int 4	Int 5
Jane					
1. Ability to describe assessment	1	2	2	2	3
2. Knowledge of purposes of summative assessment	2	3	3	3	3
3. Knowledge of what to assess	1	3	3	3	3
4. Knowledge of strategies and design	1	2	2	2	2
5. Knowledge of assessment interpretation	1	3	3	3	3
6. NCEA assessment	1	2	2	2	3
7. Preparing students for standards-based assessment	0	0	0	2	3
8. Using summative assessment formatively	1	3	3	3	3
9. Understanding assessment consequences	2	2	2	3	3
10. Fairness	1	2	2	2	2
Elizabeth					
1. Ability to describe assessment	1	2	2	3	3
2. Knowledge of purposes of summative assessment	1	3	3	3	3
3. Knowledge of what to assess	2	2	2	3	3
4. Knowledge of strategies and design	1	3	3	4	4
5. Knowledge of assessment interpretation	2	2	2	3	3
6. NCEA assessment	1	2	2	3	4
7. Preparing students for standards-based assessment	0	3	3	3	3
8. Using summative assessment formatively	2	3	3	3	3
9. Understanding assessment consequences	1	1	2	2	2
10. Fairness	1	2	2	2	3
Ryan					
1. Ability to describe assessment	1	2	2	2	2
2. Knowledge of purposes of summative assessment	1	1	2	2	3
3. Knowledge of what to assess	1	1	1	2	2
4. Knowledge of strategies and design	1	1	1	2	2
5. Knowledge of assessment interpretation	2	2	2	2	2
6. NCEA assessment	1	1	1	2	2
7. Preparing students for standards-based assessment	1	1	2	2	3
8. Using summative assessment formatively	2	2	2	2	2
9. Understanding assessment consequences	2	2	2	2	3
10. Fairness	1	1	1	2	2

shift occurred between the third and fourth data gathering points. Again this coincided with the time when teachers were on placement full time in a school under the guidance of one or two associate teachers. This raises questions about the extent to which increased competencies identified at data collection points two and four were linked to the learning and experience teachers gained in the time they spent in schools.

The scores from three of the eight teachers are presented below in Table 4 to illustrate a variety of development patterns. Radar charts for these three individual teachers were developed to present the data graphically, as shown in Figure 1.

Jane's case

Jane commenced her ITE with little confidence about her knowledge and skills about assessment. Interview 1 scores show she was at a novice level for most dimensions, although she scored 2 for *Knowledge of purposes of assessment*, and *Understanding of assessment consequences*. Jane showed significant development in her summative assessment literacy at the second data collection point after her first practicum, where there was documented evidence of improvement in 8 of the 10 dimensions, with 3 dimensions being scored at 3 (competent) surprisingly early. However, no further development was noticed in these

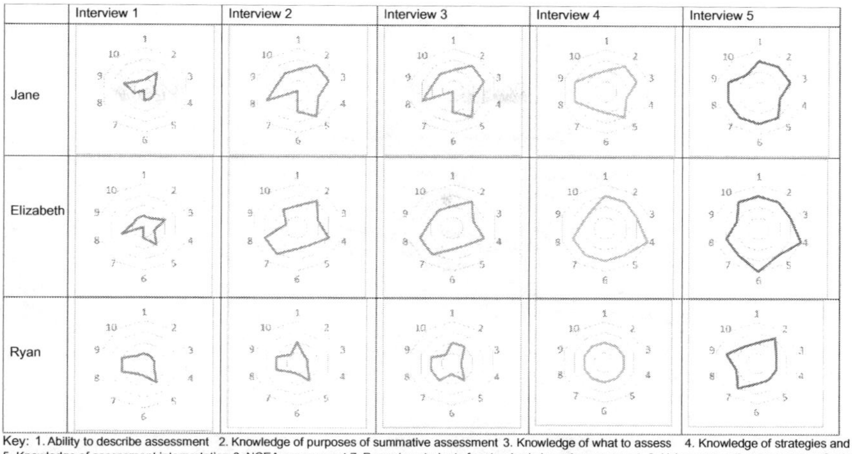

DEVELOPING TEACHERS' ASSESSMENT CAPACITY

Key: 1. Ability to describe assessment 2. Knowledge of purposes of summative assessment 3. Knowledge of what to assess 4. Knowledge of strategies and design 5. Knowledge of assessment interpretation 6. NCEA assessment 7. Preparing students for standards-based assessment 8. Using summative assessment formatively 9. Understanding assessment consequences 10. Fairness

Figure 1. Radar charts for teachers' assessment literacy development.

eight dimensions until six months into her first year of teaching. No evidence of change in dimensions 7 and 9 (*Preparing students for standards-based assessment* and *Understanding assessment consequences*) was present until near the end of her ITE programme, after her second practicum. By the end of the 20-month study, Jane was scored as competent in eight of the dimensions of the SALRubric, and at the advanced beginner level for *Knowledge of strategies and design*, and *Fairness*. Of interest was Jane's rapid development in some dimensions early in her ITE year, followed by little perceptible change for a long period of time.

Elizabeth's case

Elizabeth commenced her teacher education and was scored at a novice level for most dimensions of summative assessment literacy, scoring 2 for *Knowledge of what to assess*, and *Using summative assessment formatively*. She showed an increase in her competency levels for most dimensions by the second data collection point, and an increase in one dimension *Knowledge of assessment interpretation* at the third data collection point. At the fourth data collection point, Elizabeth was scored at competent or proficient level for all but two dimensions, and she talked confidently about assessing students in her first teaching position. By the end of the study, Elizabeth was the highest scoring of the teachers overall, with the only dimension below the competent level being *Understanding assessment consequences*.

Ryan's case

Ryan entered ITE with a very negative view of assessment based on his personal experiences of being assessed. He was scored at the novice level for 7 of the 10 dimensions and advanced beginner for the other three. Ryan showed very slow development in almost all dimensions, and by the end of the ITE year, he scored advanced beginner for all dimensions. At the final data collection point, Ryan scored 3 (competent) for 3 of the 10 dimensions. For two of the dimensions, *Knowledge of assessment interpretation* and *Understanding assessment consequences*, Ryan showed no development over the entire study.

99

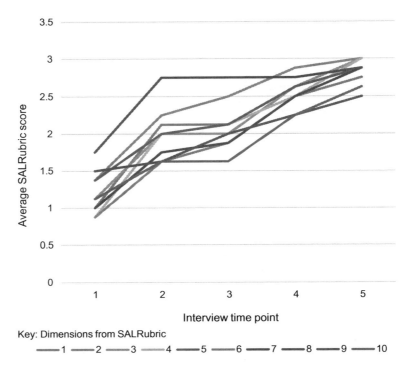

Figure 2. Average SALRubric scores for 8 teachers.

While idiosyncratic patterns were evident in teachers' development of assessment literacy, as shown for the three cases in Figure 1, some patterns were observable when scores were combined for all teachers. For example, all teachers experienced growth in assessment literacy but none of them achieved the 'expert' level on any dimensions. In order to better see these patterns, the scores generated from the rubric were averaged for the eight participants for each dimension over the five time points.

Figure 2 shows the average scores for the eight teachers for each dimension over the 20-month period. The gradients indicate the size of shift in average teacher competencies for each dimension over time. For example, the steep gradients between the first and second data gathering points, and the third and fourth data gathering points, indicate more substantive shifts for most teachers, and the lower gradient between the third and fourth data gathering points indicates smaller shifts in this time period. It is interesting to note the slower improvement in development of 'fairness' over the course of the study, perhaps indicating the difficulty teachers find in moving from a belief that to be fair everything must be equal, to understanding the complexity of fairness issues and the need for access to all and equity.

Discussion

Assessment literacy is important for effective teaching even though considered to be 'a stable but malleable characteristic of teachers' (Gotch & French, 2014, p. 14). Gauging assessment literacy has proven challenging, and despite the development and use of a number of tools, a recent review of a large range of teacher assessment literacy measures highlighted the need for increased work in this field as support for claims made based on the tools was found to be weak (Gotch & French, 2014). The use of the SALRubric to track the development of teachers' summative assessment literacy illustrates how patterns of development can be made visible. These findings raise many interesting questions for individual teachers' development and indicate the complexity of the development of assessment literacy. The findings illustrate the SALRubric as a useful and relevant way of assessing summative assessment literacy and its potential on informing teacher-educators and pre-service and novice teachers' on their practice and development.

The SALRubric is a context-specific tool developed to track summative assessment literacy for New Zealand secondary teachers. It focuses on aspects particularly pertinent to assessment literacy in the context in which it is being used. It has merits over a generic assessment literacy measurement tool designed for a very different context (many tools originate from the USA which has a very different assessment culture). In particular, the dimensions in Category II of the SALRubric are context specific. The particular requirements of NCEA and standards-based assessment, as well as the strong policy emphasis on formative assessment in New Zealand, are reflected in these dimensions. Educators in countries with different forms of summative assessment and different policy priorities may need to reconsider Category II of the SALRubric.

Recontextualising assessment tools for local settings has been reported with respect to Assessment for Learning tools (Hermansen, 2014), and a similar country-specific or jurisdiction-specific recontextualisation would mean that SALRubric could have wider applications.

For the three examples given above, it can be seen that the teachers arrived at the teacher education programme with a range of knowledge and understanding about assessment (similar to findings by DeLuca, Chavez, Bellara & Cao, 2013; Hill et al., 2013; Lyon, 2013b). It is clear from the radar charts that these teachers developed in dimensions of assessment literacy at different rates. Close examination of the development pattern for individual teachers allowed for better understanding of their strengths and areas in which they needed support. Looking forward, formative use of the SALRubric could be made for future pre-service and novice teachers, allowing more targeted and specific teaching to enable teachers to more likely become competent by the time they enter employment as teachers.

In summary, the examples in Figure 1 show that the SALRubric provided a mechanism by which teachers' assessment literacy could be monitored over time in a nuanced way. Key experiences were held in common by all teachers in the study, yet their development patterns did not always occur in parallel. The trajectories were varied, and individual teachers developed dimensions of assessment literacy in diverse and often idiosyncratic ways. When regarded holistically, development occurred over time and for a range of reasons, some known to the teachers and others probably unknown, and it appears that proposing a simple cause and effect mechanism to the development of assessment literacy would be too simplistic.

The SALRubric and associated radar charts facilitate the documentation and visual representation of the development of teachers' assessment literacy over time. The SALRubric has evidence of content validity through the use of elements of the empirically derived model of science teacher assessment literacy developed by Abell and Siegel (2011), work by Lyon (2013a), New Zealand context-specific policies, and inductively derived elements arising from the study. The use of context-sensitive tools like the SALRubric has potential to allow teacher-educators and pre-service and novice teachers to more closely monitor the development of assessment literacy in individuals for evaluative purposes. It also has potential for use as a powerful formative assessment tool to assist teachers see where they need to focus their learning with respect to summative assessment literacy.

Implications for teacher education

The examples presented were focussed on the developing summative assessment literacy of a group of New Zealand secondary teachers. However, the use of a context-specific rubric such as the SALRubric has broader applications for teacher-educators and those involved in the support of novice teachers.

Assessment literacy develops over time and has a number of dimensions. The SALRubric can indicate and measure shifts in pre-service and novice teacher assessment literacy. This can be done by considering a combination of the generally agreed attributes of assessment literacy as described in the literature, as well as context-specific policies and practices deemed important by experienced educators in the jurisdiction where the teachers work. A context-specific rubric which clearly delineates expectations for assessment literacy could then be used both as a tool to monitor shifts, and more importantly, as an instrument to aid in learning. Rubrics can be used to enhance teaching by providing educators, mentors and students with descriptions of concepts and common language to foster discussion and feedback. Studies have shown that clearly described criteria allow for better understanding of the dimensions by those being assessed, allowing for reflection on practice, facilitating communication between experienced practitioner and learner, and giving them shared language to foster feedback and discussion (Keister et al., 2012; Lasater, 2011). The strength of a context-specific rubric such as the SALRubric is that it can reflect internationally accepted dimensions of assessment literacy but at the same time it can respond to particular contextual priorities.

By using a rubric such as the SALRubric, and looking at patterns across pre-service and novice teachers' development, teacher-educators are able to pinpoint times of more rapid growth and development and times of little change. In this study, the effect of teacher education, and particularly the practicum within the teacher education programme, can be seen to be critical as considerable growth was noticeable in almost all teachers after each practicum. A backwards mapping exercise to discover what particular events and/or learning activities were aligned to growth could further inform teacher-educators and mentor teachers. By looking at the development of assessment literacy as an amalgam of dimensions rather than conflating scores to get an overall score, teacher-educators and pre-service teachers are able to use the rubric formatively, to direct feedback and adjust instruction (Lyon, 2013a). Additionally, if a formative focus is taken, pre-service and novice teachers are more likely to consider focus areas for their own development.

Limitations

The exemplars used in this paper came from a qualitative study of secondary science teachers in New Zealand. The SALRubric was developed deductively from literature sources, and inductively using multiple data sources from pre-service/novice teachers, collated over time. The SALRubric is being presented as a context-specific tool that has been shown to be useful in monitoring summative assessment literacy, rather than as a tool of high technical quality ready for general use. Its use should encourage conversations and feedback between teacher-educators and teachers. The findings reported in this paper are from a small qualitative research study, and as such, there is limited scope for making generalisations about these teachers or ITE programmes. However, the patterns of development raise a range of questions worth further investigation. No teachers in this study were at an expert level on any of the dimensions. This is not unexpected as these levels were based in part on expected performance by experienced teachers in New Zealand as outlined in the *Practising Teacher Criteria* (Education Council, 2015). However, enough evidence was gathered in this study to suggest further exploration in the area of assessment literacy development through the use of an analytical rubric such as the SALRubric is worthwhile.

Conclusion

The SALRubric contributes to work on the development of assessment capacity in pre-service and novice teachers in that it provides a tool by which summative assessment literacy can be monitored and visually represented. Although a number of studies have examined aspects of development of assessment literacy, many are based on one-off surveys or measurements. There are very few extended studies of the development of teachers' assessment literacy over time (three examples are Edwards & Cooper, 2012; Smith et al., 2014; Volante & Fazio, 2007). The SALRubric provides additional insights into the nature of teachers' development as they become more sophisticated in their assessment practices. This paper has detailed the insights gained from the design and use of SALRubric, a customised rubric, to track the development of pre-service and novice teachers' summative assessment literacy. The rubric has value in identifying key dimensions of summative assessment literacy and making these visible for teacher-educators and pre-service teachers.

Disclosure statement

No potential conflict of interest was reported by the author.

References

Abell, S. K., & Siegel, M. A. (2011). Assessment literacy: What science teachers need to know and be able to do. In D. Corrigan, J. Dillon, & R. Gunstone (Eds.), *The professional knowledge base of science teaching* (pp. 205–221). Dordrecht: Springer.

Aitken, G., Sinnema, C., & Meyer, F. (2012). *Initial teacher education outcomes: Graduate teacher standards – background paper*. Auckland: The University of Auckland.

Bakx, A., Baartman, L., & van Schilt-Mol, T. (2014). Development and evaluation of a summative assessment program for senior teacher competence. *Studies in Educational Evaluation, 40*, 50–62. doi:10.1016/j.stueduc.2013.11.004

Black, P., Harrison, C., Hodgen, J., Marshall, B., & Serret, N. (2010). Validity in teachers' summative assessments. *Assessment in Education: Principles, Policy & Practice, 17*, 215–232. doi:10.1080/09695941003696016

Bransford, J. D., Brown, A. L., & Cocking, R. (Eds.). (2000). *How people learn: Brain, mind, experience, and school.* Washington, DC: National Academy Press.

Brookhart, S. M. (1999). *The art and science of classroom assessment: The missing part of pedagogy* (ASHE-ERIC Higher Education Report No. Vol. 27, No. 1). Washington, DC: The George Washington University, Graduate School of Education and Human Development.

Brookhart, S. (2011). Educational assessment knowledge and skills for teachers. *Educational Measurement: Issues and Practice, 30*, 3–12.

Cendan, J., Hernandez, C., & Castiglioni, A. (2015). Using visual radar graph representation of learner achievement to complement the RIME framework. *Academic Medicine, 90*, 1425. doi:10.1097/ACM.0000000000000360

Chen, P. P. (2005). Teacher candidates' literacy in assessment. *Academic Exchange Quarterly, 65*, 62–66.

Christoforidou, M., Kyriakides, L., Antoniou, P., & Creemers, B. P. M. (2014). Searching for stages of teacher's skills in assessment. *Studies in Educational Evaluation, 40*, 1–11. doi:10.1016/j.stueduc.2013.11.006

Crooks, T. (2011). Assessment for learning in the accountability era: New Zealand. *Studies in Educational Evaluation, 37*, 71–77. doi:10.1016/j.stueduc.2011.03.002

DeLuca, C., Chavez, T., Bellara, A., & Cao, C. (2013). Pedagogies for preservice assessment education: Supporting teacher candidates' assessment literacy development. *The Teacher Educator, 48*, 128–142.

DeLuca, C., & Klinger, D. A. (2010). Assessment literacy development: Identifying gaps in teacher candidates' learning. *Assessment in Education: Principles, Policy & Practice, 17*, 419–438. doi:10.1080/0969594X.2010.516643

Dreyfus, S. E. (2004). The five-stage model of adult skill acquisition. *Bulletin of Science, Technology & Society, 24*, 177–181. doi:10.1177/0270467604264992

Dreyfus, H. L., & Dreyfus, S. E. (1986). *Mind over machine: The power of human intuition and expertise in the era of the computer.* New York, NY: Free Press.

Education Council New Zealand. (2015). Practising teacher criteria. Retrieved from http://educationcouncil.org.nz/content/practising-teacher-criteria

Edwards, F. C. E. (2014). Developing assessment literacy in early career New Zealand secondary teachers: Summative assessment. Presented at the European Association for Research on Learning and Instruction: SIG 1 Assessment and Evaluation Conference, August 27–29, 2014, Madrid, Spain.

Edwards, F. C. E. (2016). Tracking the development of assessment literacy: Pre-service teachers' trajectories. Paper presented at Public Scholarship to Educate Diverse Democracies AERA 2016, April 8–12, 2016, Washington, DC, USA.

Edwards, F., & Cooper, B. (2012). Developing assessment capable secondary teachers. Paper presented at European Association for Research on Learning and Instruction SIG1 Conference, August 28–31, 2012, Brussels, Belgium.

Edwards, F. C. E., & Edwards, R. J. (2016). A story of culture and teaching: the complexity of teacher identity formation. *The Curriculum Journal*, 1–22. Doi:10.1080/09585176.2016.1232200

Eyers, G. (2014). *Pre-service teachers' assessment learning: Change, development and growth* (PhD). University of Auckland, Auckland.

Furtak, E. M., Morrison, D., & Kroog, H. (2014). Investigating the link between learning progressions and classroom assessment. *Science Education, 98*, 640–673. doi:10.1002/sce.21122

Gipps, C. (1999). Socio-cultural aspects of assessment. *Review of Research in Education, 24*, 355–392.

Gotch, C. M., & French, B. F. (2014). A systematic review of assessment literacy measures. *Educational Measurement: Issues and Practice, 33*, 14–18. doi:10.1111/emip.12030

Harlen, W., & Gardner, J. (2010). Assessment to support learning. In J. Gardner, W. Harlen, L. Hayward, G. Stobart, & M. Montgomery (Eds.), *Developing teacher assessment* (pp. 15–28). Maidenhead: Open University Press.

Harris, J., Grandgenett, N., & Hofer, M. (2012). Testing an Instrument using structured interviews to assess experienced teachers' TPACK. *Teacher Education Faculty Proceedings & Presentations.* Retrieved from http://digitalcommons.unomaha.edu/tedfacproc/15

Hermansen, H. (2014). Recontextualising assessment resources for use in local settings: Opening up the black box of teachers' knowledge work. *The Curriculum Journal, 25,* 470–494. doi:10.108 0/09585176.2014.956771

Hill, M., Cowie, B., Gilmore, A., & Smith, L. (2010). Preparing assessment-capable teachers: What should pre-service teachers know and be able to do? *Assessment Matters, 2,* 43–64.

Hill, M., Smith, L., Cowie, B., Gilmore, A., & Gunn, A. (2013). *Preparing initial primary and early childhood teacher education students to use assessment.* Retrieved from http://www.tlri.org.nz/sites/default/files/projects/Hill_Final%20Summary%20Report_signed%20off.pdf

Keister, D. M., Larson, D., Dostal, J., & Baglia, J. (2012). The radar graph: The development of an educational tool to demonstrate resident competency. *Journal of Graduate Medical Education, 4,* 220–226. doi:10.4300/JGME-D-11-00163.1

Koh, K. (2014). Authentic assessment, teacher judgment and moderation in a context of high accountability. In C. Wyatt-Smith, V. Klenowski, & P. Colbert (Eds.), *Designing assessment for quality learning* (pp. 249–264). Dordrecht: Springer.

Lasater, K. (2007). Clinical judgment development: Using simulation to create an assessment rubric. *Journal of Nursing Education, 46,* 496–503.

Lasater, K. (2011). Clinical judgment: The last frontier for evaluation. *Nurse Education in Practice, 11,* 86–92. doi:10.1016/j.nepr.2010.11.013

Luft, J. A. (1999). Rubrics: Design and use in science teacher education. *Journal of Science Teacher Education., 10,* 107–121.

Lyon, E. G. (2013a). Conceptualizing and exemplifying science teachers' assessment expertise. *International Journal of Science Education, 35,* 1208–1229. doi:10.1080/09500693.2013.770180

Lyon, E. G. (2013b). Learning to assess science in linguistically diverse classrooms: Tracking growth in secondary science pre-service teachers' assessment expertise. *Science Education, 97,* 442–467. doi:10.1002/sce.21059

Maclellan, E. (2004). Initial knowledge states about assessment: Novice teachers' conceptualisations. *Teaching and Teacher Education, 20,* 523–535. doi:10.1016/j.tate.2004.04.008

Martín del Pozo, R., Porlán, R., & Rivero, A. (2011). The progression of prospective teachers' conceptions of school science content. *Journal of Science Teacher Education, 22,* 291–312. doi:10.1007/s10972-011-9233-4

McGee, J., & Colby, S. (2014). Impact of an assessment course on teacher candidates' assessment literacy. *Action in Teacher Education, 36,* 522–532. doi:10.1080/01626620.2014.977753

Mertler, C. A. (2001). Designing scoring rubrics for your classroom *Practical Assessment, Research & Evaluation, 7.* Retrieved June 20, 2016, from http://PAREonline.net/getvn.asp?v=7&n=25

Mertler, C., & Campbell, C. (2005). Measuring teachers' knowledge and application of classroom assessment concepts: Development of the assessment literacy inventory. Presented at the Annual meeting of the American Educational Research Association, Montreal, Quebec, Canada.

Moskal, B. M. (2000). Scoring rubrics: What, when and how? *Practical Assessment, Research & Evaluation, 7.* Retrieved June 20, 2016, from http://PAREonline.net/getvn.asp?v=7&n=3

Moskal, B. M., & Leydens, J. A. (2000). Scoring rubric development: Validity and reliability. *Practical Assessment, Research & Evaluation, 7*(10), 1–10.

New Zealand Qualifications Authority. (2015). *Annual report on NCEA and New Zealand scholarship data and statistics (2014).* Wellington: Ministry of Education.

Nusche, D., Laveault, D., MacBeath, J., & Santiago, P. (2012). OECD reviews of evaluation and assessment in education: New Zealand, main conclusions. Retrieved from http://www.oecd.org/education/school/49681563.pdf

Popham, W. J. (2009). Assessment literacy for teachers: Faddish or fundamental? *Theory Into Practice, 48,* 4–11. doi:10.1080/00405840802577536

Popham, W. J. (2011). Assessment literacy overlooked: A teacher educator's confession. *The Teacher Educator, 46,* 265–273.

DEVELOPING TEACHERS' ASSESSMENT CAPACITY

Pryor, J., & Crossouard, B. (2008). A socio-cultural theorisation of formative assessment. *Oxford Review of Education, 34*(1), 1–20. doi:10.1080/03054980701476386

Schneider, R. M., & Plasman, K. (2011). Science teacher learning progressions a review of science teachers' pedagogical content knowledge development. *Review of Educational Research, 81*, 530–565. doi:10.3102/0034654311423382

Shepard, L. A. (2000). The role of assessment in a learning culture. *Educational Researcher, 29*, 4–14. doi:10.2307/1176145

Siegel, M. A. (2014). Developing preservice science teachers' expertise in equitable assessment. *Journal of Science Teacher Education, 25*, 289–308.

Smith, L. F., Corkery, G., Buckley, J., & Calvert, A. (2013). Changes in secondary school pre-service teachers' concerns about teaching in New Zealand. *Journal of Teacher Education, 64*, 60–74. doi:10.1177/0022487112449019

Smith, L. F., Hill, M. F., Cowie, B., & Gilmore, A. (2014). Preparing teachers to use the enabling power of assessment. In C. Wyatt-Smith, V. Klenowski, & P. Colbert (Eds.), *Designing assessment for quality learning* (pp. 303–323). Dordrecht: Springer Netherlands. Retrieved from http://link.springer.com.ezproxy.waikato.ac.nz/chapter/10.1007/978-94-007-5902-2_19

Spillane, J. P., & Miele, D. B. (2007). Evidence in practice: A framing of the terrain. In P. A. Moss (Ed.), *Evidence and decision making* (pp. 46–73). Malden, MA: National Society for the Study of Education.

Stevens, D., & Levi, A. (2005). *Introduction to rubrics: An assessment tool to save grading time, convey effective feedback, and promote student learning.* Stirling, VA: Stylus.

Struyven, K., Dochy, F., & Janssens, S. (2008). The effects of hands-on experience on students' preferences for assessment methods. *Journal of Teacher Education, 59*, 69–88. doi:10.1177/0022487107311335

TeachNZ. (2006). *Advanced classroom expertise teacher recognition.* Retrieved from https://www.teachnz.govt.nz/home/advanced-classroom-expertise-teacher-recognition/

Timperley, H. (2013). Learning to practise: A paper for discussion. Retrieved from http://www.educationcounts.govt.nz/__data/assets/pdf_file/0014/120146/LearningTo-Practise.pdf

Volante, L., & Fazio, X. (2007). Exploring teacher candidates' assessment literacy: Implications for teacher education reform and professional development. *Canadian Journal of Education, 30*, 749–770.

Willis, J., Adie, L., & Klenowski, V. (2013). Conceptualising teachers' assessment literacies in an era of curriculum and assessment reform. *The Australian Educational Researcher, 40*, 241–256. doi:10.1007/s13384-013-0089-9

Windschitl, M., Thompson, J., Braaten, M., & Stroupe, D. (2012). Proposing a core set of instructional practices and tools for teachers of science. *Science Education, 96*, 878–903.

Appendix – Interview protocol

1. What is your understanding of assessment? Of summative assessment?
2. What purpose/s do you think assessment serves?
3. How is (summative) assessment used in secondary classrooms?
4. How, if at all, have you used (summative) assessment as a teacher? Examples?
5. What have you learnt about assessment that has surprised you so far?
6. What have you learnt about assessment from your practicum experience?
7. How has your practicum experience helped in your development as a teacher with respect to summative assessment?
8. What have you learnt about assessment from your university course experience?
9. How has your university course experience helped in your development as a teacher with respect to summative assessment?
10. How 'assessment capable' do you feel at the moment? Explain.
11. What do you need to learn about assessment?

DEVELOPING TEACHERS' ASSESSMENT CAPACITY

12. In the last interview you said …[quote of interest from previous interview]… do you want to comment on this now? [Used for any quotes that required follow-up].

Interviewees were also asked to talk about the artefacts they provided, and asked how these demonstrated their assessment literacy development. This conversation occurred either at the beginning or near the end of the interview – whenever interviewees referred to the artefacts as a natural part of the interview.

Professional controversies between teachers about their summative assessment practices: a tool for building assessment capacity

Lucie Mottier Lopez and Raphaël Pasquini

ABSTRACT

This article describes two collaborative research projects whose common goal was to explore the potential role of professional controversies in building teachers' summative assessment capacity. In the first project, upper primary teachers were encouraged to compare their practices through a form of social moderation, without prior instructor input or theoretical preparation. In the second project, lower secondary school teachers were encouraged to compare their summative assessment practices with reference to a theoretical model of curriculum alignment, under the guidance of an instructor. The findings support the potentially constructive role of professional controversies in supporting teachers' professional development for summative assessment. They highlight the status of references called upon in discussion of controversies, and their contribution to the construction of the subjects under discussion.

Introduction

Since the work of Bloom, Hasting, and Madaus (1971), formative and summative assessment of student learning have been differentiated. While most research on teacher assessment has focused on formative assessment whose goal is 'to ensure adaptation of teaching and learning activities in ways that will enable students to attain intended learning outcomes of schooling' (Laveault & Allal, 2016, p. 4), the research literature has exposed worrying findings about teachers' *summative* assessment practice, whose purpose 'is to determine the student's overall achievement in a specific area of learning at a particular time' (Moss, 2013, p. 235). In view of its impact on students' future academic pathways, achieving dependable summative assessment continues to be a major challenge for teacher professional development. Moss has noted, for example, that as far as summative assessment is concerned, 'many teachers are underprepared and insufficiently skilled. This leads to summative judgments that are often inaccurate and unreliable' (Moss, 2013, p. 251).

In most OECD countries,[1] summative assessment tends to remain traditional, focused on a limited number of cognitive outcomes, thus reducing the content of the curriculum

(Nusche, Radinger, Santiago, & Shewbridge, 2013). Other research has qualified these findings – for example, the study of Allal and Mottier Lopez (2014) revealed that professional judgement processes were in operation when teachers graded their students' work. In particular, teacher professional judgement involves a critical and ethical reflection on the benefits and risks of decisions based on assessment evidence. In this article, we focus on the construction of summative tests by teachers, among other professional skills that come into play in classroom summative assessment practice.

Among different models of teacher professional learning and development (e.g. Timperley, Wilson, Barrar, & Fung, 2007), we adopted a collaborative research approach (Desgagné, 1997; Desgagné, Bednarz, Lebuis, Poirier, & Couture, 2001; Mottier Lopez & Morales Villabona, 2016) in our explorations into the potential for building teachers' summative assessment capacity of 'professional controversies', i.e. of debates among professionals who express contradicting viewpoints, arguments and proposals (Lessard, 2012). Such intellectual debates aim at improving representations and practices whose stakes are linked to a profession (Clot, 2010).

Collaborative research 'encourages teachers to question and refine their practices and to work together on a wide range of shared problems relating to contemporary education' (Desgagné, 1997, p. 36, our translation). The double goal of this approach is to provide empirically based information about teachers' summative assessment practices, and to support their transformation seen as closely linked to collective practices of collaboration (Wenger, 1998).

This article focuses on two collaborative research projects undertaken in French-speaking Switzerland, one in the primary sector and the other in the lower secondary sector. While both projects were designed to develop teachers' summative assessment capacity, they differed in their operational choices, in particular with respect to the framework underpinning the comparison between teachers' summative assessment practices: theoretical references, actorial references and institutional references (Vanhulle, Merhan, & Ronveaux, 2007). The primary-based project relied on teachers' experience-based knowledge and their institutional points of reference to encourage the sharing and comparison of their situated assessment practices, while in the lower secondary project, collective exchanges between teachers were initiated with research-based knowledge as an added frame of reference. This difference between the two projects is characteristic of dialectical processes (bottom-up processes and top-down processes) between situated assessment practices and theoretical knowledge involved in teacher professional development designs.

The objective of the research was to study the exchanges among participants within each setting, especially when the teachers concerned *did not share* their views about their summative assessment practices. We chose this focus because the literature on teachers' professional development rarely examines potentially constructive disagreements among practitioners (e.g. Lefeuvre, Garcia, & Namolovan, 2009). In an exploratory perspective, our study examines the types of contradictions and argumentations expressed by participating teachers, and the kind of shared knowledge they co-constructed about their summative assessment in relation to the frameworks (theoretical, actorial and institutional references) valued by each research project.

We first present our general theoretical framework about teachers' professional development centred on a collaborative research approach. We follow by explaining the value of studying professional controversies in these collaborative contexts. Then, we present the theoretical bases underpinning our two specific projects (social moderation and curriculum alignment model). In the second part of the article, we present the common ground for the two projects and the methodology used to analyse the professional controversies that emerged, before offering some salient findings and reflective interpretation.

Collaborative research to support teachers' professional development

Collaborative research is popular in the French-speaking community in Switzerland, by virtue of educational policies deliberately intended to encourage partnerships between the worlds of educational research and teaching. This construction of professional knowledge and understanding is supported by negotiations and dialogues led by the collaborative research group (Desgagné, 1997, 2007; Desgagné et al., 2001; Morrissette, Mottier Lopez, & Tessaro, 2012; Mottier Lopez, 2015).

Ways of thinking about the relationship between theory and practice are quite varied in collaborative research. Some start with teachers' practices and experiences. Others favour more top-down approaches, mainly based on theoretical models offered by educational research. Despite their diversity, collaborative research projects involve teachers in the study of their own pedagogical practices, making explicit and integrating their 'internal' understanding of situations. Collaborative research can focus on the 'individual and his or her activity' (e.g. the teacher in the classroom when he or she is assessing students' work) or on a 'group of persons and their activity' (e.g. a community of teachers who collaborate to construct common assessment tools) (Lefeuvre et al., 2009).

Emphasis is often placed on the importance of collaborative interactions between members of a learning community for professional development purposes. The conflictual dimension is rarely examined. However, Lessard (2012) postulates that professional controversies can contribute to the reflectiveness of teachers, and to change in their practices. Lessard defines controversy as 'all reasoned, on-going discussion, all structured and continuous debate on an issue of interest to a particular group' (p. 128, our translation). Lessard assumes that controversies destabilise teachers, and function as a lever for greater individual and collective reflectiveness. The notion of controversy for Lessard extends this reflectiveness to 'the relationship between self and a practice, in the presence of others' (p. 123, our translation). Finally, it is this public relationship between self and the norms and practices of the teaching profession that would be critical for more effective pedagogical practices. In a work analysis perspective, Clot (2010) considers it is through controversy that the quality of a profession is envisaged and redefined by means of an individual–collective relationship. 'This "professional debate" originates in the collective and then continues, consciously or unconsciously, in the individual. Thus it becomes no longer a matter of the individual within the collective, as the collective merges into the individual' (p. 177, our translation). Lessard (2012) notes that very few studies have examined controversies as a *potential* motor for teacher professional development. It is for this reason that we chose to examine professional controversies likely to occur in collaborative research, knowing that an important limitation of our choice is that the issue rarely features in the current research literature.

To delineate our units of analysis, we drew from the pedagogical model of 'constructive controversy' proposed by Johnson (2015) in a cooperative learning perspective. 'Constructive controversy exists when one person's ideas, information, conclusions, theories, or opinions are incompatible with those of another, and the two seek to reach an agreement that reflects their best reasoned judgment'. Controversy involves discussion of the advantages and disadvantages of proposed actions. The participants assume different points of view, use arguments, counterarguments and refutations. Controversy involves inquiry to resolve the issue emerging from the critical discussion, and leads to reconceptualisation, synthesis and integration (Johnson, 2015).

In our context of teacher professional development, we are interested in this process of constructive controversy, but related to the kind of references (actorial, institutional and theoretical) called on in the exchanges to explain, to argue, to co-construct common new meaning about summative assessment, and showing individual and collective reflectiveness about the professional norms and practices linked to classroom assessment. We will call this the 'dynamics' of the professional controversy.

Context

At the time the research described here took place, a new curriculum had just been introduced into French-speaking Switzerland: the *'Plan d'études romand- PER'*.[2] Teachers are now responsible for:

- Conceiving assessment tasks according to the subject matter, linked to learning objectives defined by the curriculum and to teaching material used in class;
- Determining assessment criteria related to learning objectives and tasks;
- Developing marking and grading schemes.

The new curriculum does not, however, provide explicit standards for summative assessment, nor rubrics or assessment tasks. An assessment frame of reference is needed, according to Figari and Remaud (2014), and indeed consultations have recently been initiated by the Swiss Conference of Cantonal Ministers of Education (EDK) to create an assessment reference linked to the PER (Carulla et al., 2013). In the meantime, teachers have requested professional development for summative assessment because they have to carry out their internal assessments with reference to the PER.

For the purpose of our research into the potential role of professional controversies in helping develop teachers' summative assessment capacity, we chose to focus on one particular subject, namely mathematics (Appendix 1 presents mathematics organisation in the PER). The study of Meier, Rich, and Cady (2006) highlights the difficulties mathematics teachers face when practising criterion-referenced assessment, for example when they try to evaluate students' learning from a more qualitative perspective. In particular, because mathematics tests often comprise several different topics and themes, teachers encounter problems trying to come to an *overall* judgement about students' achievement (Klein et al., 1998).

Project A: a primary-based social moderation project

Our first project, which we here call 'Project A', was undertaken with the voluntary participation of upper primary teachers in the Canton of Geneva, and was structured in terms of social moderation from a professional development perspective (Wyatt-Smith, Klenowski, & Gunn, 2010). Social moderation entails 'multiple assessors judging performances on a specific task, and marking them using a common framework with a common standard' (Watty et al., 2014, p. 468). Exchanges in the context of social moderation aim to provide teachers with opportunities to share their assessment criteria, confront their understanding of these criteria with regard to the official curriculum and their own teaching practice, reflect on the assessment tasks that they typically develop and use and agree on marks and grades assigned to students. The goal is to build consensus on teachers' assessment choices and their interpretation of students' work (Klenowski & Wyatt-Smith, 2010).

Geneva primary schools are required to assign marks from 1 to 6^3 to students at each summative assessment event. An average mark, a numeric 'grade', is then calculated at the end of each trimester and at the end of the school year. The pass mark is 4. The individual result in this test is an integral part of the third trimester average grade. The '*Direction générale de l'enseignement obligatoire*' (DGEO) also requires teachers to insert a 'header' in each of their summative tests (Appendix 2). The items to be included are: the assessed objectives, the number of marks in total or by part of the test (by objective, for example), expected threshold marks and the scale used to convert marks into a numeric grade.

A feature of Project A was getting teachers to discuss their summative assessment practices in the light of what they normally did in class, i.e. in terms of their reference points on both actorial and institutional levels. For Vanhulle et al. (2007), the *actorial* level refers to experience-based knowledge, not always formulated, which is acquired in work situations, made up of habitus, common sense and knowledge embedded in ways of thinking and doing. As for the *institutional* level, it refers to accredited, prescribed and official knowledge, which is determined by curricula, programmes and forms of educational intervention.

Project B: a secondary-based curricular alignment project

The second research study, 'Project B', was also carried out with the voluntary participation of teachers, this time lower secondary teachers in the Canton of Vaud. A number of requirements are imposed by the Canton of Vaud in regard to assessment. First, teachers must assess the objectives laid down by the PER in terms of learning progressions. Teacher-developed summative tests are meant to assess complex learning through tasks requiring students to mobilise various cognitive resources. Marks from 1 to 6, with half marks allowed, are assigned to each summative test. The marks are compounded to provide a grade per subject at the end of each semester and at the end of the school year. An average mark of 4 indicates 'adequate'. Cantonal prescriptions require the use of established scales, both above and below 4. Teachers must let students know the learning/assessment objectives in advance, along with the assessment criteria (Cadre Général de l'Evaluation, 2015).

The study was centred on the curriculum alignment model, defined as the level of coherence between curriculum objectives and assessment, between curriculum objectives and instructional activities and between assessment and instructional activities (Anderson, 2002). The project extended the model to include marking and grading processes (McMillan & Nash, 2000). The model is situated at a *theoretical* level in the typology of Vanhulle et al. (2007). It postulates first that the quality of summative assessment has to be built on the curriculum alignment coherence. Secondly, it postulates that marking and grading cannot be decided in a mechanical way but according to pedagogical purposes.

Our research into professional controversies is *exploratory* in the sense of Groulx (1998): 'It aims to highlight and explore the various issues that reveal new situations or novel issues and changes or transformations that affect individuals and groups' (p. 33, our translation). Its purpose is *hermeneutic* (comprehensive), by studying the meanings constructed by interactive participants and their interpretations in given social contexts (Paquay, Crahay, & De Ketele, 2009) with regard to the research questions.

For both projects, our research questions were the following:

(1) What specific dimensions of assessment practice would the professional controversies reveal?
(2) What are the dynamics of those professional controversies that appeared to support potential new understandings of summative assessment practice?

Method

Project A involved 13 teachers of grades 7–8 (10–12 year-old students) from 8 primary schools with different socio-economic characteristics. Teachers were volunteered to the research. We here focus on one of the research seminars.[4] Prior to the seminar, teachers and trainers had agreed on the mathematical theme to be covered by the teachers' self-developed tests – that of mathematical applications aimed at finding logical relationships between sets of numbers. During the seminar, participants exchanged information about their tests, which had previously been taken by their students and marked.

The trainers divided the teachers into groups: three trios and a quartet from different schools. Social moderation took place without trainer intervention. This stage lasted an hour and eight minutes. Two phases were distinguished during the social moderation activity: (1) building consensus on the construction of the tests according to the curriculum, (2) building consensus on the judgement and marking of specific student work. Group interaction with instructor participation then followed (Mottier Lopez, Tessaro, Dechamboux, & Morales Villabona, 2012). The instructions given at the beginning of social moderation were: 'Look at your tests; confront your views in order to build consensus on what matters while you are creating a test (themes, objectives, assessment criteria, scale, items, etc.) and while you are marking students' task responses'. The material available was as follows:

(1) A test constructed by each teacher that had been used with one of their students (medium to low academic level) and which had already been marked;
(2) The previous year's cantonal test (external assessment) for the year group concerned (end of grade 8, 12-year olds);
(3) The PER and the requirements of the Geneva primary school authority in terms of assessment;
(4) A sheet to draft consensus points and disagreements during social moderation.

Project B was conducted in the context of the third cycle of education in the Canton of Vaud (grades 9–11: 13–15-year-old students). The case we present concerns four mathematics teachers volunteered to the study, from two schools with the same socio-economic characteristics. We here focus on one seminar of 43 min.[5] The curriculum alignment model had previously been presented to the group by the trainer, to guide members in their construction of new summative tests for classroom use, and participants were now invited to compare the tests they had produced. The main instructions for the tests' presentations were as follows: 'Please explain the approach pursued in developing your test. How did you build consistency between the objectives of the curriculum, the exercises (tasks), and the construction of the scores and mark? What elements are you satisfied with? Which bother you? Why?'. The material available was the PER, the assessment requirements of the Vaud secondary school and the teachers' curriculum material.

Our research design drew on a 'multiple case study inquiry' (Yin, 2003) using within-case (controversy's description within each project) and multiple-case analyses (comparison between both projects with respect to the research questions). We chose this method because its purpose is to investigate 'a contemporary phenomenon within its real-life context, especially when the boundaries between phenomenon and context are not clearly evident' (p. 15).

For each project, exchanges between teachers and the trainer were audio recorded and field notes were taken. Summative tests and all written records produced during the seminars were collected.

A qualitative analysis of data was carried out in three steps:

First, we made a temporal and organisational diagram of the collective moments of each research study that shows the configurations (instructions, material, etc.) created to organise the comparison of teachers' assessment practices.

Second, we carried out an analysis of the summative tests that were reviewed and compared by the teachers: choice and nature of assessed objectives, content and form of assessment tasks, selected weighting systems (criteria, points) and construction of marks (scales, thresholds).

Finally, we transcribed the verbatim exchanges that arose as tests were being compared. This enabled an interpretative analysis by way of *narrative codes* that describe the structure of talk, the narrative form of individual contributions to the interaction and the inference of the collective meaning co-constructed by the participants (Babione, 2015). We analysed:

- The dimensions characterising the 'process of constructive controversy' (Johnson, 2015): views expressed by participants; arguments and counterarguments put forward to justify participants' positions; new meanings co-constructed to resolve the intellectual conflict, integration of these in a consensus.
- The themes about summative assessment discussed during the controversy, and shifts in thematic content produced in discourse.
- The kinds of reference (Vanhulle et al., 2007) called on in negotiating positions: actorial, institutional and theoretical.

In this article, we focus in detail on two professional controversies (one per project) that revealed an *overall* process, from conflicting views to the emergence of a consensus, that we consider conducive to the construction of new professional knowledge. In Project A, only one complete controversy emerged for our observed teacher group as they were comparing their respective summative tests. In Project B, one professional controversy was also observed, inspired by the presentation of a summative test by one of the teachers, that questioned the assessment practices of the other teachers. For each controversy, we employed interpretive writing (Paillé & Mucchielli, 2016).

To verify the validity and reliability of our analyses and results, we conducted two types of triangulations, as defined by Denzin (1978) and Patton (1990), fully consistent with the case study method (Yin, 2003). For each case, a report was written by the researcher responsible for one or other of the research projects.[6] In this step, the first type of triangulation was between different data sources, the verbatim exchanges, the tests and the researcher's

DEVELOPING TEACHERS' ASSESSMENT CAPACITY

field notes in order to enhance understanding of the analysed discourse. Triangulation was essential, particularly with written records of verbal exchanges. Concretely, contents of discourse were systematically put into perspective with the summative tests involved, which were, in their turn, analysed with respect to the subject of the exchanges and to the issue of classroom assessment (see Appendices).

The second type of triangulation involved acquiring responses from more 'analysts', in the sense of 'investigator triangulation' defined by Denzin (1978). The idea was to see the different ways in which each was able to interpret the data collected from the viewpoint of the research questions. The two researchers exchanged their interpretive accounts of the controversy concerned in order to refine categories of analysis and examine possible alternative interpretations (Yin, 2003). Consultation followed, that occasionally led to a return to the recordings to refine the dimensions analysed. This procedure is coherent with the view that:

> qualitative analysis is fundamentally an iterative set of processes (…). The role of iteration, not as a repetitive mechanical task but as a deeply reflexive process, is key to sparking insight and developing meaning. Reflexive iteration is at the heart of visiting and revisiting the data and connecting them with emerging insights, progressively leading to refined focus and understandings. (Srivastava, 2009, p. 77)

In this perspective, triangulations were aimed at deepening and widening data interpretation and not only at validation. The researchers assumed a reflexive and critical stance about their qualitative data analysis and interpretation (Mauthner & Doucet, 2003).

Findings

Professional controversy in Project A: why and for whom should one establish standards of competence by objective/task?

The controversy discussed below concerns four teachers: Ariane, Arthur, Daniel and Valentine.[7] During the first 15 min, the teachers sought to identify the common aspects of their tests. They seemed anxious to avoid contrasts between them that were too marked. They protected each other, presenting a positive and attractive image (Goffman, 1973) of their assessment practices. In so doing, they readily established initial elements of consensus, but without going into any depth. Yet, a response from Ariane sparked an interactive dynamic that led to a controversy.

This started with the definition of pass marks in a test. In earlier discussions, the teachers had drawn up a list of common elements that they included in the header of their test, following the requirements of the DGEO. Among these elements was the pass mark. Ariane said she did not necessarily fix a pass mark for each task. In her test, it was indeed clear that she did not do so, unlike her colleagues. No further exchanges about this subject took place at this point in the proceedings. The threshold question came after some 200 turns to speak, when teachers were systematically comparing their tests. Ariane thought that indicating the sum of allocated marks was sufficient. None of her colleagues picked up on this point. Subsequent exchanges turned to the formulation of qualitative feedback for the student. The controversy emerged from the 519th turn to speak onwards.

Ariane said: *'I forgot the pass mark … well, they* (the students) *know that it is 4 anyway … usually I put it, the total marks …. We more or less agree, even if I don't indicate the marks by criterion'.* Arthur said he did not do so systematically (although in his test the thresholds

115

by objective were indicated). As for Daniel, he said he did it all the time and argued: '*It also helps to write the school reports … in the comments, when you meet the parents and then you look back at the tests, it allows you to be more focused … we assessed applications and then you see that he still has trouble reading a table … that cannot be wrong in sessions, especially meetings with parents*'. These arguments were directly related to his pedagogical action. Valentine agreed. For her, it was important to know which type of task a student succeeded in. Daniel went on to say that he was aware that often students, as well as parents, tended to take only the overall mark into account. Finally, for everyone, the indication of the thresholds by objective/task was helpful, to have a performance profile for each student and to justify the overall mark.

Having heard Daniel's arguments, Arthur justified not systematically fixing a threshold per task: '*For example, the cantonal test, there are no thresholds … there is a global pass mark*'. The reference here was institutional. The external test served as a model. Arthur continued, '*In some situations, it is difficult to set a threshold … it can be a trap*'. Ariane added: '*I think it's very difficult because when you have only 2 marks, do you set your threshold at 2 or 1 … I wonder what that means?*'. Arthur agreed. For him, it made no sense to fix a threshold when there were so few marks available and then pronounce work insufficient in such a case.

The discussion of the number of marks available per task refocused the debate on the technical question of whether to establish thresholds for every task or just globally. In the Canton of Geneva, the norm had long been to fix the pass mark at two-thirds of marks achieved. Daniel explained that even if he fixed pass marks by task or objective, he sometimes weighted them such that the overall pass mark was around two-thirds. Valentine protested, referring to the cantonal regulations:

> In the service document, they said that this business of two-thirds was over! … in a period of awareness building, consolidation (of learning) … we can have an expected pass mark that is different. For example, for students in grade 7, we may not have the same requirements as in grade 8 on the same theme.

Arthur believed that it was easier to stick to this reasoning when there were many marks available for each task. All agreed. They went no further on the subject, not raising the question of setting thresholds by task rather than by PER objective or component, which encouraged grouping several tasks, for example.

Ariane, who had said little during this discussion, but who had been at the origin of the controversy, (finally) put forward her arguments. If she did not enter the thresholds in the header, it was because she considered that this header was first and foremost for the student. Making reference to her experience-based knowledge, Ariane said that in the past she had not given marks to students.[8] Instead of thresholds in the header, there was a self-assessment that students were required to provide for each defined objective. This viewpoint moved her colleagues and redirected the discussion. They wondered about how to involve students in summative assessment. Daniel explained that in his school, teachers worked together to initiate a new practice in summative assessment. His three colleagues then asked him pragmatic questions about how he took into account the provision of help in summative assessment, and what marks were attributed in those tasks where help was provided. The later analysis of exchanges indicated that the teachers agreed that students should have access to material resources during summative assessments. They felt entitled to do this because it was allowed in external tests. The teachers drew up a list of resources they made available to students, and those differentiated measures applied to students with special educational needs during summative assessments.

In general, the controversy analysis revealed that teachers argued primarily from actorial references, that is educational activities they valued in their teaching. When it came to justifying their assessment practices, they called upon institutional references: the cantonal guideline and the external test seen as operationalising the prescriptions defined by the canton. We note that the teachers at no time mentioned the PER, even outside the controversy discussion. They did not seem to feel the need to refer to the new curriculum to make their assessment decisions, which appeared rooted in their experience-based knowledge and cantonal prescriptions.

Professional controversy in project B: how do we build a mark that reflects the nature of students' mathematics learning?

Three summative tests were presented. The first was jointly developed by two teachers, Catherine and Philemon, the second by Paul and the third by Fernando.[9] The controversy emerged during the last – Fernando's – presentation. The test focused on isometrics and the properties of polygons. It addressed students of 9th VP[10] (12–13 years). On the first page of the test (see Appendix 3), a PER objective is mentioned: '*MSN31 – Ask and solve problems to model both plane and space*'. The objective is made up of four PER components, for example: '*... defining two-dimensional figures by some of their geometric properties*'. The scale conversion used to fix the mark is indicated to students. Fernando added marks for '*respecting the instructions*' and for '*precision and care taken*'. The test consisted of four problems (called '*exercises*') next to each of which were indicated the total marks available. In the test, no components or assessment criteria were linked to the problems or to the marks attributed to the problems, as in the headers elaborated by the primary teachers in Project A. There was no institutional requirement to do so.[11]

Fernando prepared an additional document for the seminar in the form of two specification tables. By doing so, he attested to the impact of discussions held during the first seminar on curriculum alignment. In the first table (Appendix 4), Fernando related the four components with different parts of the mathematical problems (a, b, c, etc.) to see how many marks were awarded to each component. The same component could feature in more than one problem. In the second specification table (Appendix 5), Fernando changed logic. He attempted to determine the overall mark for the test based on a threshold mark he set for each component. The first table was implemented with his students. He wished to submit the second table to the group for their opinion. Our analysis of the overall discussion in seminar 2 shows that the controversy did not suddenly emerge with Fernando's presentation – it was present implicitly in two previously presented documents. Philemon and Catherine reflected on a form of assessment that is not limited to a simple mechanical counting of marks awarded. Philemon said he sometimes fixed his scale prior to marking, reflecting on the desired threshold for each task. During the second presentation, Paul explained that usually he worked with the 'federal scale'.[12] He said he had some difficulty fixing his scale before correcting students' work. By consistently using the federal scale, he avoided situations in which a predetermined pass mark was too demanding, or the contrary. It was the presentation of both specification tables proposed by Fernando that sparked the controversy. Below, we provide an extract of the exchange and underline the reference points called upon by participants.

Fernando explained his second table:

> We are no longer strictly adding marks. So do we give one or more marks, and how do we handle the transition between awarding marks for each component? Specifically, if a student passes on one component, but not on another, that student cannot have 4. Can we assume that?

This questioning indicates prior thought about the meaning of an overall mark that covers different mathematical themes, without being able to be explicit about what it is composed of. To be consistent, Fernando wondered whether a mark by component could be considered. If not, an alternative would be to require the student to attain a threshold mark for each component.

If, in theory, these solutions appeared attractive to the teachers, they seemed difficult to operationalise in their assessment practices. Catherine said: '*Yeah, difficult!*'. Philemon, in contrast, was enthusiastic. He returned to his own test: '*It's really interesting. We wanted to go in that direction with our assessment when we thought of our 4 from a qualitative point of view, but we didn't allow ourselves to do so*'. Philemon used the concept of 'quality score', a theoretical notion presented earlier by the trainer, to signify that the mark, even as a number, should refer to meaningful qualitative elements directly linked to the mastery of specific mathematical content and learning. This approach would require linking 'marks' and 'tasks' as Philemon did. But Catherine expresses serious doubts, based on pragmatic constraints. '*But this is madness, for an assessment, we would need four pages of explanation …*'. To which Fernando replied: '*we should start by removing half marks*', challenging institutional prescriptions (mark range of 1 to 6, with half marks). At the beginning of this extract, we noted that the references evoked in the controversy belonged to different levels: the actorial (experience and common sense, Catherine), institutional (official knowledge requirements, Fernando) and theoretical (concepts based on scientific research, Philemon) levels. But it seems impossible to reconcile the use of curricular alignment to improve the quality of assessment with some institutional requirements. This observation marks a turning point in the professional controversy. It becomes epistemic (specific to the professional development being undertaken, and referred to a theoretical model), rather than interpersonal (driven by people who argue different points of view emerging from their experiences). The same teacher expressed opposing points of view, aware of the dilemma he was confronted with.

To move the reflection forward, the trainer suggested a compromise: '*What if this logic allowed you to fix the pass mark (4/6), even if you then drew up traditional scales?*'. Philemon's reaction was categorical: '*No one would understand*'. Fernando clarified: '*Yes, it is possible, if the contract with students is clear from the beginning*'. Catherine concluded: '*So, right from the beginning, we need to be clear what is fundamental to our teaching in terms of content, and, as a result, for the assessment*', an argument that corresponded to one of the major objectives of curricular alignment (Biggs, 1999) that would return several times in the collective discourse.

The debate continued for another 10 minutes. Several dimensions of assessment practice were addressed, including specific difficulties, mainly: understanding the curriculum (PER) and its use for constructing tests; the nature of mathematical knowledge taught to make informed choices about marks to be awarded by component and by task in the summative assessment.

Limitations

The main shortcoming of the study is its focus on a limited number of practical confrontations associated with only two collaborative research studies. While the size of transcripts analysed was considerable (about 1700 turns to speak), the fact remains that the number of cases presented in this article is small. Further collaborative research configurations will be required before the study can claim a strong form of generalisation. Because of the exploratory nature of our study, there are very few comparisons with findings from prior research. Furthermore, the comparison between the classroom contexts involved in both projects is not optimal because Project A concerns the second cycle of education, whereas Project B concerns the third cycle. Another limitation is the fact that the interpretative hypotheses about professional development associated with controversies were based solely on the collective discourse analysed, but nevertheless produced from traces of classroom practice. In both research projects, additional procedures were implemented to collect data on teachers' practices in their classes, before and after the seminars. These will be analysed in due course to explore the extent to which effective transformations of summative assessment practices took place.

Conclusion and discussion

In this conclusion, we end by putting the two research projects into perspective with respect to our research questions, and then we consider some prospects.

> (1) What specific dimensions of assessment practice would the professional controversies reveal?

In Project A, the analysis of professional controversy shows that teachers addressed the following dimensions of their assessment practice:

- Mechanically fixing thresholds according to a given ratio (two-thirds) or according to pedagogical reflection;
- Communicating with students and parents about the results of the summative assessment. A criteria-based profile of results with thresholds by objective/task enables better communication about students' learning achievements and difficulties. This information is also useful for teachers to adjust their forthcoming teaching;
- The students' involvement in summative assessment and the formative resources at their disposal during this assessment.

In doing so, teachers discussed the communication process at the heart of learning assessment (Weiss, 1991), as well as ways and means to support students' learning that could be associated with summative assessment (Harlen, 2012). We note that teachers appeared sensitive to the need to ensure consistency between their teaching and the summative tests they designed.

As for Project B, teachers specifically addressed the following dimensions:

- The subject-based content that is assessed and its specificity; constructing the mark with respect to the specific dimensions of the learning assessed;
- The new curriculum to define this content and the related assessment rubrics, including the limits of this curriculum as a reference for assessment;

DEVELOPING TEACHERS' ASSESSMENT CAPACITY

- The consistency of assessment, in terms of curriculum alignment; understanding the mark in a more qualitative way.

Fundamental dimensions of assessment were debated, namely the apprehension of the 'value' of the students' learning according to the subject matter prescribed by the curriculum, the assessment tasks, the criteria and mark scales decided by the teachers related to their teaching.

(2)   In view of each project design, what are the dynamics of those professional controversies that appear to support potential new understandings of summative assessment practice?

The exploratory nature of our study precludes generalisation. However, our analyses revealed interesting observations with respect to project designs. In the first step of Project A, teachers only called on actorial and institutional references for justifying their viewpoints and practices. None of them used results or theoretical frameworks, even if they had been trained at university to do so. The dynamics of the professional controversy is based on the confrontation of two main positions. We postulate that in Project A the controversy probably strengthened the pedagogical use of summative assessment (to better inform students and parents, to use the results to adjust teaching, to allow students to use resources during the summative assessment). In doing so, the controversy had a potential effect on representations of summative assessment and its links to teaching and learning. But from the viewpoint of fixing thresholds, 'standard setting', which was at the origin of the controversy, it did not really better equip teachers. The teachers did not question the relationship between thresholds and students' learning, as tested by the tasks with reference to the curriculum. At no time was this mentioned in the social moderation session. It should be noted that it is not sufficient to set up tools, such as the header and a curriculum, for teachers to make use of the reasoning underpinning them.

The second step of Project B encouraged the teachers to cross the three reference frameworks defined by Vanhulle et al. (2007): actorial (by presenting their own summative tests and their use in their classrooms), institutional (by stressing their schools' requirements for classroom assessment) and theoretical (by objectifying their summative tests in the light of the curriculum alignment conceptual units). The teachers explained and compared their different choices for constructing their summative tests. That is the encounter with the theoretical model led the four teachers to express different viewpoints on an intra-personal level, while being conscious of institutional constraints and feasibility. The professional controversy becomes epistemic.

It would seem that teachers underwent an about-face in envisaging the consistency of their assessments. Although based on the allocation of marks, the teachers' evaluative reasoning became more qualitative. We assume that the controversy likely contributes to make teachers more aware of the importance of critical reflection about the specific mathematical content in their summative assessments. As such, the work gave more meaning to the new curriculum, which took on the status of a reference. Our analysis, however, indicates that the passage from allocated marks to an overall mark/grade remains problematic, especially because institutional requirements leave little room for deciding the overall mark in a more qualitative approach. This confirms research findings on marking which show that, from a qualitative perspective, it is not so much the mark but the scope of the mark scale that is a problem (Walvoord & Johnson Anderson, 2009).

DEVELOPING TEACHERS' ASSESSMENT CAPACITY

To end, our study shows draft results that are coherent with larger research about summative classroom assessment practices. For instance, Zhang and Burry-Stock (2003) demonstrate that 'knowledge in testing has a significant impact on teachers' self-perceived assessment skills regardless of their teaching experience. This is particularly true in terms of [...] revising teacher-made tests' (p. 335). In this view, professional controversies may have a role to play in supporting teachers' professional development. The teachers in our two projects called on actorial and institutional references because both research designs solicited their experience-based knowledge linked to their situated assessment practices. But if the design doesn't also plan theoretical resources for sustaining exchanges and confrontation between teachers, we can postulate that the professional controversy has more difficulty being epistemic on both inter-personal and intra-personal levels. As Lessard (2012) observed, there are too few empirical results on professional controversies and more study is needed. Future results could lead us to use professional controversy as an *explicit tool* for teacher professional development articulated with existing approaches for assessment education, such as social moderation and the curriculum alignment model.[13]

Notes

1. http://www.oecd.org/about/membersandpartners/list-oecd-member-countries.htm.
2. For more information, consult https://www.plandetudes.ch/web/guest/PG2-contexte. New common curricula have also been introduced into the German- and Italian-speaking regions.
3. This was the case at the time of this research (2012–2014). Recently, teachers in Geneva have been obliged to use a mark scale that includes half marks, as used in the Canton of Vaud.
4. The seminar described in this article is part of wider research which included classroom observation time before and after the seminars. This research was supported by the Swiss National Research Fund, subsidy n° n°100013–143453/1. Thanks to the teachers and to Lionel Dechamboux, Laurent Filliettaz, Fernando Morales Villabona and Walther Tessaro.
5. The seminar described in this article is part of wider research presented in Pasquini (2014) which included successive constructions of summative tests experienced in classrooms and discussed during several seminars.
6. In Project A, several trainers were involved, including the principal investigator who has co-authored this article. In Project B, the trainer was also the researcher and co-author of this article.
7. Pseudonyms.
8. In the Canton of Geneva, during the early 2000s, several schools, said to be 'renovated', gave no marks for summative assessments. Renovation took the form of novel teaching practices and innovative school organisation with an emphasis on collaborative projects. Marks were reintroduced in 2006.
9. Pseudonyms.
10. The VP stream is the most demanding in the Vaud education system.
11. Reminder, this was a Canton of Geneva requirement that did not apply in the Canton of Vaud.
12. The 'federal scale' is a standard way to fix the overall mark (or numeric grade) by applying the following calculation: 'numeric grade = (marks obtained by the student/total marks available) $\times$ 5 + 1'.
13. We sincerely thank Sandra Johnson and the experts for their very formative comments.

Disclosure statement

No potential conflict of interest was reported by the authors.

References

Allal, L., & Mottier Lopez, L. (2014). Teachers' professional judgement in the context of collaborative assessment practice. In C. Wyatt-Smith, V. Klenowski, & P. Colbert (Eds.), *Designing assessment for quality learning* (pp. 151–165). London: Springer (The Enabling Power of Assessment).

Anderson, L. W. (2002). Curricular alignment: A re-examination. *Theory Into Practice, 41*, 255–260.

Babione, C. (2015). *Practitioner teacher inquiry and research* (Kindle Edition). San Francisco, CA: Jossey-Bass

Biggs, J. (1999). What the student does: Teaching for enhanced learning. *Higher Education Research & Development, 18*, 57–75.

Bloom, B. S., Hasting, J. T., & Madaus, G. F. (1971). *Handbook on formative and summative evaluation of student learning*. New York, NY: McGraw-Hill.

Cadre Général de l'Evaluation. (2015). Etat de Vaud, Département de la formation, de la jeunesse et de la culture [General evaluation framework]. Retrieved from http://www.vd.ch/fileadmin/user_upload/organisation/dfj/dgeo/fichiers_pdf/CGE2015.pdf

Carulla, C., Corti, D., de Pietro, J.-F., Kassam, S., Roth, M., Sanchez Abchi, V., & Singh, L. (2013). *Quoi et comment évaluer en référence au Plan d'études romand (PER): premières pistes (Rapport scientifique intermédiaire)* [What to assess and how with reference to the Swiss French regional curriculum: First steps (Intermediate report)]. Neuchâtel: IRDP.

Clot, Y. (2010). *Le travail à cœur. Pour en finir avec les risques psychosociaux* [The work to heart. To put an end to psychosocial risk]. Paris: La Découverte.

Denzin, N. K. (1978). *The research act: A theoretical introduction to sociological methods*. New York, NY: McGraw-Hill.

Desgagné, S. (1997). Le concept de recherche collaborative: L'idée d'un rapprochement entre chercheurs universitaires et praticiens enseignants [The concept of collaborative research: The idea of a rapprochement between educational researchers and practising teachers]. *Revue des sciences de l'éducation, 23*, 371–393.

Desgagné, S. (2007). Le défi de coproduction de savoir en recherche collaborative : Autour d'une démarche de reconstruction et d'analyse de récits de pratique enseignante [The challenge of knowledge co-construction in collaborative research: Around a process of reconstruction and analysis of teachers' accounts of their practical experience]. In M. Anadon (Ed.), *La recherche participative : Multiples regards* [Participant research: Multiple perspectives] (pp. 89–121). Québec: Presses de l'Université du Québec.

Desgagné, S., Bednarz, N., Lebuis, P., Poirier, L., & Couture, C. (2001). L'approche collaborative de recherche en éducation: un nouveau rapport à établir entre recherche et formation [The collaborative approach to research in education: Towards a new relationship between research and training]. *Revue des sciences de l'éducation, 27*, 33–64.

Figari, G., & Remaud, D. (2014). *Méthodologie d'évaluation en éducation et formation* [Assessment methods in education and training]. Bruxelles: De Boeck.

DEVELOPING TEACHERS' ASSESSMENT CAPACITY

Goffman, E. (1973). *La mise en scène de la vie quotidienne* [The presentation of self in everyday life]. Paris: Edition de Minuit.

Groulx, L.-H. (1998). Sens et usage de la recherche qualitative en travail social [Meaning and use of qualitative research in social work]. In J. Poupart, L.-H. Groulx, R. Mayer, J.-P. Deslauriers, A. Laperrière, & A. P. Pires (Eds.), *La recherche qualitative. Diversité des champs et des pratiques au Québec* [Qualitative research. Diversity of fields and practice in Québec] (pp. 1–50). Montréal: Gaëtan Morin.

Harlen, W. (2012). On the relationship between assessment or formative and summative purposes. In J. Gardner (Ed.), *Assessment and learning* (pp. 87–102). London: Sage.

Johnson, D. W. (2015). *Constructive Controversy: Theory, research, practice*. Cambridge: Cambridge University Press (Kindle version).

Klein, S. P., Stecher, B. M., Shavelson, R. J., McCaffrey, D., Ormseth, T., Bell, R. M., ... Othman, A. R. (1998). Analytic versus holistic scoring of science performance tasks. *Applied Measurement in Education, 11*, 121–137.

Klenowski, V., & Wyatt-Smith, C. (2010). Standards, teacher judgement and moderation in contexts of national curriculum and assessment reform. *Assessment Matters, 2*, 107–131.

Laveault, D., & Allal, L. (2016). Implementing assessment for learning: Theoretical and practical issues. In D. Laveault & L. Allal (Eds.), *Assessment for learning: Meeting the challenge of implementation* (pp. 1–18). London: Springer.

Lefeuvre, G., Garcia, A., & Namolovan, L. (2009). Les indicateurs de développement professionnel [Indicators of professional development]. *Questions vives recherches en éducation, 5*, 277–314.

Lessard, C. (2012). Controverses éducatives et réflexivité: quant-à-soi personnel ou professionnalisation [Educational controversies and reflexivity: Self-sufficiency or professionalisation]. In M. Tardif, C. Borges, & A. Malo (Eds.), *Le virage réflexif en éducation. Où en sommes-nous 30 ans après Schön?* [The reflexive turn in education. Where are we 30 years on from Schön?] (pp. 123–142). Bruxelles: De Boeck.

Mauthner, N. S., & Doucet, A. (2003). Reflexive accounts and accounts of reflexivity in qualitative data analysis. *Sociology, 37*, 413–431.

McMillan, J. H., & Nash, S. (2000). *Teacher classroom assessment and grading practices decision making (Report)*. (ERIC Document Reproduction Service No. ED447195).

Meier, S. L., Rich, B. S., & Cady, J. (2006). Teacher's use of rubrics to score non-traditional tasks: Factors related to discrepancies in scoring. *Assessment in Education: Principles, Policy & Practice, 13*, 69–95.

Morrissette, J., Mottier Lopez, L., & Tessaro, W. (2012). La production de savoirs négociés dans deux recherches collaboratives sur l'évaluation formative [The production of negotiated knowledge within two collaborative research projects concerned with formative assessment]. In L. Mottier Lopez & G. Figari (Eds.), *Modélisations de l'évaluation en éducation: questionnements épistémologiques* [Models of educational assessment: Epistemological issues] (pp. 27–43). Bruxelles: De Boeck.

Moss, C. (2013). Research on classroom summative assessment. In J. McMillan (Ed.), *Sage handbook of research on classroom assessment* (pp. 235–255). Thousand Oaks, CA: Sage.

Mottier Lopez, L. (2015). Au cœur du développement professionnel des enseignants, la conscientisation critique. Exemple d'une recherche collaborative sur l'évaluation formative à l'école primaire genevoise [Critical consciousness at the heart of teachers' professional development. An example of collaborative research on formative assessment in Geneva primary schools]. *Carrefours de l'éducation, 39*, 119–135.

Mottier Lopez, L., & Morales Villabona, F. (2016). Teachers' professional development in the context of collaborative research: Toward practices of collaborative assessment for learning in the classroom. In D. Laveault & L. Allal (Eds.), *Assessment for learning: Meeting the challenge of implementation* (pp. 161–180). London: Springer (The Enabling Power of Assessment).

Mottier Lopez, L., Tessaro, W., Dechamboux, L., & Morales Villabona, F. (2012). La modération sociale : un dispositif soutenant l'émergence de savoirs négociés sur l'évaluation certificative des apprentissages des élèves [Social moderation: A design that supports knowledge's negotiation on certificative assessment of students' learning]. *Questions vives recherches en éducation, 6*, 159–175.

Nusche, D., Radinger, T., Santiago, P., & Shewbridge, C. (2013). *Synergies for better learning: An international perspective on evaluation and assessment*. Paris: OCDE.

DEVELOPING TEACHERS' ASSESSMENT CAPACITY

Paillé, P., & Mucchielli, A. (2016). *L'analyse qualitative en sciences humaines et sociales* [Qualitative analysis in the humanities and social sciences] (6th ed.). Paris: Armand Colin.

Paquay, L., Crahay, M., & De Ketele, J.-M. (Eds.). (2009). *L'analyse qualitative en éducation. Des pratiques de recherche aux critères de qualité* [Qualitative analysis in education. From research practice to quality criteria]. Bruxelles: De Boeck.

Pasquini, R. (2014). *Le développement des pratiques évaluatives certificatives chez des enseignants en exercice: une question d'alignement curriculaire élargi* [The development of certification assessment practices for practising teachers: A question of broader curriculum alignment] (PhD Canevas). Geneva: University of Geneva.

Patton, M. Q. (1990). *Qualitative evaluation and research methods.* (2nd ed.). Newbury Park, CA: Sage.

Srivastava, P. (2009). A practical iterative framework for qualitative data analysis. *International Journal of Qualitative Methods, 8*, 75–84.

Timperley, H., Wilson, A., Barrar, H., & Fung, I. (2007). *Teacher professional learning and development: Best evidence synthesis iteration.* Wellington: Ministry of Education. Retrieved November 26, 2016, from http://educationcounts.edcentre.govt.nz/goto/BES

Vanhulle, S., Merhan, F., & Ronveaux, C. (2007). Du principe d'alternance aux alternances en formation des enseignants et des adultes [From principle to practice in dual systems of teacher and adult education]. In F. Merhan, C. Ronveaux, & S. Vanhulle (Eds.), *Alternances en formation* [Alternating between classroom and workplace in education and training] (pp. 7–45). Bruxelles: De Boeck.

Walvoord, B. E., & Johnson Anderson, V. J. (2009). *Effective grading: A tool for learning and assessment.* San Francisco, CA: Jossey Bass.

Watty, K., Freeman, M., Howieson, B., Hancock, P., O'Connell, B., de Lange, P., & Abraham, A. (2014). Social moderation, assessment and assuring standards for accounting graduates. *Assessment & Evaluation in Higher Education, 39*, 461–478.

Weiss, J. (Ed.). (1991). *L'évaluation: problème de communication* [Assessment: A problem of communication]. Cousset Neuchâtel: DelVal-IRDP.

Wenger, E. (1998). *Communities of practice: Learning, meaning, and identities.* Cambridge: Cambridge University Press.

Wyatt-Smith, C., Klenowski, V., & Gunn, S. (2010). The centrality of teachers' judgement practice in assessment: A study of standards in moderation. *Assessment in Education: Principles, Policy & Practice, 17*, 59–75.

Yin, R. K. (2003). *Case study research: Design and methods* (3rd ed.). Los Angeles, CA: Sage.

Zhang, Z., & Burry-Stock, J. A. (2003). Classroom assessment practices and teachers' self-perceived assessment skills. *Applied Measurement in Education, 16*, 323–342.

Appendices

Appendix 1: Example of the organisation of mathematics in the PER

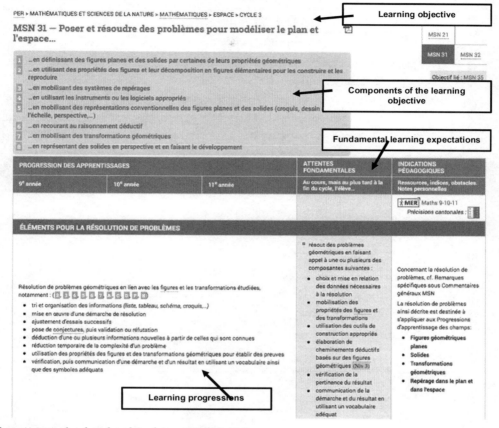

http://www.plandetudes.ch/web/guest/MSN_31/

Appendix 2: Example of test header (Arthur, Project A)

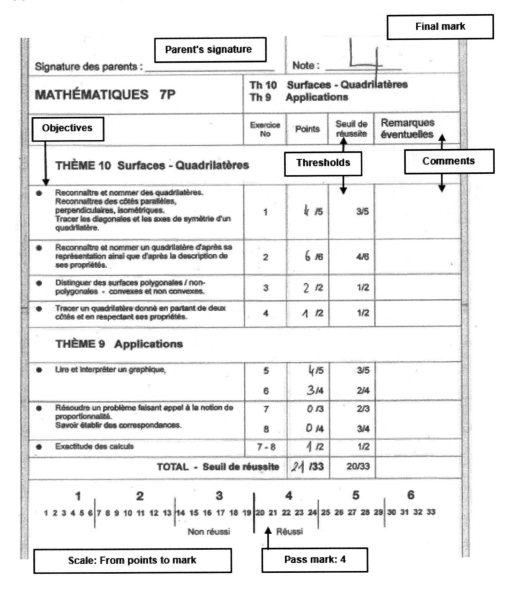

DEVELOPING TEACHERS' ASSESSMENT CAPACITY

Appendix 3: First page of Fernando's test (Project B)

Mathématique

Evaluation significative

Prénom : ....

Date : ....

Classe : ....

Géométrie | Theme

PER components: Objectives

MSN 31 - Poser et résoudre des problèmes pour modéliser le plan et l'espace ...

... en définissant des figures planes par certaines de leurs propriétés géométriques ;

... en utilisant des propriétés des figures et leur décomposition en figures élémentaires pour les construire et les reproduire ;

... en utilisant les instruments appropriés ;

...en mobilisant des transformations géométriques

Scale: From points to mark

Echelle :

40	à	38.5	6	28	à	25	4	14.5	à	12	2
38	à	35	5.5	24.5	à	22	3.5	11.5	à	8.5	1.5
34.5	à	32	5	21.5	à	18.5	3	8	à	0	1
31.5	à	28.5	4.5	18	à	15	2.5				

Remarques : | Comments

....

....

Nota bene.

Pour les 3 premiers exercices il y a un point par exercice pour le respect de la consigne.

Pour chaque dessin il y a un point pour la précision et le soin apporté à sa réalisation

Appendix 4: First specification table proposed by Fernando (Project B)

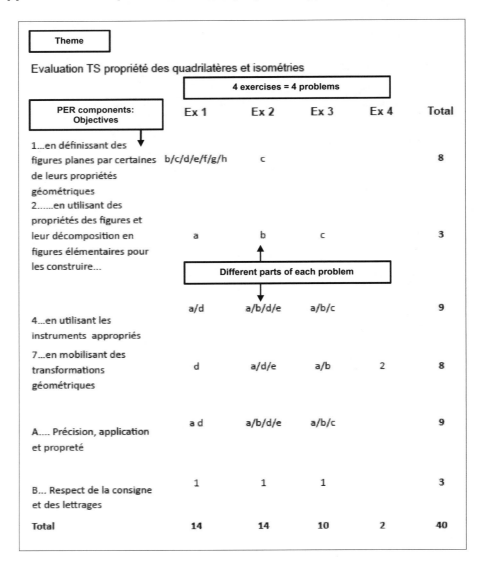

DEVELOPING TEACHERS' ASSESSMENT CAPACITY

Appendix 5: Second specification table proposed by Fernando (Project B)

PER components: Objectives	Scale: From points to mark										
	6	5.5	5	4.5	4	3.5	3	2.5	2	1.5	1
	Thresholds by objective										
1…en définissant des figures planes par certaines de leurs propriétés géométriques	7/8	6/8	6/8	5/8	5/8	4/8	4/8	3/8	2/8	1/8	0/8
2……en utilisant des propriétés des figures et leur décomposition en figures élémentaires pour les construire…	3/3	3/3	3/3	2/3	2/3	1/3	1/3	1/3	1/3	0/3	0/3
4…en utilisant les instruments appropriés	9/9	8/9	8/9	7/9	6/9	5/9	4/9	3/9	2/9	2/9	1/9
7…en mobilisant des transformations géométriques	7/8	6/8	5/8	4/8	3/8	3/8	2/8	2/8	1/8	1/8	0/8
A…. Précision, application et propreté	8/9	7/9	5/8	4/8	3/8	3/8	2/8	2/8	1/8	1/8	0/8
B… Respect de la consigne et des lettrages	3/3	3/3	2/3	2/3	1/3	1/3	1/3	1/3	0/3	0/3	0/3
Total pour comparaison avec l'échelle pratiquée **Total**	37	33	29	24	20	17	14	12	7	4	1

Standards of practice to standards of evidence: developing assessment capable teachers

Claire Wyatt-Smith, Colette Alexander, Deanne Fishburn and Paula McMahon

ABSTRACT
Teacher education is a hotly debated policy area in higher education and schooling portfolios, with increasing emphasis on standards and accountability. It is in this environment that *The Standards Project* (2013–2015) presented in this article began. It has at its core a three-part commitment: first, to undertake a comprehensive audit and analysis of all teacher education programmes in the state of Queensland, Australia, to establish the approaches and practices Universities relied on to preparing beginning teachers as assessment capable; second, to take account of multiple perspectives and approaches in initial teacher education to integrating data into how beginning teachers are prepared to source and use evidence for improving learning and teaching; and further, to develop new principles, policy and practices for reviewing and moderating teacher education programmes against professional standards. The paper proposes a move beyond the discourse of professional standards of practice towards a complementary discourse of standards of evidence. In our collaboration we drew on two fields, namely the writing on teacher education including reviews, and the field of assessment, both considered within broader sociocultural theory applied to assessment.

Introduction

The research presented in this article is a descriptive case study of beginning teacher assessment preparation addressed through inter-agency collaboration in Australia. Begun in 2013 and continuing, *The Standards Project* was stimulated by three related phenomena: (i) the now widespread recognition of the need for quality classroom assessment to promote student learning (Black & Wiliam, 1998; Stiggins, 2008); (ii) the increasing interest in teachers' assessment literacy, and the related issues in initial teacher education (ITE) raising concern in several countries including Wales, Scotland, England and Australia about how and how effectively beginning teachers are prepared and (iii) the strengthening interest in Professional Standards for teacher classroom practice, including assessment. The research has relied heavily on collaboration across agencies. By way of introduction, to date, collaborators include Deans and Heads of School from all universities and higher education providers in Queensland, Australia (N:11); senior personnel in the state's Teacher Registration Authority with responsibilities for ITE programme appraisal in line with professional standards for teacher registration; employing authorities in the schooling sectors (Catholic, Independent and State Schooling), and university researchers.

Internationally, there are differences across the iterations of Professional Standards in different educational and geographic contexts (Wyatt-Smith & Looney, 2016). There are also differences among the identified action areas and recommendations in the numerous ITE reviews completed in the last five years, discussed later in this article. These include, but are not restricted to, the relative emphases given to specific assessment practices (e.g. feedback and moderation), and the approaches taken to developing teacher dispositions or attitudes to learning and learners. However, common across the standards and reviews is the complex capacity building, knowledge and relational issue of how the ITE academic programme and school-based professional experience components work together. In Australia, the *Teacher Education Ministerial Advisory Board (*Craven et al., 2014*) Review of ITE* identified as one of the highest priorities the need for Education Faculties and Schools of Education to prepare beginning teachers who are classroom ready and assessment literate. This is taken to include content and curriculum knowledge and skills, and capabilities in aligning teaching, learning and assessment for purposeful assessment, both formative and summative. The review gave particular attention to how pre-service teachers are being prepared to collect, infer meaning from and use data to improve student learning and inform in-the-moment instructional decision-making. It also highlights how teachers use data to monitor the impact of teaching on learning and diverse learners over time.

It was in this context that the Queensland College of Teachers (QCT)[1] began a significant initiative in professional standards, working in partnership with higher education institutions and other providers responsible for ITE. The primary aim of the case study was to examine the nature and extent of the opportunities in ITE programmes that sought to develop beginning teachers' assessment knowledge, skills and capabilities, as well as the formation of their assessment identities. From the beginning, it had at its centre the *Australian Professional Standards for Teachers* (APST), and Focus Area 5.4 in particular. This focus, discussed in more detail below, enabled concentration on the professional knowledge, skills and expertise in assessment that teacher education students are expected to develop to be ready for practice. This includes their developing abilities to use data[2] to improve teaching and learning. The stimulus for the work came from the increasing recognition of the need for assessment-capable teachers on entry to the profession, recognising that professional learning would be ongoing throughout the career.

Background one: teacher education in the broader context of reform and standards

The future development of the teaching profession has high prominence in education policy in many countries. This is not a new development. It reflects the now widespread and increasingly influential discourse that constructs teacher education as a problem, even an entrenched and consequential problem that cannot be fixed from within. There are reported concerns in many countries including Australia, Northern Ireland, Wales, Scotland and the United States, to name a few, that ITE as a field lacks a strong evidence base, needs

DEVELOPING TEACHERS' ASSESSMENT CAPACITY

reform and overall, is not well led (see e.g. Furlong, 2015, referring to Wales; Sahlberg, Broadfoot, Coolahan, Furlong, & Kirk, 2014, referring to Northern Ireland; Craven et al., 2014, referring to Australia). While context is undoubtedly important in policy attempts at educational change and improvement, as suggested, there are some issues that appear to be common in reviews of ITE relevant to the research presented here and completed in the last decade. These include, but are not restricted to: entry requirements and pathways into teaching; the relationship between respective academic programmes and in-school professional practice components; the increasing interest in standards for qualified teacher status and career progression; and the development of measures for gauging the impact of ITE on school and individual student achievement.

Wyatt-Smith and Looney (2016) have noted that the emergence of standards is not new. Indeed, 'standards or prescriptions intended to govern teachers' classroom practice, general demeanour and behaviour at school and beyond the classroom have existed in the developed world since teachers were first employed and paid' (p. 805). What is new, however, is the policy-driven interest in standards as drivers for teacher education reform, and more than this, the interest in standards as driving measurable improvement in ITE and 'teacher/teaching quality' more generally.

Internationally, professional standards codify professional practice in teacher education and these codes are increasingly being used to identify and evaluate quality teachers and teaching (Wyatt-Smith & Looney, 2016; see also Craven et al., 2014; Furlong, 2015; Sahlberg et al., 2014). Amongst the many meanings attributed to the term 'standard', its relationship to manufacturing and prescription of a single statement of acceptable parameters for production, albeit at national levels, is not insignificant. In the case of products and industries, for example, standards can be set as minimum requirements, and the expectation prescribed and legally enforced, with penalties, where breaches occur. Within the context of professional standards for teachers, however, three features of standards across national and international jurisdictions are worth noting: (i) the multiplicity of codified components of the task of teaching; (ii) the identification of incremental steps in the proficiency of practice of the standards as progression markers; and (iii) how degree of quality is captured in the terms used to convey the standards. Amongst this multiplicity, the complexity of teaching is politicised by policy that uses professional standards as the arbiter of quality teaching (Cochran-Smith, Piazza, & Power, 2013). Despite the political assumptions made about the link between standards of practice and quality teachers, there is both a paucity of evidence to support the claimed link and a growing critical analysis of the claims (Connell, 2009; O'Neill & Adams, 2014).

How professional standards for teaching are conceptualised, including in relation to ITE, and how they are expected to function, are key issues with significant implications. This holds not only for the approach to developing the teaching workforce, but also for shaping perceptions of the status of teaching profession. Referring to Wales, Furlong (2015) recognised the significance of Standards for Qualified Teacher Status (QTS), writing that, 'it is perhaps not surprising that in many cases [the standards] have become a de facto curriculum in many teacher education programmes' (p. 12) (italics in original). In his exploration of options for the future of ITE in Wales, he identified the difficulties associated with standards conceptualised as, 'a set of behaviourally based "competences": things that newly qualified teachers "must know and do"' (p. 12). Further, he contrasts this conceptualisation of standards with the alternative conceptualisation of teacher learning in a developmental

132

way whereby teachers are prepared, 'to be active professionals, with their own judgements to make and with their own responsibilities as leaders of children's learning' (p. 12).

The APST, including Standard 5 with its focus on assessment, adopts this alternative conceptualisation. Focus Area 5.4 calls for beginning teachers to demonstrate the judgements they make and the responsibilities they take up in interpreting assessment data for the purposes of evaluating student learning and modifying teaching practice to improve learning. Further, the standard seeks to align the contribution of ITE to teachers' long-term professional development. *The Standards Project* had at its centre Focus Area 5.4. It was deliberately ambitious in concentrating attention on how ITE programmes develop beginning teachers to be active professionals capable of making evidence-informed judgements necessary to lead students' learning. The discussion that follows examines the approach taken to moderate the submissions from Faculties and Schools of Education within a formal collaboration with the QCT.

Background two: the move to a national process in quality assuring teacher preparation: the choice of assessment as a priority area

The QCT is the regulatory authority for the teaching profession in Queensland, established on 1 January 2006 under the *Education (Queensland College of Teachers) Act 2005* (the Act). The main objectives of the organisation are to uphold the standards of the teaching profession, maintain public confidence and protect students in schools by maintaining a register of qualified and suitable teachers.

Since the 1970s, Queensland has a well-established history of teacher registration and the accreditation or approval of ITE programmes. The QCT and the preceding authorities of the Board of Teacher Education and the Board of Teacher Registration have worked collaboratively with providers and stakeholders to ensure that programmes remain current, reflect research and meet the needs of teacher employers, schools and the profession. Using a standards-based approach via the *Professional Standards for Queensland Teachers* (Queensland College of Teachers [QCT], 2006) and a set of requirements outlined in the *Programme Approval Guidelines* (Queensland College of Teachers [QCT], 2007/2009/2011), ITE programmes are routinely considered by the QCT for two-phased cyclic review. Phase One Approval granted initial endorsement of the intended curriculum and assessment of an ITE programme, while Phase Two Approval reviewed the enacted curriculum with consideration given to how the standards are applied in practice (QCT, 2007/2009/2011, p. 23).

In 2012, Australia introduced national standards for teaching and teacher education and a national approach to the accreditation of ITE programmes. This move disrupted the existing QCT review cycles. The national approach is outlined in the *Accreditation of Initial Teacher Education Programmes in Australia: Standards and Procedures,* endorsed by the Ministerial Council for Education, Early Childhood Development and Youth Affairs (Australian Institute for Teachers & School Leadership [AITSL], 2011). While the process is undertaken by state and territory jurisdictions, such as the QCT, the national system facilitates an agreed national process to support consistency and quality assurance in teacher preparation.

With the commencement of the national approach, there was early recognition by the QCT of a loss of continuity in reviewing the intended, taught and assessed curriculum of state-based programmes while transitioning to the new system. ITE programmes were considerably redeveloped to meet the APST and new accreditation requirements and therefore, all programmes sought initial accreditation under this process. It became apparent that this would result in programme outcomes not being interrogated by the QCT for an extended period, in some cases, for a decade.

In this context of ITE policy change, attention turned to available levers to support continuous improvement as well as to ensure a QCT regulatory presence across the life of a programme. While Section 230h of the Act enables the QCT to approve and monitor ITE programmes, by 2012 the monitoring function had not been fully activated. Higher education institutions were required to submit an annual statement about their programmes. This was to include relevant data on, for example, key changes made to the ITE programmes over time, and a statement about student outcomes. However, given the discontinuity of standards (professional and programme), the intensifying government interest in teacher quality and data-driven decision-making in the education portfolio at state and federal levels, and the increasingly loud calls for ITE reform, the QCT moved to develop a sharper focus on monitoring the quality of programme implementation.

Early in 2013, the Professional Standards Committee (PSC) of the QCT endorsed the design of an innovative monitoring strategy. This was subsequently carried forward into action as *The Standards Project*. There were two key drivers of this initiative: (i) a commitment to a collaborative approach to continuous improvement in programmes informed by the APST; and (ii) the opportunity to identify and disseminate exemplars of quality practice that meet the requirements of the standards. A key decision point was the choice of priority area. The approach was to take a systematic analysis of a deep slice of the enacted curriculum in ITE, delving deeper into the application of professional standards to academic programmes. This involved going beyond the broad scope of evaluation that occurs in the initial accreditation phase. The priority area chosen for this deep slice was assessment and specifically, Standard 5, which encompasses: teacher understanding of assessment, the agency to provide feedback, make judgements and moderate them, and use of student data for teaching and learning improvement and reporting purposes. Within this broader standard, the chosen priority area was Focus Area 5.4 with its focus on interpreting student data, mentioned earlier (see Appendix 1 for the standard in full). This decision took account of the responsibilities of the QCT for monitoring university programmes against the professional standards, and the political and employer clamour for improved teacher quality in the area of assessment.

Two areas considered critical for designing the project were: risk-based regulation and practice-informed policy, and moderation as professional accountability. These are addressed next.

Key considerations in project design

Risk-based regulation and practice-informed policy

Internationally ITE as a field of research is in its infancy, emerging in an uncertain decision-making environment characterised by what Fullan and Quinn (2016) refer to as 'fragmentation' and 'policy churn' (p. 13). In such an environment, the project worked from the position that, 'managers in the public sector are better off adopting explicitly exploratory approaches in which goals and intended outcomes are fairly fluid, efforts are redirected

DEVELOPING TEACHERS' ASSESSMENT CAPACITY

Table 1. Fullan and Quinn's right drivers.

Original right drivers (Fullan, 2011)	Right drivers in action (Fullan & Quinn, 2016)
Systemness (coordinated policies)	Focusing direction
Collaboration (development of social capital)	Cultivating collaborative cultures
Pedagogy	Deepening learning
Capacity building for results (knowledge, skills and capabilities)	Securing accountability

as learning advances, and overly hierarchical command and control systems are avoided' (Matthews, Lewis, & Cook, 2009, p. 7). Consequently, the core task of government and policy-makers is twofold: (i) to identify harms and control them effectively; and (ii) to ensure that policies and procedures are minimally intrusive (Sparrow, 2008). The potential harm identified in designing *The Standards Project* was that beginning teachers could commence working with students without the requisite knowledge, skills and dispositions to undertake teaching and assessment as a complex activity involving professional judgement and decision-making.

An additional dimension of monitoring a high-risk component of teaching practice – in this case, teachers' use of actual student learning data (Focus Area 5.4) – was undertaken to provide further confidence about the overall quality of ITE programmes. To minimise intrusion in providers' programme design and decision-making, the regulatory authority needed to 'design for participation', 'build a simple system and let it evolve' and 'lower the barriers to experimentation' (Hannon, Patton, & Temperley, 2011, p. 19).

Choosing to focus on the development of assessment-capable teachers and in particular, how graduates are being prepared to demonstrate the capacity to interpret assessment data to evaluate student learning and modify teaching practice (Focus Area 5.4) addressed these priorities for policy-makers. It also engaged with the indications from employers of graduates across the three schooling sectors (Catholic, Independent and State schooling) that assessment is a complex area of teaching and in need of strengthening in ITE programmes. More specifically, the chosen Focus Area related to beginning teachers' abilities to use data. It is one of the practice-oriented graduate level standards that goes beyond knowledge and understanding to application. As such, it is potentially of higher risk.

For this reason attention was given to the *right drivers* in action, to use the categories of Fullan (2011) and Fullan and Quinn (2016). These are taken to be historical social constructs subject to change. The drivers regarded by the case study participants and researchers to be *right* were aligned with those identified in Table 1. This reflects the authors' understanding that designing of policy is designing 'not as a rational problem-solving activity but as a socially based, collective activity for generating solutions to complex problems and challenges' (Hobday, Boddington, & Grantham, 2012, p. 278).

The intent was for transformation to be emergent during the Project, made possible by structuring processes for conversation, collaborative learning and innovation through implementation first, and drafting policy and regulations later (Heilmann, 2008). Attention now turns to moderation and quality assurance.

Moderation as professional accountability

Broadly speaking, research has tended to focus on the use of moderation as quality assurance that determines the equivalence of outcomes for students and graduates (Sanderson et al., 2011). In Australia, attention on the use of moderation for accountability has been a response to federal intervention in the assurance of academic standards. (Readers are invited to see Recommendation 23: Bradley review – Australian Government, 2008; Tertiary Education Quality & Standards Authority [TEQSA], 2015). While standards-referenced assessment and external moderation for accountability has been practised in senior schooling assessment in some Australian states for several decades, it has not been the subject of systematic and sustained research in higher education or senior schooling, with very limited engagement in ITE involving cross-institutional review. Much of the broader research activity in moderation has had an institutional lens and cross-border studies. These have included studies across institutional faculties, trans-national delivery, full-time and casual academics, and private providers (Crimmins et al., 2015; Krause et al., 2013; Sanderson et al., 2011; Tuovinen, Dachs, Fernandez, Morgan, & Sesar, 2015). Research into the use of moderation in ITE is very limited (see e.g. Adie, Lloyd, & Beutel, 2013), with the focus on its implications for higher education rather than teacher education in particular.

The range of moderation practices and purposes engaged in higher education can be categorised into two broad approaches represented in the literature (Bloxham, Hughes, & Adie, 2015). These are a low-stakes approach which focuses on the professional learning of academics in making consistent and comparable judgements (Crimmins et al., 2015; Tuovinen et al., 2015); and a high-stakes accountability approach (Krause et al., 2013; Sanderson et al., 2011). The Tertiary Education Quality Standards Authority requirements identified that moderation can be used to 'support consistency and reliability of assessment and grading' (cited by Adie et al., 2013; p. 969). In the context of heightened concerns in Australia about teacher quality, moderation for accountability has gained prominence. As a consequence, the role of moderation has moved towards verifying educational standards as a key measure of course and institutional success. Issues with other means of verifying educational standards, such as self-reported graduate outcomes and standardised-exit testing (Krause et al., 2013), has further emphasised the need to sharpen the focus of moderation in higher education away from professional learning to professional accountability.

However, studies of standards and moderation in schooling (Wyatt-Smith, Klenowski, & Colbert, 2014), have shown that this balancing of professional learning and system accountability is a delicate one, involving sustained system support (Adie et al., 2013; Sadler, 2013). It involves sustained professional conversations about the meaning of standards as expectations of quality, and the development of shared understandings of how these apply in practice. From this vantage point, the application of standards and participation in moderation typically involve calibrating judgement processes. Such calibration involves attuning judgement using various exemplars chosen as illustrating the requirements of the standards, commentaries revealing how compensations or trade-offs are made in arriving at judgement and time for moderation meetings where the focus is on talk and interaction of assessors who come together to reach agreement about the assessed work assessed against the standards.

Attention now turns to *The Standards Project*, its design features, data and methods used to monitor how programmes engaged with the requirements of Focus Area 5.

Methods: data and design

The methods used in *The Standards Project* to facilitate monitoring of ITE programmes were built around two broad principles that promoted learning for all participants. These principles were: (i) the engagement of stakeholders in collaborative learning relationships; and (ii) a series of learning activities designed to facilitate the monitoring of Focus Area 5.4 and shared understanding of the relevant standards.

During 2013, consultation with the PSC of the QCT and negotiations with the Queensland Deans of Education Forum (QDEF) used these principles to design and implement an approach for the first monitoring cycle, discussed below. This cycle was described as a pilot used for participative policy-making through a continuous cycle of collaboration, action, evaluation, iteration and diffusion (Albury, 2011; Christiansen & Bunt, 2012; Maffei, Mortati, & Villari, 2013).

The following discussion presents the design of the project, the data collected and related methods of analysis and findings. While the investigation is necessarily context-specific, the approach and findings have potential relevance and application to other jurisdictions inquiring into ITE with a focus on assessment literacy.

The data in overview

The data collected and analysed included all ITE Provider Evidence Reports and Expert Panel Feedback Reports collated across the monitoring cycle. In total, 11 Schools of Education reported on 52 approved ITE programmes. The programmes included four-year undergraduate and one-year and two-year postgraduate programmes covering early childhood, primary and secondary sectors. They represented 70% of the approved programmes offered in Queensland in 2013/2014. Across these programmes, ITE providers identified 164 individual assessment tasks as contributing to Focus Area 5.4. The Evidence Reports identified and discussed aspects of programmes intended to develop assessment capabilities and relevant exemplars of these. Also included were sample programme assessment tasks, including task descriptions and accompanying statements of criteria used for making judgements about ITE students' achievement. Assessment criteria were provided for 110 tasks (67% of the total sample). Evidence in the form of student work samples was provided for 21 of the submitted tasks (13%).

Five main activities were designed for examining the approach taken by ITE providers to develop assessment-capable teachers. A purpose-built intervention model was designed whereby educational stakeholders could participate in Core Activities deliberately linked across stages. These are discussed in more detail in the following section, though it is worth mentioning here that the Core Activities were: (i) the development of shared understandings of the focus area and rationale for this choice of focus. Participants in this were ITE Faculty Deans and Heads of Schools across the 11 participating sites; (ii) ITE-led moderation of institutional evidence of pre-service teachers' assessment capabilities; (iii) ITE providers' preparation of evidence reports; (iv) moderation by an expert panel; and (v) the provision of feedback reports to the providers.

This purpose-designed intervention model was informed by ITE research pointing to the critical need for explicit and agreed roles and responsibilities in ITE (Caldwell & Sutton, 2010; Kenny, 2012), genuine collaboration among partners involved in the academic

DEVELOPING TEACHERS' ASSESSMENT CAPACITY

Table 2. Engagement of stakeholders across stages.

Stage		QCT	QDEF	ITE provider	Other
1	Development of shared understandings	X	X	X	X
2	ITE-led moderation – 6 July 2014 (*purpose:* professional learning)		X	X	
3	Preparation of evidence reports		X	X	
4	Expert moderation (1) – 15 Sept. 2014 (*purpose:* professional accountability)	X			X
5	Provision of institutional feedback (1)	X		X	
6	Preparation of second evidence reports		X	X	
7	Expert moderation (2) – 5 May 2015 (*purpose:* professional accountability)	X			X
8	Provision of institutional feedback (2)	X		X	
9	Preparation of third evidence report (to be submitted in March, 2016)		X	X	

and school-based professional experience components of programmes (Kruger, Davies, Eckersley, Newell, & Cherednichenko, 2009; Turner, 2008), mentioned earlier, and responsiveness to the needs of the profession (Le Cornu, 2012; Martinez & Coombs, 2001). Five Core Activities were intended to maximise engagement and ownership of *The Standards Project*. They were used iteratively across nine stages. See Table 2 *Engagement of stakeholders across stages*. In the table, 'X' indicates partner engagement at a particular stage. This iterative approach provided both feedback and feedforward loops to inform next-stage action by all partners in the process.

Development of shared understandings (Stage one: February–October 2013)

Stage one developed shared understandings about what counts as evidence of developing assessment capabilities in both the academic and school-based experience components of ITE. The relationship of these components of ITE programmes was deliberately put to the fore from the beginning. This *joined-up approach* took account of the findings in ITE reviews (Caldwell & Sutton, 2010) and research showing the critical role of enduring school and university partnerships and the commitment to reciprocal learning relationships (Darling-Hammond, 2006; Peters, 2011; Roberts-Hull, Jensen, & Cooper, 2015). The actions undertaken across this stage included the commissioning of new research to inform stakeholders about best practice in school assessment (Renshaw, Baroutsis, van Kraayenoord, Goos, & Dole, 2013), and a forum event to disseminate to ITE providers and other stakeholders the initial findings of this research. The forum also provided an opportunity for sectors and employers to articulate expectations of the assessment capabilities of beginning teachers for their respective workforces.

ITE-led moderation (Stage two: meeting 6 July 2014)

In July 2014, the respective Deans or Heads of Education and ITE providers worked together and in consultation with the QCT on the moderation of practices relating to Focus Area 5.4, the development of a template for preparing evidence and the identification of a set of best practice principles in assessment for ITE. The QDEF hosted a workshop for academic staff across all ITE providers. Representatives from institutions were asked to bring and share evidence from their programmes of how they were developing pre-service teachers' assessment capabilities in using data to modify teaching practices. They were also asked to moderate this evidence against the requirements of Focus Area 5.4, looking for comparability of graduate outcomes across institutions. This stage brought to light the need for a common reporting template, informed by a research-informed set of best practice principles, discussed in stage three. A draft monitoring template was provided to the QCT and subsequently refined and distributed to all ITE providers in preparation for the third stage.

Preparation of evidence reports (Stage 3: July–August 2014; Stage 6: November 2014–March 2015; Stage 9: continuing, July 2015–March 2016)

The QDEF and the QCT agreed that the evidence reports prepared by ITE providers for stage three would comprise three components. Parts one and two provided evidence relating to all approved programmes with student enrolments in 2013/2014. These were a *programme map* and *supporting evidence* for each approved programme. The map was a visual representation of the spread of opportunities to demonstrate Focus Area 5.4, including interpretation of student assessment data, evaluation of student learning and modification of teaching practice, as well as opportunities for adjustments in assessments for inclusion purposes. The supporting evidence was to include task descriptions, guides used for making judgements and examples of pre-service teacher work. Stage three asked ITE providers to prepare an institutional response to the best practice principles identified during stage two. This statement was intended to demonstrate alignment between ITE practices and these principles, thereby demonstrating the quality of that practice. These best practice principles were as follows:

- Assessment tasks demonstrate the understanding that data come in multiple forms for multiple purposes.
- Assessment tasks that are authentic and contextual.
- Assessment tasks are underpinned by a theoretical framework which provides students opportunities to develop the language of critique.
- Assessment tasks that are inclusive of the core underpinning skills of data use, such as collect, organise, analyse, infer meaning or interpret, and act upon.
- Assessment tasks that are underpinned by ethical principles and regard for diversity and inclusion.

At stages six and nine, ITE providers were asked to submit additional programme maps and supporting evidence based on the findings of the expert panel. This included requests for evidence about the 30% of programmes that were not included in the initial stage three evidence reports and requests for additional evidence about the programmes and tasks that had been reported. As such, these additional reporting stages were deliberately specific to institutional contexts and responses.

Expert moderation (Stage 4: September 2014; Stage 7: May 2015)

For stages four and seven an expert panel was convened by the QCT and tasked with examining and evaluating the evidence reports submitted by ITE providers. Members of the expert panel included QCT officers, sector/employer representatives and an academic expert in

DEVELOPING TEACHERS' ASSESSMENT CAPACITY

the field of assessment who acted as Chair. The QCT prepared an Analysis and Feedback Tool (see Appendix 2) to guide the expert panel's judgements about ITE evidence reports.

At stage four, the expert panel developed assessment criteria that represented expectations of beginning teachers in Focus Area 5.4. These criteria covered the development of knowledge and understanding of both formative assessment and summative assessment, with an emphasis on fitness-for-purpose and the desired ability to:

- design diagnostic tools to determine what students know and can do;
- develop and use a variety of assessment strategies to gather sufficient evidence to make sound judgements about student learning;
- infer meaning from the range of data collected and modify learning experiences and teacher pedagogy in response; and
- engage in ongoing evaluation throughout the teaching and learning cycle as part of teaching and learning practice.

The approach taken to moderation at both stages four and seven was to identify and consider the learning and experiential opportunities provided for pre-service teachers in relation to these criteria and to link decision-making about the quality of programmes to evidence of these criteria as representative of Focus Area 5.4. The common point of reference used for each ITE provider's Evidence Report was back to these criteria as guiding discussions about developing assessment-capable teachers. That is to say, the approach taken in moderation was itself criteria- and standards-referenced, rather than norm-referencing or ranking of submissions. Concurrently, attention focused on identifying good practice for sharing exemplars to disseminate approaches to preparing assessment-capable teachers as feed forward to ITE providers and other stakeholders. In this action, the expert panel recognised that Standard 5 (Assessment) and Focus Area 5.4 were presented as verbal descriptors and therefore remained open to interpretation. The aim was that the exemplars returned to ITE providers would provide concrete referents of the intent of the standard.

Provision of institutional feedback (Stage 5: November 2014; Stage 8: July 2015)

Following each meeting of the expert panel, feedback reports were prepared for both the QCT and ITE providers. These reports provided general feedback about the outcomes of the expert moderation of programmes, identified points of good practice for Focus Area 5.4 and the quality of submissions, and provided recommendations for programme and submission improvements across ITE providers. Alongside the general feedback, the expert panel provided targeted feedback in relation to each ITE provider's submission and programmes. This included feedback about programme sequencing, partnerships with schools and the depth of simulation of learning experiences and assessment tasks. The greatest depth or authenticity was achieved when beginning teachers were prepared for and undertook inquiry projects into student learning. At their fullest, these involved collecting, collating, analysing actual classroom evidence and using this in the design and implementation of interventions intended to improve student learning. In effect, the classroom data were used to inform the beginning teachers' own learning about learning and about their teaching effectiveness.

As a consequence of the outcomes of the planned moderation at stage four, further iterative feedback loops were engaged. ITE providers were asked to respond to the stage five feedback through annual reporting in March 2015. This was to include how the feedback had been shared with the ITE staff, changes made as a consequence of the feedback and the provision of requested additional evidence. With the provision of stage eight feedback in July 2015, two cycles of evidence, moderation and feedback had been completed. The monitoring process was extended to a third submission of evidence in March 2016, with the findings from the full set of submissions from the commencement of *The Standards Project* presented next.

Findings and discussion

The Standards Project generated key findings relating to: (i) evidence of quality practices in the implementation of Focus Area 5.4; and (ii) evidence of quality monitoring submissions. Aspects of both were identified by the Expert Panel at its first meeting.

Evidencing Focus Area 5.4

In relation to Focus Area 5.4, the panel identified and reported that quality programmes could be characterised as those that engaged in:

- developing pre-service teachers' assessment identity through a discrete course/unit on assessment, preferably early in the programme;
- demonstrated the use of data across a range of teacher practices and data sets, including:
    - collection and use of data to diagnose and cater for an individual student's learning needs,
    - analysis of a range of class data to inform lesson planning, and
    - analysis of data to inform modifications to units of work to meet identified learning goals. Quality monitoring submissions were identified as those that provided thorough coverage of the enacted curriculum, that told a narrative of the implementation of Focus Area 5.4, and included both descriptions and evidence of teaching, learning and assessment tasks.

This project did not set out to collect data on the relative merit of discrete or stand-alone assessment courses or units, as distinct from embedded assessment across courses or units. It is clear however that the former provided more dedicated time and focused opportunities to develop a repertoire of assessment knowledge, skills and capabilities not otherwise possible when assessment was one learning area competing with other areas for time and attention.

Another key finding related to the point raised earlier regarding the extent to which the beginning teacher's engagement with assessment data could be described as a thick (as distinct from thin) simulation (Heap, 1991). As applied in the context of ITE, the distinction is a useful one insofar as in the main, thick simulations typically represent more authentic learning opportunities or opportunities that could be expected in schools. Overall, the evidence across the various reports analysed show that ITE providers were not well placed to provide a range of data types for analysis in academic programmes. While schools and systems (Catholic, Independent and State) routinely hold assessment data of various types, the project identified historic data access restrictions for ITE providers. As discussed in the conclusion, an outcome of the Project is joint action on these.

The evidence also showed that an optimum mix in developing assessment-capable teachers is a stand-alone assessment course as well as a sharp focus on assessment practices during in-school professional experience. This combination appears optimum in offering the mix of research-informed learning in the academic programme about assessment as well as authentic practice opportunities in schools to collect, collate and use data through to the point of classroom action. This action could include, for example, diagnosing learning difficulties or needs, monitoring progress and making assessment adaptations or adjustments for students for inclusion purposes.

A related finding is that stronger partnerships between stakeholders are necessary to better enable ITE programmes to engage fully with professional standards relating to assessment, and evidence of using data for improvement, in particular. The partnerships between ITE providers, the responsible registration authority (in this case the QCT), schools and education statutory authorities at system level are required to ensure that assessment capabilities are developed as part of developing expertise in teaching and learning in situated practice. A more systematic approach is called for, if pre-service teachers are to be provided with suitable opportunities to learn and practice assessment techniques in a range of settings, and develop skills to interpret data and determine what the information means for their teaching, in a *context of mutuality*. In this context, on-campus activities in the academic programme would be integrally linked with professional experience placements in schools. In order to facilitate practical learning experiences within the on-campus component of ITE programmes, there is a critical need for authentic or actual student learning data at class and cohort levels.

Evidencing the enacted curriculum

A further key finding from the analysis of both the ITE Provider Evidence Reports and Expert Panel Feedback Reports stemmed from identified issues associated with the standard of evidence provided across the submissions that were analysed. The expert panel expressed concerns about the sufficiency or completeness of the information provided about programme delivery and assessment in the Focus Area, and a narrow or reductive perspective of student data that did not reflect contemporary practice in schools.

Analysis of the Evidence Reports and Expert Panel Reports identified four categories of approach to the monitoring process by ITE providers that were characterised as:

- *Capstone submissions:* included descriptions and/or evidence of culminating task/s without considering the narrative of the enacted curriculum that lead to that task.
- *Generic submissions:* included descriptions and/or evidence relating to Standard 5 more generally, rather than specifically about the use of data for improvement.
- *Hypothetical submissions:* described the intended curriculum as required for accreditation without evidence of the enacted curriculum or classroom practice.
- *Political submissions:* responded to the issue without descriptions and/or evidence of either the intended or enacted curriculum.

This analysis resulted in four recommendations for improving monitoring processes. These incorporated the development of guidelines for ITE providers as a means of clarifying expectations of the process to improve the standard of evidence provided for moderation. First, supporting the needs of ITE providers to understand and implement the monitoring process is essential. Given the in-depth nature of monitoring in identified priority areas, different individuals from ITE providers will likely be engaged in the process for each monitoring process. Ongoing support will therefore need to be provided as part of an overall communication and engagement strategy surrounding the continued monitoring of ITE programmes.

Second, clarity about the expected evidence, and more specifically, the standard of evidence is essential. This would ensure that the expectations of the evidence to be provided are public, open to scrutiny and further, able to support teacher educators' own developing understandings of professional standards. In part, this involves engaging the Panel Chair much earlier in the process to build in more effective processes of ITE-led moderation, as described in the section above.

Third, the articulation of the intended curriculum in ITE academic programmes into the enacted curriculum is an area for ongoing attention. The relevant aspects of the enacted curriculum to be included in future monitoring templates are: the teaching, learning and assessment cycle; outcomes for pre-service teachers; and approaches to curriculum evaluation and review.

Finally, the monitoring process needs to differentiate between aspirational practice and minimum requirements. While both of these can and should be encouraged, there needs to be clear lines between the two in order to avoid what we have referred to as 'standards creep' towards extremely high expectations as the minimum requirements for any one Focus Area. Arguably, a focus on *aspirational expectations* could also serve to promote professional excellence for ITE providers and their graduates.

Standards of evidence and evidence of standards

The key finding from this research concerns the distinction between evidence of standards (showing how the design of ITE academic programmes meets stated requirements) and standards of the evidence (showing the quality and impact of actual teacher preparation in assessment). Many of the issues identified by the expert panel were the result of limited evidence presented by ITE providers about how they prepared pre-service teachers to connect assessment of students' learning and teaching. Consequently, in some cases, the expert panel had difficulty making on-balance judgements about how the requirements of the Focus Area were being satisfied. The judgements made by the expert panel were that the standard of evidence provided was such that it could not always be used to make judgements about the standard of programmes. In short, in some cases, it lacked fitness-for-purpose. For the monitoring of Focus Area 5.4, this resulted in further feedback loops. For future monitoring processes, it was shown that the development of practice and policy itself needed to improve the standard of evidence collected for moderation by expert panels.

Further, the reliability of the on-balance judgements made by the expert panel concerning the quality of a programme is dependent upon the content validity of the evidence that is available to the expert panel. For the outcomes of the monitoring process to be credible and dependable, such that decision-making about the quality of programmes is both valid and reliable, shared understandings of appropriate standards of evidence must be developed. This represents new terrain in ITE in Australia. One possibility in progressing research in ITE is to develop and publish suitably targeted exemplars chosen to illustrate how the requirements of professional standards have been met. Assessment researchers have previously pointed to how standards, together with actual work samples or exemplars (Sadler, 1989), and an accompanying explanatory statement or 'cognitive commentary' (Wyatt-Smith & Gunn, 2009; Wyatt-Smith & Klenowski, 2013) is the optimum mix for illustrating the meaning of standards. One advantage of this combined approach to illustrating standards is that it acknowledges assessment as situated practice. It can also accommodate the diversity of ITE and school contexts in which pre-service teachers complete their preparation.

Conclusion

The results of *The Standards Project* confirmed the benefits of adopting an iterative and collaborative approach to ITE monitoring for improving principles, practices and policy in the provision of quality teacher preparation that connects the work of ITE providers with the sector they purport to serve. Moving beyond consultation to participation (Maffei et al., 2013) in policy building, and focusing on capacity building and accountability as a strengthening process (Fullan & Quinn, 2016), has successfully shifted practices in both the regulation of ITE in Queensland and the preparation of assessment-capable teachers for Queensland schools.

Using a model of practice-informed policy development enabled the regulator to explore and identify what quality evidence of the enacted ITE curriculum looks like, and subsequently, to develop a comprehensive and workable monitoring policy. Alongside policy, a practice-oriented supporting template was developed, comprising stronger scaffolding to: (i) support ITE staff in thinking through a quality submission; and (ii) facilitate a standards-referenced approach to moderation for cycle two (see Appendix 3).

Building policy in a participatory way has not been without challenges: distributed leadership and variable (and in some cases, limited) evidence provided in relation to Focus Area 5.4 has required negotiation, openness to experimentation and learning. These challenges, however, have been far outweighed by a range of benefits for ITE providers and the profession in the designing of policy. These have included: the development of negotiated understandings of professional knowledge and practice in the selected Focus Area across providers and stakeholders; the dissemination of good practice in a selected Focus Area; a broader range of ITE provider staff involved in regulatory processes (through the rotation of selected focus areas); and furnishing of evidence that is useful to ITE providers in meeting other regulatory requirements, including annual reporting, reaccreditation and higher education benchmarking. At the time of writing, a second monitoring cycle – focusing on pre-service teachers' understanding of numeracy teaching strategies and their application in learning areas – is underway and is already demonstrating more substantial and systemic evidence of positive change.

The unanticipated positive impact of stakeholder collaboration throughout *The Standards Project* is that it has created space for previously unknown challenges and systemic issues affecting the outworking of Focus Area 5.4 to emerge. As mentioned above, historic access restrictions (including various ethics and privacy concerns), mentioned earlier, have previously limited the agency of ITE providers and pre-service teachers in developing assessment skills relating to using data for teaching and learning.

An outcome from the research is that stakeholder commitment to collaborative projects has been roused and action taken to address data access restrictions and develop data-related resources. This includes access inside ITE providers and programmes to sector learning management systems, curriculum achievement standards, varied assessment technologies and authentic student achievement data for diagnostic, intervention and monitoring purposes.

Furthering the relationship between the on-campus learning experiences in assessment and school-based professional experience in developing assessment-capable teachers remains a high priority for sustained inquiry through research, policy and practice.[3] Building on the evidence generated from *The Standards Project*, a new study is underway on the design and implementation in Australian universities of an authentic, culminating assessment known as the *Graduate Teacher Performance Assessment* that pre-service teachers complete over a sustained period in their final professional experience. The outcomes from this work will generate a corpus of common evidence for the application professional standards in moderation. It also has potential to advance inquiry into standards of evidence necessary to demonstrate teacher education graduates to be assessment capable. Readers interested in this work are asked to contact the first author.

Notes

1. The Queensland College of Teachers is the regulatory authority for the teaching profession in Queensland.
2. The term data is taken to refer to the assessment evidence that teachers collect and interpret for the purposes of critically reflecting on teaching effectiveness and using system data including large-scale standardised test data for improvement.
3. The next stage of the research reported in this article includes the development of a research-informed assessment curriculum in ITE. The aim is to develop beginning teachers' assessment identities by (i) embedding studies in assessment in both academic programmes and professional experiences and (ii) building resilience through attention to teacher attributes/dispositions and underpinning principles of assessment.

Disclosure statement

No potential conflict of interest was reported by the authors.

References

Adie, L., Lloyd, M., & Beutel, D. (2013). Identifying discourses of moderation in higher education. *Assessment & Evaluation in Higher Education, 38*, 968–977. doi:10.1080/02602938.2013.769200.

Albury, D. (2011). Creating the conditions for radical public service innovation. *Australian Journal of Public Administration, 70*, 227–235. doi:10.1111/j.1467-8500.2011.00727.x

Australian Government. (2008). *Transforming Australia's higher education system: Review of Australian higher education – Final report* (D. Bradley, Chair). Canberra: Department of Education, Employment and Workplace Relations.

Australian Institute for Teachers and School Leadership [AITSL]. (2011). *Accreditation of initial teacher education programs in Australia: Standards and procedures.* Carlton South: Education Services Australia.

Black, P., & Wiliam, D. (1998). Assessment and classroom learning. *Assessment in Education: Principles, Policy & Practice, 5*, 7–74.

Bloxham, S., Hughes, C., & Adie, L. (2015). What's the point of moderation? A discussion of the purposes achieved through contemporary moderation practices. *Assessment & Evaluation in Higher Education, 41*, 638–653. doi:10.1080/02602938.2015.1039932

Caldwell, B., & Sutton, D. (2010). *Review of teacher education and school induction: First report – Full report.* Brisbane: Department of Education and Training, Queensland Government.

Christiansen, J., & Bunt, L. (2012). *Innovation in policy: Allowing for creativity, social complexity and uncertainty in public governance.* Retrieved from http://www.nesta.org.uk/sites/default/files/innovation_in_policy.pdf

Cochran-Smith, M., Piazza, P., & Power, C. (2013). The politics of accountability: Assessing teacher education in the United States. *The Educational Forum, 77*, 6–27. doi:10.1080/00131725.2013.739015

Connell, R. (2009). Good teachers on dangerous ground: Towards a new view of teacher quality and professionalism. *Critical Studies in Education, 50*, 213–229. doi:10.1080/17508480902998421

Craven, G., Beswick, K., Fleming, J., Fletcher, T., Green, M., Jensen, B., ... Rickards, F. (2014). *Action now: Classroom ready teachers.* Retrieved from http://www.studentsfirst.gov.au/teacher-education-ministerial-advisory-group

Crimmins, G., Nash, G., Oprescu, F., Alla, K., Brock, G., Hickson-Jamieson, B., & Noakes, C. (2015). Can a systematic assessment moderation process assure the quality and integrity of assessment practice while supporting the professional development of casual academics? *Assessment & Evaluation in Higher Education, 41*, 427–441. doi:10.1080/02602938.2015.1017754

Darling-Hammond, L. (2006). Assessing teacher education: The usefulness of multiple measures for assessing program outcomes. *Journal of Teacher Education, 57*, 120–138. doi:10.1177/0022487105283796

Fullan, M. (2011, April). *Choosing the wrong drivers for whole system reform* (Seminar Series 204). Melbourne: Centre for Strategic Education.

Fullan, M., & Quinn, J. (2016). *Coherence: The right drivers in action for schools, districts, and systems* [Adobe Digital Editions version]. Retrieved from https://play.google.com/store/books/details?id=STjrCQAAQBAJ

Furlong, J. (2015). *Teaching tomorrow's teachers. Options for the future of initial teacher education in Wales* (Report to Huw Lewis, Minister for Education and Skills). Oxford: Oxford University.

DEVELOPING TEACHERS' ASSESSMENT CAPACITY

Hannon, V., Patton, A., & Temperley, J. (2011). *Developing an innovation ecosystem for education: White paper*. Retrieved from https://www.cisco.com/web/strategy/docs/education/ecosystem_for_edu.pdf

Heap, J. (1991). A situated perspective on what counts as reading. In C. D. Baker & A. Luke (Eds.), *Towards a critical sociology of reading pedagogy* (pp. 103–140). Amsterdam: John Benjamins.

Heilmann, S. (2008). Policy experimentation in China's economic rise. *Studies in Comparative International Development, 43*(1), 1–26. doi:10.1007/s12116-007-9014-4

Hobday, M., Boddington, A., & Grantham, A. (2012). Policies for design and policies for innovation: Contrasting perspectives and remaining challenges. *Technovation, 32*(5), 272–281. doi:10.1016/j.technovation.2011.12.002

Kenny, J. D. (2012). University–school partnerships: Pre-service and in-service teachers working together to teach primary science. *Australian Journal of Teacher Education, 37*, 57–82. doi:10.14221/ajte.2012v37n3.1

Krause, K., Scott, G., Aubin, K., Alexander, H., Angelo, T., Campbell, S., … Vaughan, S. (2013). *Assuring final year subject and program achievement standards through inter-university peer review and moderation*. Retrieved from http://www.olt.gov.au/resource-assuring-learning-teaching-standards-inter-institutional-peer-review

Kruger, T., Davies, A., Eckersley, B., Newell, F., & Cherednichenko, B. (2009). *Effective and sustainable university–school partnerships: Beyond determined efforts by inspired individuals*. Acton: Teaching Australia, Australian National University.

Le Cornu, R. J. (2012). School co-ordinators: Leaders of learning in professional experience. *Australian Journal of Teacher Education, 37*, 18–33. doi:10.14221/ajte.2012v37n3.5

Maffei, S., Mortati, M., & Villari, B. (2013). Making/design policies together. *10th European Academy of Design Conference – Crafting the Future*. Retrieved from http://www.academia.edu/3341210/Making_Design_Policies_Together

Martinez, K., & Coombs, G. (2001). Unsung heroes: Exploring the roles of school-based professional experience coordinators in Australian preservice teacher education. *Asia Pacific Journal of Teacher Education, 29*, 275–288. doi:10.1080/13598660120091874.

Matthews, M., Lewis, C., & Cook, G. (2009). *Public sector innovation: A review of the literature*. Retrieved from http://www.anao.gov.au/uploads/documents/Suppliment_Literature_Review.pdf

O'Neill, J., & Adams, P. (2014). The future of teacher professionalism and professionality in teaching. *New Zealand Journal of Teachers' Work, 11*(1), 1–2.

Peters, J. (2011). Sustaining school colleagues' commitment to a long-term professional experience partnership. *Australian Journal of Teacher Education, 36*(5), 1–15. doi:10.14221/ajte.2011v36n5.2

Queensland College of Teachers (QCT). (2006). *Professional standards for Queensland teachers*. Toowong: Author.

Queensland College of Teachers (QCT). (2007/2009/2011). *Program approval guidelines for preservice teacher education*. Toowong: Author.

Renshaw, P., Baroutsis, A., van Kraayenoord, C., Goos, M., & Dole, S. (2013). *Teachers using classroom data well: Identifying key features of effective practices. Final report*. Brisbane: The University of Queensland.

Roberts-Hull, K., Jensen, B., & Cooper, S. (2015). *A new approach: Teacher education reform*. Melbourne: Learning First.

Sadler, D. R. (1989). Formative assessment and the design of instructional systems. *Instructional Science, 18*, 119–144. doi:10.1007/BF00117714

Sadler, D. R. (2013). Assuring academic achievement standards: From moderation to calibration. *Assessment in Education: Principles, Policy & Practice, 20*, 5–19. doi:10.1080/0969594X.2012.714742

Sahlberg, P., Broadfoot, P., Coolahan, J., Furlong, J., & Kirk, G. (2014). *Aspiring to excellence. Final report of the international review panel on the structure of initial teacher education in Northern Ireland* (Report to the Minister for Employment and Learning). Belfast: Department for Employment and Learning.

Sanderson, G., Yeo, S., Mahmud, S., Briguglio, C., Wallace, M., Hukam-Singh, P., & Thuraisingam, T. (2011). *Moderation for fair assessment in transnational learning and teaching*. Retrieved from http://www.olt.gov.au/resource-library?text=Moderation+for+fair+assessment+in+TNE

DEVELOPING TEACHERS' ASSESSMENT CAPACITY

Sparrow, M. (2008). *The character of harms*. Cambridge: Cambridge University Press.

Stiggins, R., (2008, September 8). Assessment FOR learning, the achievement gap, and truly effective schools. *Educational Testing Service and College Board conference, Educational Testing in America*, Washington, DC.

Tertiary Education Quality and Standards Authority (TEQSA). (2015). *A risk and standards based approach to quality assurance in Australia's diverse higher education sector.* Retrieved from http://www.teqsa.gov.au/sites/default/files/publication-documents/RiskStandardsSectorPaperFeb2015.pdf

Tuovinen, J., Dachs, T., Fernandez, J., Morgan, D., & Sesar, J. (2015). *Developing and testing models for benchmarking and moderation of assessment for private higher education providers.* Retrieved from http://www.olt.gov.au/resource-library?text=Developing+and+testing+models+for+benchmarking+moderation

Turner, W. (2008). Developing and sustaining perpetual school university partnerships. *Proceedings of the EDU-COM 2008 international conference. Sustainability in higher education: Directions for change.* Perth, WA: Edith Cowan University.

Wyatt-Smith, C., & Gunn, S. (2009). Towards theorising assessment as critical inquiry. In C. Wyatt-Smith & J. Cumming (Eds.), *Educational assessment in the 21st century* (pp. 83–102). Dordrecht: Springer.

Wyatt-Smith, C., & Klenowski, V. (2013). Explicit, latent and meta-criteria: Types of criteria at play in professional judgement practice. *Assessment in Education: Principles, Policy and Practice, 20*, 35–52.

Wyatt-Smith, C., Klenowski, V., & Colbert, P. (2014). *Designing assessment for quality learning* (Foundation book in the series: The enabling power of assessment). Dordrecht: Springer.

Wyatt-Smith, C. & Looney, A. (2016). Professional standards and the assessment work of teachers. In L. Hayward & D. Wyse (Eds.), *Handbook on curriculum, pedagogy and assessment* (pp. 805–820). London: Routledge.

Appendix 1

Australian professional standards for teachers – graduate

Standard 5 – Assess, provide feedback and report on student learning

Focus Area 5.1 Assess student learning
Demonstrate understanding of assessment strategies, including informal and formal, diagnostic, formative and summative approaches to assess student learning.

Focus Area 5.2 Provide feedback to students on their learning
Demonstrate an understanding of the purpose of providing timely and appropriate feedback to students about their learning.

Focus Area 5.3 Make consistent and comparable judgements
Demonstrate understanding of assessment moderation and its application to support consistent and comparable judgements of student learning.

Focus Area 5.4 Interpret student data
Demonstrate the capacity to interpret student assessment data to evaluate student learning and modify teaching practice.

Focus Area 5.5 Report on student achievement
Demonstrate understanding of a range of strategies for reporting to students and parents/carers and the purpose of keeping accurate and reliable records of student achievement.

Appendix 2

Focus area 5.4 Monitoring Report – Analysis and Feedback Tool

5.4 – Interpret student data – Demonstrate the capacity to interpret student assessment data to evaluate student learning and modify teaching practice.
Key informing questions:

(1)   Where/how is 5.4 covered in course content?
(2)   To what extent/how/where are pre-service teachers assessed as being able to demonstrate 5.4?

University Name: _____

Approved/Accredited Programme _____

Aspects	Requirements to be met	Yes	No	Comments/ notes
Programme structure	How is assessment addressed in the programme? • In a course dedicated to assessment (identify by name) • And/or in a number of ways across the programme (identify where/how) Are there sufficient learning opportunities, and are these scaffold-ed developmentally, across the programme? Does the programme address high stakes testing regimes (e.g. NAPLAN) as well as assessment for learning?			
Assessment (and examples of student work)	Does the programme formally assess students' capacity to interpret and use student assessment data to inform teaching and learning? Have sample assessment tasks and student responses been supplied? Do the course tasks and assessment criteria (marking guide) clearly articulate the expectations of Focus area 5.4? If this is assessed during professional practice, are students and supervising teachers supported appropriately?			
Best PracticePrin-ciples	Do the assessment tasks reflect best practice principles? • demonstrate the multiple forms and purposes for data • are authentic and contextual • are underpinned by a theoretical framework (language of critique) • are inclusive of core skills (collect, organise, analyse and interpret, and act upon) • are underpinned by ethical principles			

University Name: _____

Approved/Accredited Programme _____

Commendations:
Recommendations (Suggestions for improvement):

• Are you satisfied that graduate teachers from this institution will have learnt about and are assessed on 5.4?
• If not, why not; and how could the situation be improved?

Appendix 3

Annotated Monitoring Template

<u>Graduate Career Stage</u>: Focus Area 5.4: Interpret student data – Demonstrate the capacity to interpret student assessment data to evaluate student learning and modify teaching practice.

DEVELOPING TEACHERS' ASSESSMENT CAPACITY

Program Map

Add, delete or merge cells as appropriate.

Assessment Criteria	Year 1		Year 2		Year 3		Year 4	
	Sem. 1	*Sem. 2*	*Sem. 1*	*Sem. 2*	*Sem. 1*	*Sem. 2*	*Sem. 1*	*Sem. 2*
a) understanding of the purpose of assessment for learning								
b) understanding of the purpose of assessment of learning	These 'assessment criteria' were taken from the report of the Expert Panel Meeting – 15 September and are relevant to Focus Area 5.4.							
c) ability to:								
i) develop and use diagnostic tools to determine what students already know and can do					Demonstrate the scope and sequence of learning opportunities provided to preservice teachers. List only the unit/course codes and names relevant to preservice teachers' achievement against each 'success criteria'.			
ii) develop and use a variety of assessment strategies (both formal and informal) to gather sufficient evidence to make sound judgements about student learning								
iii) infer meaning from a range of data collected regarding student learning and modify learning experiences and teacher pedagogy in response								
iv) engage in ongoing evaluation throughout the teaching and learning cycle (closing the loop)								

Supporting Evidence

Complete one table for each unit/course listed in the program map. Copy the table as many times and needed. Add, delete and merge cells as necessary.

Assign a Unit/Course Number:	Start with 1. and use this to number all related attachments.
Unit/Course Code and Name:	*Name the unit/course and list all relevant programs. Where applicable identify if it is a core or elective unit/course.*
Relevant Programs:	
Assessment Criteria:	*Copy the relevant 'assessment criteria'. Add or delete columns as necessary.*
Curricular Evidence:	
Curriculum Intentions:	*Identify and list the learning outcome/s relevant to each assessment criteria.*
Teaching and Learning:	*List content topics relevant to the assessment criteria and provide a narrative of relevant teaching and learning experiences. Where possible, attach illustrative examples of materials and/or activities that provide evidence.*
Assessment:	*Identify tasks and the criteria relevant to the assessment criteria. Attach task descriptions and criteria as provided to preservice teachers (PST).*
*Illustrative PST Examples:**	*Attach evidence of student work assessed at a passing standard against the relevant assessment criteria. Evidence of best practice performance by students may also be provided.*
Curriculum Review:	*As appropriate, provide a narrative of curriculum revisions or changes relevant to improving practice.*

*One student example may be used to illustrate more than one assessment criteria.

150

Scaling up, *writ small*: using an assessment for learning audit instrument to stimulate site-based professional development, one school at a time

Zita Lysaght and Michael O'Leary

ABSTRACT

Exploiting the potential that Assessment for Learning (AfL) offers to optimise student learning is contingent on both teachers' knowledge and use of AfL and the fidelity with which this translates into their daily classroom practices. Quantitative data derived from the use of an Assessment for Learning Audit Instrument (AfLAI) with a large sample ($n = 594$) across 42 primary schools in the Republic of Ireland serve to deprivatise teachers' knowledge and use of AfL and the extent to which AfL is embedded in their work. The data confirm that there is urgent need for high-quality teacher professional development to build teacher assessment literacy. However, fiscal constraints coupled with the fractured nature of current provision renders it impossible to offer sustained support on a national scale in the immediate term. In response, this paper proposes the adoption of a design-based implementation research approach to site-based collaborations between researchers, teachers and other constituent groups, such as that engaged in by the authors over recent years, as a mechanism for addressing teachers' needs in a manner that also supports other participants' professional interests.

Introduction

An emerging theme from review of large-scale implementation research in Assessment for Learning (AfL) is that summative assessment and accountability measures in national policy frameworks influence the nature and extent to which AfL takes hold (Hopfenbeck & Stobart, 2015). Examination-focused education systems linked with powerful high-stakes national and international testing regimes have proven highly resistant to change (Apple, 2013; Birenbaum et al., 2015; Fullan, 2015), albeit they are known to be 'only marginally useful for guiding day-to-day instructions and supporting student learning' (Shute & Kim, 2014, p. 312). Further 'reform overload or previous attempts to reform assessment practices that have been unsuccessful' (Carless, 2005, p. 52) often accentuate existing resistance to change.

Challenges notwithstanding, there are increasing calls for more balanced assessment systems (Chappuis, Commodore, & Stiggins, 2016), coupled with a growing awareness that a combination of factors are required to motivate deep lasting change. These include, but are

DEVELOPING TEACHERS' ASSESSMENT CAPACITY

not limited to, sustained, high-quality teacher professional development in the principles and practices of AfL (Trumbull & Lash, 2013), coupled with 'mechanisms for supporting its introduction' (Hopfenbeck & Stobart, 2015, p. 1). Important, too, is awareness that teachers are not passive or neutral recipients of mandated policy change; they are 'change agents' whose 'moral purpose' is intimately bound up with their 'life and career' histories (Day, 2002, p. 15). Hence, while professional development (PD) is a potentially important enabler of policy change and implementation, models that purposively engage the hearts and minds of teachers and frame AfL as 'part of a comprehensive system' of assessment and evaluation (Bennett, 2011, p. 5) are more likely to bring about change in classroom practice, albeit sustained time and effort are required (Leahy & Wiliam, 2009; Lysaght, 2013). Further, given that 'sustained change in day-to-day practice is inherently local' (McLaughlin & Talbert, 2006, p. 26), PD is needed that is responsive to the 'reciprocal influences' of three subsystems: the teacher, the school and the learning activity (Opfer & Pedder, 2011, p. 276).

In response, this paper advances the argument that in Ireland currently, when fiscal resources are limited and the need to develop teacher assessment literacy is acute, small-scale, site-based, research partnerships with teachers warrant closer attention. It is proposed that if the challenge of designing scalable models of continuous professional development (CPD) for teachers in assessment is framed as a design-based implementation research (DBIR) issue, the possibility presents to galvanise valuable, but typically fragmented and incidental, professional support currently provided to individual schools. As described (Penuel, Fishman, Cheng, & Sabelli, 2011), DBIR brings key actors in education together, including teachers, researchers, curriculum specialists and policy-makers for example, to systematically and iteratively research, design, implement and review workable solutions to vexing problems. In the light of calls nationally (The Teaching Council, 2016; Irish National Teachers' Organisation [INTO], 2014) and internationally (OECD, 2013a, 2013b, 2013c) to employ emergent, collaborative, approaches to the development of scalable models of professional development (PD), DBIR is worthy of consideration.

The paper is in three parts. It begins by considering briefly identified challenges at primary level in Ireland regarding assessment and teacher professional development. The sustained prioritisation of standardised assessment in recent years, coupled with legacy problems in the development and provision of high-quality PD opportunities for teachers, serves to contextualise the authors' work with schools in AfL. The second section introduces the Assessment for Learning Audit Instrument (AfLAi), data from which have helped quantify the nature and extent of the teachers' understanding and use of AfL (Lysaght & O'Leary, 2013), and spawned calls from schools for site-based PD. A detailed account of the support provided to one school is provided. The concluding section advances some ideas about how work of this kind with schools, that confirm benefits on both the researchers and teachers involved, might be reframed as DBIR projects to broaden their scope, value and appeal.

Section 1: the status quo in Ireland *vis a vis* assessment and CPD

In keeping with global trends as described by Wiseman (2010), greater accountability in Ireland is often accompanied by a commitment to evidence-based or evidence-informed policy. As stated in *Ireland's education and training sector: Overview of service delivery and reform* (Department of Education and Skills [DES], 2015) report, the aspiration is for Ireland to create '... an internationally recognised education and training system based on evidence informed policies designed to anticipate and respond to the changing needs of learners, society and the economy' (p. 2). In response, the DES (2015) has identified four 'whole system reform' goals to include 'all learners, all teachers and all schools and colleges' (p. 11), one of which is 'improving quality and accountability' (p. 3). This is to be achieved by engaging a range of strategies including reform of initial teacher education, implementation of new models of school inspection, developing teachers as professionals, introduction of school self-evaluation and improvements of the assessment and reporting of students' progress (DES, 2015, pp. 20–27).

In a related policy document, colloquially referred to as the *Literacy and Numeracy Strategy* (see DES, 2011), described by the Chief Inspector as 'ground breaking for the Irish system' (Hislop, 2013, p. 8), reference is made to exiting assessment and evaluation systems at primary level that inform policy and practice. These include the National assessments of English Reading and Mathematics at second and sixth classes, and international assessments – principally, the Progress in International Reading Literacy Study (PIRLS) and Trends in International Mathematics and Science Study (TIMMS). As argued (Looney, 2016), the availability to Ireland of these data, and PISA data in particular, fills a vacuum identified over two decades ago in a Government *White Paper* (1995). At that time, internationally acceptable benchmarks were called for to enable greater comparative scrutiny of educational outcomes and impact. Shiel, Kavanagh and Millar's (2014, p. v) observation that 'lack of improvement' in National Assessments since the early 1980s in literacy and numeracy and 'lower-than expected performance' in these areas in PISA 2009 informed the *Literacy and Numeracy Strategy* evidences the weight now attributed to these national and international data of student achievement. Further, the DES (2015, pp. 24–25) acknowledges that these data inspired a 'new self-evaluation model' in primary schools based on '… a clear set of standards for schools' geared at 'school improvement'. Their expectation that 'standardised tests will enable schools to track how children are progressing …' and allow the DES to '… track progress at a national level' (DES, 2015, pp. 24–25) echoes worryingly of high-stakes assessment regimes internationally and the attendant challenges to the low-stakes AfL that these bring.

While some of the initiatives mentioned have been in train for some time (e.g. school self-evaluation – albeit with mixed results, see Sheehan, 2016), others, including the requirement that schools return the aggregated data from standardised testing annually to the DES represent a significant policy shift. Further, Hislop's description of the inclusion of 'very specific targets for improvements in students' learning' in the *Literacy and Numeracy Strategy* as 'novel' (2013, p. 8) is an under-estimation of the policy shift that this represents. It is noteworthy that it took Ireland almost 14 years to move from a position where '… an extensive use of attainment tests …' was deemed 'inappropriate … and … especially prejudicial to the needs of disadvantaged pupils' (Primary Education Review Primary Education Review Body, 1990, pp. 80–81) to the announcement by the DES of what was described as 'a controversial and unexpected proposal to introduce standardised testing in literacy and numeracy for all in compulsory education' (Looney, 2006, p. 351). The National Council for Curriculum and Assessment (NCCA, 2005c) cautioned the government at the time against prioritising standardised testing or attaching 'stakes' to attendant scores and their advice that such testing be restricted to two (or, more recently, three) times during a child's primary school years was heeded until 2011.

DEVELOPING TEACHERS' ASSESSMENT CAPACITY

While many would concur with the view that, in the absence of national tests or examinations, 'assessment is far less contested in the primary context in Ireland', to conclude that 'therefore the boundary between assessment of and for learning can be more permeable' (Looney, 2016, p. 126) seems more aspirational than probable currently. If, as argued (Birenbaum et al., 2015, p. 135), 'it is the overarching policy context' that ultimately provides 'the necessary zeitgeist for success' of AfL reform in nation states, then the incremental reliance on standardised assessment data is a concern. Despite the stated intention to 'use standardised tests, but with safeguards against an over-reliance on their outcomes' (Hislop, 2013, p. 13), recent communications from the DES (Circular 0034/2016; The Action Plan for Education, 2017) might be interpreted as suggesting otherwise. Of particular import to schools is the DES reminder that it '… is considering potential revisions to the existing system of allocating Resource Teaching/Learning Support resources to schools' and 'that standardised test data being returned may be used in the future to inform the development of a proposed revised model' (Circular 0034/2016, p. 3). Further, from a policy perspective, the fact that there is no mention of AfL in the 84 page *Action Plan* that 'confirms the vision and ambition to create the best education and training service in Europe by 2026' (DES, 2016b, p. 5) is confirmation that AfL is not a priority issue.

In this context, Hislop's exhortation of the need to 'examine deliberately how we want the essential components of an evaluation and assessment framework to develop in a coherent way' (2013, p. 8) deserves serious attention. The OECD has made similar calls (2013c, 2015a, 2015b) identifying such a framework as a mechanism to strengthen school self-evaluation, teacher appraisal and assessments for improvement and 'improve teaching and student outcomes' (OECD, 2013a, p.4) in Ireland. However, they caution that 'securing effective links to classroom practice is a key policy challenge in the design of evaluation and assessment frameworks' (OECD/CERI, 2008, p. 4) in the absence of which 'evaluation and assessment frameworks have no value' (OECD/CERI, 2008; p. 3). As acknowledged, this is contingent on the provision of 'focused support for teachers in classrooms …' (OECD/CERI, 2008, p. 4).

Data from the AfLAi Lysaght & O'Leary (2013) indicate that AfL is neither well understood nor used widely at primary level in Ireland currently. Hall and Kavanagh's (2002) finding that policy reports dating back to the 1990s inappropriately coupled teachers' use of diagnostic assessment at that time with an assumption that '… since teachers (were) already engaged in teacher assessment for formative purposes capacity to promote learning … further guidance (was) unnecessary' (p. 262) suggests a serious legacy weakness in the appropriate use of AfL. Subsequent investigations and evaluation reports of teaching, learning and assessment at primary level (e.g. Eivers, Shiel, & Shortt, 2004; the DES Inspectorate, 2005a, 2005b; the National Council for Curriculum and Assessment [NCCA], 2005a, 2005b) confirmed that teachers needed support in relation to classroom assessment. The DES (2005a) called for 'significant attention and improvement' in assessment practices (p. 62) and identified the need to clarity '… what should be assessed, and specify the assessment tools that can be used' (DES, 2005b, p. 54).

While the publication in 2007 of the *Guidelines on assessment in the primary school in Ireland* (NCCA, 2007) went some way to addressing these legacy weaknesses, failure to provide the promised professional development to teachers undermined their import. In keeping with previous commentary on weaknesses in policy development in assessment, research on CPD in Ireland, over many years, has repeatedly identified the fractured nature of provision. There have been iterative calls, in response, for systemic coordination and coherence in the design of CPD and the proactive engagement of teachers in the process by, among others, Burke (2004), Conway, Murphy, Rath, and Hall (2009), Granville (2005), Loxley, Johnston, and Murchan (2007) and Sugrue (2002). More recently, in the light of their review of the factors influencing teachers' participation in CPD in Ireland, Banks and Smyth (2013) called for further research in two areas, both of which have import for this paper. The first is the evaluation and assessment of the quality and relevance of CPD content for teachers and, in particular, the nature and extent of alignment between content and teachers' day-to-day work. The second relates to teacher access to, and participation in, informal CPD in Ireland and the need to investigate approaches to address the vexing issue of making time for professional development during the school year.

At first glance, the extensive promises made in the *Programme for government* (Government of Ireland, 2016) to 'promote excellence and innovation in schools' (p. 90) signal that change is imminent. There is reference to supporting school leaders to 'drive up educational standards, particularly in the fundamental of reading, writing and arithmetic'. A 'Schools Excellence Fund' is to be established to reward 'new approaches driven by teachers and parents'. Newly appointed principals are to 'take a preparation course' and there is the intention to 'incentivise voluntary school participation in new 'Local Education Clusters ....' However, in the absence of any clear implementation roadmap, it is not unreasonable to suggest that the programme is deserving of the same criticism levelled against the 1999 *Revised primary curriculum* (Government of Ireland) and, more recently, Education Minister's manifesto on the future development of education in Ireland (Quinn, 2012). The first was said to be 'stronger on progressive sentiment and much more vague on what this would look like in practice' (Sugrue, 2004, p. 197) while the latter invited the comment that it puts us at risk 'of putting a bush in every gap and camouflaging existing inadequacies, rather than bringing about sustainable improvements' (Sugrue, 2012, p. 153).

While it might legitimately be argued that the *Literacy and Numeracy* Strategy document provides greater detail of the nature and extent of CPD to be offered to teachers across the continuum (see DES, 2011, pp. 34–37), scrutiny of the commitments made suggests that the proposed support is quite limited. As the section *Actions to improve the development and improvement of teachers' skills in the teaching, learning and assessment of literacy and numeracy* indicates, CPD in assessment is intimately bound up with literacy and numeracy in this policy document rather than being conceptualised as a body of knowledge warranting independent study. Further, because there is a perceived need to provide support to teachers at multiple levels (including pre-service), the limitations of the planned CPD package for practicing teachers is easily missed. In reality, what is being proposed is –

> ... Access to approved, high-quality professional development courses of at least twenty hours' duration in literacy, numeracy and assessment (as discrete or integrated themes, provided incrementally or in block) every five years (as an element of the continuing professional development that teachers require to maintain their professional skills). (DES, 2011, p. 36)

In the light of the increasing focus on summative and high-stakes assessment noted previously, and notwithstanding strong statements in support of AfL in the *Literacy and Numeracy Strategy*, it is unlikely that a balanced assessment framework will develop in Ireland in the absence of purposeful timely intervention. The teachers' union cautions that 'current policy rhetoric is about encouraging schools to be learning communities ...' but 'rhetoric must be supported by action' (INTO, 2014, p. 7). The next section describes an approach that might be taken in response.

Section 2: empirical findings from the AfLAi and linked work with schools

For the past six years, the authors have supported primary schools in Ireland (and elsewhere, e.g. Norway) to collect data about AfL knowledge, skills and practices in their schools in order to identify their professional development needs and develop realistic plans to expand incrementally their use of AfL in the classroom. Comprehensive accounts of the history and development of the AfL audit (AfLAi) used by the teachers in this study and the AfL measurement (AfLMi) instruments are provided elsewhere (Lysaght, 2012; Lysaght & O'Leary, 2013; O'Leary, Lysaght & Ludlow, 2013). Hence, save for an initial description of the AfLAi, account in this section of the paper is deliberately restricted to more detailed review of the professional development provided to individual schools.

The assessment for learning audit instrument

The AfLAi consists of a five-page document, the first of which seeks demographic information from the respondent, with each of the remaining four focusing on one formative assessment strategy (e.g. classroom questioning and discussion). Table A1 lists each strategy, its associated acronym and the number of statements related to it in the audit. In total, 58 statements about classroom practices, identified within the literature as indicative of formative assessment practices, (see Thompson & Wiliam, 2008, for explanation of *The One Big Idea*, associated strategies and techniques), are included – distributed across four scales.

When responding to the set of statements linked to each AfL strategy, teachers are requested to employ a five-point rating scale to indicate the extent to which they believe the statement reflects their classroom practice:

Embedded   (Happens 90% of the time)

Established   (Happens 75% of the time)

Emerging   (Happens 50% of the time)

Sporadic   (Happens 25% of the time)

Never   (Never happens)

For the purposes of quantitative analyses, numerical values were assigned to each of the scale points (e.g. 5, the highest score, was assigned to an 'embedded' practice; 1, the lowest score, to the statement 'never'). When factor analysis was applied to the four scales, scree plots revealed the presence of one large factor in each case with eigenvalues ranging in size from 4.5 Feedback (FB) to 7.2 Learning Intentions and Success Criteria (LISC). The variance explained for the first factor was 45, 38, 37 and 39% for LISC, Questioning and Classroom Discussion (QCD), FB and (Peer and Self-Assessment) PSA, respectively. Cronbach alpha reliabilities were above .84 (LISC = .92; QCD = .89; F = .84; PSA = .88) in each of the four cases and all six Pearson correlations between the four scales ranged in value from .57 (LISC and PSA) to .66 (FB and QCD). All these findings are consistent with the analyses conducted previously (Lysaght & O'Leary, 2013), and confirm that the underlying structure of the relationships between the statements within each of the four scales remains coherent with the increase in sample size. Further, in keeping with the theoretical framework employed originally when constructing the instrument, it is clear that the constructs being measured are different but related as anticipated[1] (see appendices).

Sample details and respondent profiles

The numbers of schools engaging in this process has steadily increased over time and in this section of the paper, an updated analysis of the original data-set to include the 118 teachers across 8 schools with whom the authors have collaborated over the past three years is provided. The teachers involved represent a large convenience sample (n = 594 teachers across 42 schools) most of whom were familiar with one or both of the authors and our work and who were either invited or sought personally to become involved following publication about the project in an article in a national teachers' journal (Lysaght, 2010).

With the exception of a Dublin geographical bias, most demographic data collected as part of the study reflect population statistics for Irish primary schools and teachers in terms of the range of school types included (single and mixed gender, disadvantaged and non-disadvantaged, urban and rural and Irish-speaking schools – called *Gaelscoileanna* in the Irish language). The majority of respondents (85%) are females working as mainstream classroom teachers or teaching principals (70%), with approximately 33% (compared with the population value of approximately 25% [Department for Education and Skills, 2011]) of the respondents indicating that they work as special educators. It is noteworthy that data analyses revealed no significant difference between the reported AfL practices of mainstream and special educators. In terms of years of teaching experience, the sample is distributed between teachers with 5 years or less (34%), between 6 and 20 years (37%) and those with more than 20 years of teaching experience (28%), respectively, with approximately equal numbers of respondents teaching at each class level from Junior Infants to Sixth Class.

To illustrate how the AfLAi acts as a catalyst to site-based professional development in AfL, the detail of one school's involvement with the project is now presented. Isolating one school in this manner facilitates presentation of the nature and extent of the initial engagement with schools who seek professional help following completion of the AfLAi. The pseudonym Hillside is used to protect the school's identity.

Professional development: the case of hillside

Hillside is a mixed gender school with an enrolment of almost 500, and is located in a middle-class suburb of Dublin. The staff comprises 26 teachers, 24 of whom took part in the study. The gender balance in the school is 4:1 in favour of females, a ratio reflective of the population of primary teachers in Ireland. While the majority of teachers (16) were working in mainstream classes from Junior Infants to Sixth Class, 7 fulfilled the roles of either learning support and/or resource teachers in the school. The staff could be described as relatively experienced, with just three having been teaching for less than five years.

In June 2015, the principal of the school contacted one of the authors by telephone requesting input on assessment for learning for the staff. She explained that while a Whole School Evaluation (WSE)[2] (see appendices) had resulted in a very good report for the school, practice in the area of assessment for learning had been highlighted as an area requiring improvement. As a result, professional development time after school hours[3] (see appendices) was being set aside to address the issue. Following discussion, it was agreed that each staff member would be invited to complete a hard copy, scannable, version of the AfLAi and return it, via the principal, to the authors in individually sealed envelopes. Once scanned, the data were aggregated and, in September 2015, a short report was sent to the principal. Soon afterwards, and following a brief review of the data with the principal conducted over the telephone, the authors were invited to visit the school to work with the staff during one of their professional development events. A two-hour slot at the end of a school day in October 2015 was agreed upon. In almost all respects, this is typical of the process of how most schools become involved in the AfLAi project, with the outcomes of a WSE or the interest of a principal or staff member often being an important catalyst for action.

Engagement framework

The engagement framework described here is informed by two sources: (a) organisation of the Teacher Learning Communities that participated in the Keeping Learning on Track project in the US (Thompson & Wiliam, 2008) and (b) experiences and lessons learned from working with schools in the very early stages of the project (Lysaght, 2009, 2012).

Step 1: Ten minute PowerPoint presentation outlining the learning intentions for the session, identifying the key big idea underlying AfL and highlighting the four strategies used in the AfLAi and some of the techniques associated with them.

Step 2: Five minute explanation of the rationale for the AfLAi (as a boundary crossing object) and explanation of how data derived from the instrument are interpreted.

Step 3: Five minute review of the LISC scale by teachers working in groups of three or four: their task, using the *Two Stars and a Wish* technique, was to identify two aspects of AfL that were working well in the school and one that needed to be improved.

Step 4: Fifteen minute plenary discussion on the outcomes of the group work using AfL techniques such as wait time ……

Step 5: Five minute review and fifteen minute plenary for the QCD scale

Step 6: Ten minute break

Step 7: Five minute review and fifteen minute plenary for the FB scale

Step 8: Five minute review and fifteen minute plenary for the PSA scale

Step 9: Twenty minute plenary on action steps that should be taken to improve AfL practices in the school

Step 10: Five minute discussion of success criteria linked to learning intentions identified in step 1.

Use of AfLAi data to inform PD

The AfLAi data for Hillside, which were shared on the day with teachers, are provided in separate tables for each scale (Tables A2–A5 inclusive; see appendices). While the statements are numbered according to how they appeared in the original instrument, they are rank-ordered in the tables, starting with the AfL practices reported by the teachers as being most embedded/established in their classrooms. It should be noted that the scale utilised implies that the closer the mean rating is to 5, the more embedded the practice. Smaller mean ratings signify that the practice is either sporadic or never happens (closer to 1). Moreover, since all teachers did not respond to every statement across the four scales, the number of responses (n) recorded in the tables is sometimes less than 24. In the case of each, while the data are explained fully during the opening stages of the PD, later stages deliberately afford teachers the opportunity to critically review, what are in effect, their self-reported perceptions of the extent to which they use AfL in practice. Further, in response to teachers' queries regarding the extent to which AfL practices in their school mirror those of other teachers nationally, we share the data displayed in Table A6 (see appendices).

Throughout our work with the Hillside school, we explain explicitly that, rather than assuming a deficit perspective of the teachers' existing knowledge and skill in AfL, we are purposefully adopting a sociocultural approach to our work with them in order to reinforce two key messages. First, the professional learning they engage in with us is socially rather than individually based. This is because we know from experience that when teachers engage in critical, collective review and discussion of their aggregated AfL data, they begin to ask questions and share stories about their individual classroom practices and their beliefs about what, how, when, where and why teaching, learning and assessment are practised in their school. This represents a crucial first step in deprivatising their classroom practice and the beliefs and mental models that underpin them. Second, we stress that this kind of mutual interrogation with their colleagues will support them in identifying and celebrating the diversity of their professional knowledge, experiences and resources (including, for example, the physical architecture of available learning spaces). Collectively, this constitutes their shared professional capital to be leveraged subsequently in the pursuit of objectives they set to advance AfL in their school. Throughout, we try to reinforce teachers' belief in themselves as the front-line workers, the gatekeepers and the street-level bureaucrats (Lipsky, 2010) with the insight and authority to determine how AfL can be incrementally promoted and embedded in their daily planning and practice. This spurs conversations about key policies, such as the *Literacy and Numeracy Strategy* (2011), the implementation opportunities and challenges that present for teachers in their particular context and the PD that might be needed. It is at this point when schools like Hillside look to us for additional, dedicated, guidance and support that the challenge of scaling up PD presents. Significantly, using DBIR as a lens through which to review additional supports which we have provided to a smaller number of schools in recent years has helped crystalise ideas about how PD in assessment might be expanded.

Section 3: 'scaling up' with design-based implementation research: challenges and opportunities

Building on the work of Odom (2009) and Coburn (2003), the term 'scaling up' is used here to refer to a process, typically undertaken by researchers and/or policy-makers, to implement systemically validated research-based or informed interventions. Successful scaling is determined by the extent to which the resulting implementations demonstrate depth, sustainability, spread and a shift in ownership (Coburn, 2003). If, as is the case here, the objective is transformational learning (Spillane, 2013) in assessment that significantly impacts teachers' classroom practice – something that cannot be achieved by simply tinkering at the surface level (Cuban, 1993) – an approach is required that engages teachers as fully as possible at each stage and level. As elaborated by Fishman, Penuel, Allen, Cheng, and Sabelli (2013), DBIR – which is based on the following four guiding principles – meets these requirements. It assumes:

> (1) a focus on persistent problems of practice from multiple stakeholders' perspectives; (2) a commitment to iterative, collaborative design; (3) a concern with developing Design-Based Implementation Research; and (4) a concern with developing capacity for sustaining change in systems. (p. 137)

Elsewhere (Lysaght, 2009, 2012), detailed description is provided of PD in AfL provided to a school as part of a doctoral study that extended over the period of the academic school year 2008–2009. While it was this research that led to the development of the AfLAi and, in turn, site-based support to schools like Hillside, the potential that in-depth CP of this kind offers to provide CPD in AfL at scale, if conceptualised in DBIR terms, has only recently emerged. The original PD model employed an activity systems frame (Tsui & Law, 2007) to conceptualise and describe collaborative inquiry involving the first author, four teachers in the base school in which the doctoral research took place and a member of the NCCA. Participation in the PD demanded that each constituent group (researcher, teacher and NCCA policy officer) cross their respective professional 'boundaries' (Engestrom & Tuomi-Grohn, 2003) in an attempt to support the teachers to embed AfL in their day-to-day teaching and learning. A range of 'boundary tools' (including lesson plans, video vignettes of the teachers using AfL in their classroom practice, research articles and policy guidelines) were used by the group to inform collective discussion, problem-solving, decision-making and iterative review. As depicted in Figure 1, this allowed for '… a group of actors with divergent viewpoints' (Star, 1989, p. 46) to work collaboratively for both mutual and independent professional gain.

Reflection on this work in the light of growing calls from school like Hillside, which have used the AfLAi to determine their baseline needs in AfL and received initial support of the

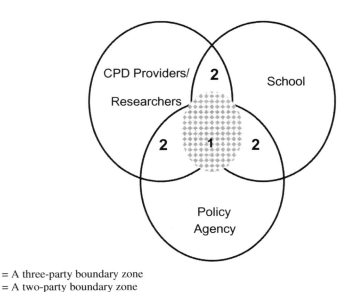

1 = A three-party boundary zone
2 = A two-party boundary zone
⋮ = Video

Figure 1. Boundary crossing by different groups involved in site-based CPD.

kind described in Section 2, prompted consideration of how to provide PD at scale. This is where DBIR shows promise. The first principle of DBIR, 'focus on persistent problems of practice from multiple stakeholders' (Fishman et al., 2013, p. 137) is congruent with the activity systems frame of Tsui and Law (2007). However, pprinciples two, three and four of DBIR extend significantly the potential of systems theory by affording greater scope to researchers, teachers and policy-makers to work together in ways that are both individually and collectively rewarding. From a teacher's perspective, adoption of a DBIR approach ensures that PD is tailored to address the specific problems encountered on site. From the researcher's/university teacher's perspective, it affords the opportunity to synchronise the community service role they are expected to fulfill with the expectation that they are research active. From the policy-maker's perspective, it affords a unique window into the process of policy implementation generally, while also providing information on challenges and opportunities relating to specific policies as they are being 'rolled-out'. Further, as an emerging research approach that is gaining traction internationally, DBIR offers the support of an active research community that sees the potential of cross-disciplinary engagement and is developing strategies and tools to make this happen. A key challenge for DBIR is to ensure that focus extends beyond '… one organisational level, such as the macro, environmental level or the micro, classroom level …' (p. 296). The ambition is to develop research that simultaneously '… highlights particular sites and processes of policy implementation' while shedding light on 'other potential conditions and interactions that may be instrumental in how policy plays out (p. 296). Consequently, it is proposed that DBIR offers the potential to elevate isolated site-based PD for teachers in AfL, such as that described in this paper, to another level, one that legitimises the time and effort exerted by the various constituent members in an attempt to improve teaching and learning.

Scaling up of this kind is not unproblematic, however, as the 'warts and all' account of the challenges that presented during the year-long research project in AfL attest (Lysaght, 2009). Carless' (2017) use of Coburn's (2003) four-dimensional scaling model to categorise the types of challenges that typically present is very useful in this context, particularly as it relates specifically to the scaling of PD in AfL. Among the key challenges observed is weak assessment capacity which can result in an absence of, or diminution in, trust; in response, Carless (2017) calls for 'at least minimising distrust' (p. 12) so that innovation in assessment is encouraged.

Conclusion

This paper calls for a futures thinking approach to the development of teacher assessment capacity enabled by synergies of effort and will. In the context of performance- and accountability-driven agendas nationally and internationally, schools and teachers must adapt to change. To be successful, they need to learn '… not just different ways of doing things, but very different ways of thinking about the purposes of their work, and the skills and knowledge that go with those purposes' (Elmore, 2000, p. 35). Central to this adaptation is the shift from heroic, hierarchical leadership and antiquated models of school organisation to 'reconfigured and reconceptualised' (Harris, 2004, p. 11) models of leadership and teacher agency, built on, and committed to, distributed leadership throughout schools (Spillane, 2013). This is crucial if, as Rigby, Woulfin and März (Rigby, Woulfin, & März, 2016) argue, structural and agency reform are to be coupled meaningfully.

Against this backdrop, and in the absence of teacher capacity linked to traditionally 'evolutionary' (Hislop, 2015, p. 2) approaches to structuring PD in Ireland, we believe that it is important, where possible, to promote and support organic and emergent calls from teachers for PD. In using the AfLAi, we are trying to actively privilege a transformative (as distinct from a transmission) approach to PD (Kennedy, 2005, 2014) that celebrates and seeks to maintain the unique and particular of, and, within each individual teacher and each individual school community. It is underlined by an understanding of teaching as a 'complex social craft' rather than an 'invariable, technical endeavour' (Spillane, 2013, p. 63) that is readily amenable to one size fits all, scalable models of PD currently awaiting 'discovery'. Engagement with teachers typically occurs at 'the 'micro' level ecosystem of learning and teaching' (OECD, 2013b, p. 14). In that context, it is significant that the AfLAi is also being used for PD purposes by individual teacher researchers as well as members of the inspectorate in Ireland as a tool to encourage change in assessment at the local level. Moreover, our lived experience in schools convinces us that by deliberately shifting focus from macro, mandated PD models and courses to site-based, micro-level engagement, teachers are positioned at the nexus of their own professional development, a key feature associated with success. This confers on them both attendant rights (to identify and/or co-design professionally relevant and valuable PD) and responsibilities (to engage fully with, and use, PD to improve their own knowledge, skill and practice). In the light of the Teaching Council's (2016, p. 11) call for PD for Irish teachers across four 'key dimensions of teachers' learning' ('formal/informal, personal/professional, collaborative/individual, school-based/external to the school or workplace'), this approach warrants serious consideration.

Notes

1. It should be noted that in previous publications, a different rating scale was used, one that ranged from 6 (*Embedded*) to 1 (*Do not understand*). This has been revised to provide a more construct coherent scale. Due to the fact that very small numbers of responses were attributable to the *Do not understand* option, differences in the findings from the data of the respective scales are negligible.
2. WSEs are carried out by a team of inspectors from the Department of Education and Skills (DES) with a focus particularly on the quality of the school management and leadership, the quality of teaching, learning and assessment and the school's own planning and self-review. At the end of the inspection, schools are provided with oral feedback and a written report which is published on the DES website (http://www.education.ie/en/Publications/Inspection-Reports-Publications/Whole-School-Evaluation-Reports-List/).

   In keeping with previous published comments from the inspectorate about the need to improve how assessment is used to support teaching and learning in Irish primary classrooms (e.g. DES, 2005b, 2005c), many WSEs feature recommendations such as '... there is a need for ongoing development of assessments across all curriculum areas on a whole-school basis. ... a whole-school policy on formative assessment is required to guide teachers and ensure consistency across the school. Further self and peer-assessment will give pupils greater confidence in their learning'.
3. In 2011, as part of a Public Service agreement between the DES and the Irish National Teachers Organisation (known as the Croke Park agreement), provision was made for primary teachers in Ireland to work an additional 36 h per school year outside of normal school opening times. The idea was that this time would be used and 'to significantly eliminate the erosion of class contact time' and to meet the requirements of school planning, continuous professional development, induction, pre- and post-school supervision, policy development, staff meetings and nationally and locally planned in-service (See DES Circular Number 0008/2011 available at: https://www.education.ie/en/Circulars-and-Forms/Active-Circulars/cl0008_2011.pdf).

Disclosure statement

No potential conflict of interest was reported by the authors.

References

Apple, M. W. (2013). *Education and power*. New York, NY: Routledge.

Banks, J., & Smyth, E. (2013). *Continuous professional development among primary teachers in Ireland: A report compiled by the ESRI on behalf of the Teaching Council*. Retrieved November 2016, from http://www.teachingcouncil.ie/en/Publications/Research/Documents/Continuous-Professional-Development-Among-Primary-Teachers-in-Ireland.pdf

Bennett, R. E. (2011). Formative assessment: A critical review. *Assessment in Education: Principles, Policy and Practice, 18*, 5–25.

Birenbaum, M., DeLuca, C., Earl, L., Heritage, M., Klenowski, V., Looney, A., & Wyatt-Smith, C. (2015). International trends in the implementation of assessment for learning: Implications for policy and practice. *Policy Futures in Education, 13*, 117–140.

Burke, A. (2004). *Teacher education in the Republic of Ireland: Retrospect and prospect*. Dublin: Standing Conference on Teacher Education North and South (SCoTENS).

Carless, D. (2005). Prospects for the implementation of assessment for learning. *Assessment in Education: Principles, Policy & Practice, 12*, 39–54.

Carless, D. (2017). Scaling up assessment for learning: progress and prospects. *Scaling up Assessment for Learning in Higher Education* (pp. 3–17). Singapore: Springer.

Chappuis, S., Commodore, C., & Stiggins, R. (2016). *Balanced assessment systems: Leadership, quality and the role of classroom assessment*. Thousand Oaks, CA: Corwin Press.

Coburn, C. (2003). Rethinking scale: Moving beyond numbers to deep and lasting change. *Educational Researcher, 32*(6), 3–12.

Conway, P., Murphy, R., Rath, A., & Hall, K. (2009). *Learning to teach and its implications for the continuum of teacher education: A nine country cross national study*. Dublin: The Teaching Council.

Cuban, L. (1993). *How teachers taught: Constancy and change in American classrooms, 1890–1990*. New York, NY: Teachers College Press.

Day, C. (2002). *Developing teachers: The challenges of lifelong learning*. London: Routledge.

Department of Education and Science. (2005a). *An evaluation of curriculum implementation in primary schools: English, Mathematics and Visual Arts*. Dublin: Stationery Office.

Department of Education and Science. (2005b). *Chief inspector's report, 2001–2004*. Dublin: Stationery Office.

Department of Education and Science. (2005c). *Literacy and numeracy in disadvantaged schools: Challenges for teachers and learners: An evaluation by the inspectorate of the Department of Education and Science*. Dublin: Stationery Office.

Department of Education and Skills. (2011). *Literacy and numeracy for learning and for life: The national strategy to improve literacy and numeracy among children and young people 2011–2020*.

Retrieved July 2016, from https://www.education.ie/en/Publications/Policy-Reports/lit_num_strategy_full.pdf

Department of Education and Skills. (2015). *Ireland's education and training sector: Overview of service delivery and reform.* Retrieved July 2016, from https://www.education.ie/en/Publications/Corporate-Reports/Irelands-Education-and-Training-Sector-Overview-of-service-delivery-and-reform.pdf

Department of Education and Skills. (2016a). Information in relation to standardised testing and other matters academic year 2015/16 and Subsequent Years, Circular 0034/2016. Retrieved January 2017, from https://www.education.ie/en/Circulars-and-Forms/Active-Circulars/cl0034_2016.pdf

Department of Education and Skills. (2016b). Action plan for education 2017. Retrieved February 2017, from http://www.education.ie/en/Publications/Corporate-Reports/Strategy-Statement/Action-Plan-for-Education-2017.pdf

Eivers, E., Shiel, G., & Shortt, F. (2004). *Reading literacy in disadvantaged primary schools.* Dublin: Educational Research Centre.

Elmore, R. (2000). *Building a new structure for school leadership.* The Albert Shanker Institute. Retrieved November 2016, from http://www.shankerinstitute.org/sites/shanker/files/building.pdf

Engestrom, Y., & Tuomi-Grohn, T. (Eds.). (2003). *Between school and work: New perspectives on transfer and boundary crossing.* London: Pergammon Press.

Fishman, B. J., Penuel, W. R., Allen, A. R., Cheng, B. H., & Sabelli, N. (2013). *Design-based implementation research: An emerging model for transforming the relationship of research and practice.* Retrieved November 2016, from https://www.sri.com/sites/default/files/publications/fishman_penuel_allen_cheng_sabelli_2013.pdf

Fullan, M. (2015). *The new meaning of educational change* (5th ed.). New York, NY: Teachers' College Press.

Government of Ireland. (2016). *A programme for a partnership government.* Retrieved July 2016, from http://www.merrionstreet.ie/MerrionStreet/en/ImageLibrary/Programme_for_Partnership_Government.pdf

Granville, G. (2005). *An emergent approach to teacher professional development: Final evaluation report on the experience and impact of the second level support service.* Dublin: Unpublished Report.

Hall, K., & Kavanagh, V. (2002). Primary assessment in the Republic of Ireland. *Conflict and consensus, Educational Management and Administration, 30*(3), 261–274.

Harris, A. (2004). Distributed leadership and school improvement: Leading or misleading. *Educational Management Administration and Leadership, 32*, 11–24.

Hislop, H. (2013). *Current policy trends and issues in teacher education and curricular reform.* Paper presented at the Cohort PhD Education Public Symposium University College Cork. Retrieved May 2016, from https://education.ie/en/Press-Events/Speeches/2013-Speeches/SP13-02-22.html

Hislop, H. (2015). *Reflections on leadership challenges in Irish schools.* Address by Dr Harold Hislop, Chief Inspector, to the Annual Conference of European Network for Improving Research and Development in Education Leadership and Management. Retrieved November 2016, from https://www.education.ie/en/Press-Events/Speeches/2015-Speeches/Address-by-Dr-Harold-Hislop-Chief-Inspector-Reflections-on-Leadership-Challenges-in-Irish-Schools.pdf

Hopfenbeck, T., & Stobart, G. (2015). Large-scale implementation of assessment for learning. *Assessment in Education: Principles, Policy & Practice, 22*(1), 1–2.

Irish National Teachers' Organisation. (2014). Learning communities. Discussion document and proceedings of the consultative conference on education 2010. Retrieved January 2017, from https://www.into.ie/ROI/Publications/LearningCommunities.pdf

Kennedy, A. (2005). Models of continuing professional development: A framework for analysis. *Journal of In-service Education, 31*, 235–250.

Kennedy, A. (2014). Understanding continuing professional development: The need for theory to impact on policy and practice. *Professional Development in Education, 40*, 688–697.

Leahy, S., & Wiliam, D. (2009, April). From teachers to schools: Scaling up professional development for formative assessment. Paper presented at the American Educational Research Association conference, San Diego, CA.

Lipsky, M. (2010). *Street-level bureaucracy: Dilemmas of the individual in public services*. New York, NY: Russell Sage Foundation.

Looney, A. (2006). Assessment in the Republic of Ireland. *Assessment in Education: Principles, Policy & Practice, 13*, 345–353.

Looney, A. (2016). Ireland: The intersection of international achievement testing and educational policy development. In L. Volante (Ed.), *The intersection of international achievement testing and educational policy development: Global perspectives on largescale reform* (pp. 75–90). New York, NY: Routledge.

Loxley, A., Johnston, K., & Murchan, D. (2007). The role of whole-school contexts in shaping the experiences and outcomes associated with professional development. *Journal of In-Service Education, 33*, 265–285.

Lysaght, Z. (2009). *From balcanisation to boundary crossing: Using a teacher learning community to explore the impact of assessment on teaching and learning in a disadvantaged school*. Unpublished Doctoral Dissertation, St. Patrick's College, Drumcondra, Dublin.

Lysaght, Z. (2010). Assessment for learning and teacher learning communities: Warranted strategies worthy of consideration. *InTouch, 112*, 49–51.

Lysaght, Z. (2012). Using an activity systems lens to frame teacher professional development. In B. Boufoy-Bastick (Ed.), *Cultures of professional development for teachers: Collaboration, reflection, management and policy* (pp. 129–158). Strasbourg: Analytics.

Lysaght, Z. (2013). The professional gold standard: Adaptive expertise through assessment for learning. In F. Waldron, J. Smith, M. Fitzpatrick, & T. Dooley (Eds.), *Re-imagining initial teacher education: Perspectives on transformation* (pp. 155–176). Dublin: The Liffey Press.

Lysaght, Z., & O'Leary, M. (2013). An instrument to audit teachers' use of assessment for learning. *Irish Educational Studies., 32*, 217–232.

McLaughlin, M. W., & Talbert, J. E. (2006). *Building school-based teacher learning communities: Professional strategies to improve student achievement*. Columbia, SC: Teachers' College Press.

National Council for Curriculum and Assessment (NCCA). (2005a). *Primary curriculum review phase 1: Summary of findings and recommendations*. Dublin: NCCA.

NCCA. (2005b). *The primary curriculum in schools: Joint DES/NCCA seminar: The proceedings*. Dublin: NCCA.

NCCA. (2005c). *Standardized testing in Irish primary schools*. Dublin: NCCA.

NCCA. (2007). *Assessment in the primary school curriculum: Guidelines for schools*. Dublin: NCCA.

O'Leary, M., Lysaght, Z., Ludlow, L. (2013). A measurement instrument to evaluate teachers' assessment for learning classroom practices. *The International Journal of Educational and Psychological Assessment, 14*, 40–62.

Odom, S. L. (2009). The tie that binds: Evidence-based practice, implementation science, and outcomes for children. *Topics in Early Childhood Special Education, 29*(1), 53–61.

OECD. (2013a). *Education policy outlook: Ireland*. Retrieved July 2016, from http://www.oecd.org/edu/EDUCATION%20POLICY%20OUTLOOK%20IRELAND_EN.pdf

OECD. (2013b). *Leadership for 21st century learning, educational research and innovative*. OECD publishing.

OECD. (2013c). *Synergies for better learning: An international perspective on evaluation and assessment*. Retrieved July 2016, from http://www.oecd.org/edu/school/synergies-for-better-learning.htm

OECD. (2015a). *Education at a glance: Ireland*. Retrieved July 2016, from http://www.keepeek.com/Digital-Asset-Management/oecd/education/education-at-a-glance-2015/ireland_eag-2015-62-en#.V7WldvmAOko

OECD. (2015b). *Education policy outlook 2015: Making reforms happen*. Retrieved July 2016, from http://dx.doi.org/10.1787/9789264225442-en

OECD/CERI. (2008). *Assessment for learning: Formative assessment*. Retrieved July 2016, from http://www.oecd.org/site/educeri21st/40600533.pdf

Opfer, V. D., & Pedder, D. (2011). Conceptualizing teacher professional learning. *Review of Educational Research, 81*, 376–407.

Penuel, W. R., Fishman, B. J., Cheng, B. H., & Sabelli, N. (2011). Organizing research and development at the intersection of learning, implementation, and design. *Educational Researcher, 40*, 331–337.

DEVELOPING TEACHERS' ASSESSMENT CAPACITY

Primary Education Review Body. (1990). *Report of the primary education review body*. Dublin: Stationery Office.

Quinn, R. (2012). (2008). *The future development of education in Ireland*. Retrieved July 2016, from https://www.studiesirishreview.ie/2012/summer-2012

Rigby, J. G., Woulfin, S. L., & März, V. (2016). Understanding how structure and agency influence education policy implementation and organisational change: Editorial introduction. *American Journal of Education, 122*, 295–302. Retrieved November 2016, from http://www.journals.uchicago.edu/doi/pdfplus/10.1086/685849

Sheehan, A. M. (2016). *Assessment in primary education in Ireland*. University College Cork: Unpublished PhD Thesis. Retrieved June 2016, from https://cora.ucc.ie/handle/10468/2625

Shiel, G., Kavanagh, L., & Millar, D. (2014). *The 2014 national assessments of English reading and mathematics. Volume 1: Performance report*. Dublin: Education Research Centre.

Shute, V. J., & Kim, Y. J. (2014). Formative and stealth assessment. In *Handbook of research on educational communications and technology* (pp. 311–321). New York, NY: Springer.

Spillane, J. (2013). The practice of leading and managing teaching in educational organisations. *Leadership for 21st century learning, Educational Research and Innovative Leadership in 21st Century Learning* (pp. 59–82). Paris: OECD.

Star, S. L. (1989). The structure of ill-structured solutions: Boundary objects and heterogeneous distributed problem solving. In M. Huhs & L. Gasser (Eds.), *Distributed artificial intelligence* (pp. 37–54). UK: Morgan Kaufmann Publishers Inc.

Sugrue, C. (2002). Irish teachers' experience of professional learning: Implications for policy and practice. *Journal of In-service Education, 28*, 311–338.

Sugrue, C. (2004). Whose curriculum is it anyway? Power, politics and possibilities in the construction of the revised primary curriculum. In C. Sugrue (Ed.), *Curriculum and ideology: Irish experiences, international perspectives* (pp. 167–208). Dublin: The Liffey Press.

Sugrue, C. (2012). Reflections on the Minister's 'manifesto'. *Studies: An Irish Quarterly Review, 101*, 153–166.

The Teaching Council. (2016). *Cosan: Framework for teachers' learning*. Maynooth: Author. Retrieved February 2017, from http://www.teachingcouncil.ie/en/Publications/Teacher-Education/Cosan-Framework-for-Teachers-Learning.pdf

Thompson, M., & Wiliam, D. (2008). Tight but loose: A conceptual framework for scaling up school reforms. In C. E. Wiley (Ed.), *Tight but loose: Scaling up teacher professional development in diverse contexts*. Retrieved November 2016, from https://www.ets.org/Media/Research/pdf/RR-08-29.pdf

Trumbull, E., & Lash, A. (2013). *Understanding formative assessment: Insights from learning theory and measurement theory*. San Francisco: WestEd.

Tsui, A. B. M., & Law, D. Y. K. (2007). Learning as boundary-crossing in school-university partnership. *Teaching and Teacher Education, 23*(8), 1289–1301.

Wiseman, A. W. (2010). The uses of evidence for educational policymaking: Global contexts and international trends. *Review of Research in Education, 34*(1), 1–24.

DEVELOPING TEACHERS' ASSESSMENT CAPACITY

Appendices

Table A1. The AfLAi: scales, acronyms and statements.

AfL strategy	Number of statements	Acronym
Learning Intentions and Success Criteria	16	LISC
Questioning and Classroom Discussion	16	QCD
Feedback	12	FB
Peer and Self-Assessment	14	PSA

Table A2. Learning intentions and success criteria practices in Hillside school

	N	Mean
3. Pupils are reminded about the links between what they are learning and the *big learning picture* (e.g. *'We are learning to count money so that when we go shopping we can check our change'*).	23	4.2
2. Learning intentions are stated using words that emphasise knowledge, skills, concepts and/or attitudes i.e. what the pupils are learning NOT what they are doing.	24	4.1
1. Learning intentions are shared with pupils at appropriate times during lessons (e.g. *Halfway through the lesson, the teacher might say: 'Remember, we are learning to distinguish between 2D and 3D shapes'*).	23	3.7
4. Pupils are provided with opportunities to internalise learning intentions by, for example, being invited to read them aloud and/or restate them in their own words.	22	3.6
6. Success criteria related to learning intentions are differentiated and shared with pupils.	23	3.5
10. Samples of work are used to help pupils develop a *nose for quality*.	24	3.3
5. Child-friendly language is used to share learning intentions with pupils (e.g. *'We are learning to make a good guess (prediction) about what is likely to happen next in the story'*).	23	3.2
9. Success criteria are differentiated according to pupils' needs (e.g. *the teacher might say, 'Everyone must complete parts 1 and 2 …; some pupils may complete part 3'*).	24	3.2
11. Assessment techniques are used to assess pupils' prior learning (e.g. concept mapping…).	24	3.1
13. Learning intentions are available throughout lessons in a manner that is accessible and meaningful for all pupils (e.g. *written on the black/whiteboard and/or in pictorial form for junior classes*).	24	2.9
14. Pupils' progress against key learning intentions is noted and/or recorded as part of lessons	24	2.9
15. Pupils demonstrate that they are using learning intentions and/or success criteria while they are working (e.g. *checking their progress against the learning intentions and success criteria for the lesson displayed on the blackboard or flipchart, for example*).	24	2.9
7. Pupils are involved in identifying success criteria.	24	2.6
12. Pupils are reminded of the learning intentions during lessons.	23	2.5
16. Pupils are given responsibility for checking their own learning against the success criteria of lessons.	24	2.4
8. Prompts are used to signal learning intentions and success criteria with pupils (e.g. *using WALTS and WILFs in junior classes*).	24	2.0

Table A3. Questioning and classroom discussion in Hillside school

	N	Mean
3. Questions are used to elicit pupils' prior knowledge on a topic.	23	4.2
2. Assessment techniques are used to facilitate class discussion (e.g. b*rainstorming*).	24	4.1
1. When planning lessons, key, open-ended questions are identified to ensure that pupils engage actively in lessons (e.g. *'If we put a coat on our snowman in the school yard, do you think the snowman last longer?'*).	23	3.7
4. During lessons, hinge questions are used to determine pupils' progress in lessons (e.g. *'We have been learning to sort 3D shapes that stack and roll. Now, if you were given a choice, would you build a tower with spheres or cubes?'*).	22	3.6
6. Assessment techniques are used to encourage all pupils to engage with questions (e.g. *no hands up, names out a hat, etc.*).	23	3.5
10. The pace of class discussions is deliberately slowed down to encourage pupils to think before responding (e.g. *using wait time*).	24	3.3
5. Assessment techniques are used to activate pupils /get them thinking during discussions and/or questioning (e.g. *using think-pair-share or talk partners*).	23	3.2
9. Questioning goes beyond the one right answer style (*where the focus is often on trying to guess the answer in the teacher's mind*) to the use of more open-ended questions that encourage critical thinking.	24	3.2
11. Pupils are asked to explore their own ideas with others, using *think-pair-share*, for example.	24	3.1
13. Pupils' incorrect responses are used to guide teaching and learning (e.g. *a pupil is asked to explain why he/she gave a particular answer*).	24	2.9

(Continued)

DEVELOPING TEACHERS' ASSESSMENT CAPACITY

Table A3. *Continued*

	N	Mean
14. Pupils are asked to evaluate their peers' responses to questions (e.g. *'Fiona, do you agree with what Regina has said and why?'*).	24	2.9
15. Pupils can explain to others what they are learning (e.g. *if a visitor came to the classroom, pupils could articulate what they are learning in terms that identify the knowledge, skills, concepts and/or attitudes being developed*).	24	2.9
7. Pupils are encouraged to share the questioning role with the teacher during lessons (e.g. *the teacher routinely invites pupils to question their peers' contributions to discussions*).	24	2.6
12. Individual answers to questions are supplemented by pupils taking an answer round the class so that a selection of responses from the pupils is used to build a better answer.	23	2.5
16. Pupils are asked to explain why they are undertaking particular tasks (e.g. *the teacher might ask, 'Why are we completing this worksheet/what are we learning by doing it?'*).	24	2.4
8. Assessment techniques are used to encourage questioning of the teacher by pupils (e.g. *using hot-seating or a Post-its challenge*).	24	2.0

Table A4. Feedback in Hillside school

	N	Mean
5. Teacher-made tests are used diagnostically to identify strengths and needs in teaching and learning (e.g. *identifying common mistakes in the addition of fractions*).	23	3.7
4. Teachers' praise of pupils' work (e.g. *'that's excellent; well done'*), is deliberately and consistently supplemented with feedback that specifies the nature of the progress made (e.g. *'Well done Kate, this paragraph helps me to visualise the characters in the story because of the adjectives you use'*).	23	3.4
1. Feedback to pupils is focused on the original learning intention(s) and success criteria (e.g. *'Today we are learning to use punctuation correctly in our writing and you used capital letters and full stop correctly in your story, well done John'*).	22	3.3
6. Diagnostic information from standardised tests is used to identify strengths and needs in teaching and learning (e.g. *common errors in the comprehension section of the MICRA-T are identified and used in teaching*).	23	3.2
3. Written feedback on pupils' work goes beyond the use of grades and comments such as 'well done' to specify what pupils have achieved and what they need to do next.	23	3.1
10. When providing feedback, the teacher goes beyond giving pupils the correct answer and uses a variety of prompts to help them progress (e.g. *scaffolding the pupils by saying: 'You might need to use some of the new adjectives we learned last week to describe the characters in your story'*).	23	3.1
8. Feedback focuses on one or two specified areas for improvement at any one time (e.g. *in correcting written work, punctuation errors may not be marked if the primary focus of the writing is on the use of adjectives*).	23	3.0
2. Assessment techniques are used during lessons to help the teacher determine how well pupils understand what is being taught (e.g. *thumbs up-thumbs-down and/or two stars and a wish*).	23	3.0
12. Pupils are provided with information on their learning on a *minute-by-minute, day-by-day* basis rather than end of week/month/term.	22	2.9
11. In preparing to provide pupils with feedback on their learning, the teacher consults their records of achievement against key learning intentions from previous lessons (e.g. *the teacher reviews a checklist, rating scale, or anecdotal record that s/he has compiled*).	22	2.3
7. Pupils are involved formally in providing information about their learning to their parents/guardians (e.g. *portfolios or learning logs are taken home*).	23	2.2
9. *Closing-the-gap*-feedback is used to focus pupils' attention on the next step in their learning.	13	2.0

Table A5. Peer- and self-assessment in Hillside school

	N	Mean
3. Lessons on new topics begin with pupils being invited to reflect on their prior learning (e.g. *pupils complete a mind map or concept map or brainstorm a topic*).	24	2.9
5. Pupils assess and comment on each other's work (e.g. *they are taught how to use the success criteria of a lesson to judge another pupil's piece of work*).	24	2.6
8. Time is set aside during lessons to allow for self- and peer-assessment.	24	2.5
6. Pupils are encouraged to use a range of assessment techniques to review their own work (e.g. *a rubric, traffic lights, thumbs up/down, two stars and a wish*).	24	2.4
11. Pupils use each other as resources for learning (e.g. *response/talk partners who comment on each others' work and discuss how it can be improved*).	24	2.3
4. Pupils are provided with opportunities to reflect on, and talk about, their learning, progress and goals.	24	2.2

(Continued)

DEVELOPING TEACHERS' ASSESSMENT CAPACITY

Table A5. *Continued*

	N	Mean
10. When pupils have difficulty in their learning, they are encouraged to draw on a range of self-assessment strategies and techniques to help them overcome the problem (e.g. *they consult with an exemplar on the bulletin board*).	24	2.0
9. Assessment techniques are used to create an environment in which pupils can be honest about areas where they are experiencing difficulty (e.g. *talk partners are used to facilitate conversations between pupils about the challenges they face in their learning*).	24	1.9
1. Pupils are given an opportunity to indicate how challenging they anticipate the learning will be at the beginning of a lesson or activity (e.g. *using traffic lights*).	24	1.8
7. A visual record of pupils' progress is maintained to celebrate pupils' learning and show areas of/for development (e.g. *a bulletin board displaying progression in story writing over a term*).	22	1.7
13. Pupils use differentiated success criteria to self- and/or peer-assess (e.g. *pupils can distinguish between what must be achieved to be successful on a task and what might be done to gain extra credit*).	21	1.7
14. Pupils have ready access to exemplar materials showing work at different levels of achievement across a range of subject areas (e.g. *pupils use examples of collage on the Art display board when advising peers on how to improve their work*).	22	1.6
2. Pupils are encouraged to record their progress using, for example, learning logs.	24	1.5
12. Time is set aside during parent/guardian-teacher meetings for pupils to be involved in reporting on some aspects of their learning (e.g. *pupils select an example of their best work for discussion at the meeting*).	24	1.0

Table A6. National data.

AfL Strategies: From most to least embedded	N	Mean	SD
Questioning and Classroom Discussion	593	3.36	.67
Feedback	590	3.27	.71
Learning Intentions and Success Criteria	594	3.23	.75
Peer and Self-Assessment	591	2.29	.69

Developing teachers' capacities in assessment through career-long professional learning

Kay Livingston and Carolyn Hutchinson

ABSTRACT
In a context of increasing demand for quality and equity in education and a sharp focus on accountability, classroom teachers are also expected to support and improve learning outcomes for pupils in response to their individual needs. This paper explores three issues: how teachers understand assessment in relation to their students' learning, the curriculum and their pedagogical choices; how teachers' capacity to use assessment to improve students' learning can be developed through career-long professional learning (CLPL); and how teachers' learning can be implemented and sustained in schools, both locally and nationally. In considering these issues, recent thinking about learning and assessment and CLPL are considered alongside empirical evidence from the development and implementation of assessment processes and approaches to professional development in Scotland. The paper emphasises the importance of a dynamic framework of CLPL that recognises the individuality of teachers' learning needs and the consequent need for tailored professional learning opportunities with different combinations of support and challenge at school, local and national levels.

Introduction

In the context of an increasing demand for quality and equity in education to meet economic and social challenges, many countries now see assessment and evaluation as playing a central strategic role in developing education policy. An OECD review of evaluation and assessment in education, *Synergies for Better Learning: An International Perspective on Evaluation and Assessment* (Organisation for Economic Cooperation & Development [OECD], 2013), identified the main trends. They include increasing focus on measuring pupil outcomes and allowing comparisons between schools and regions and over time. The review also points out that many countries now publish a national curriculum, embracing twenty-first-century learning theories, and set associated progressive performance 'standards' (or 'levels') for what pupils should know and be able to do at different stages in their learning. This has encouraged the use of national assessments to determine the extent to which pupils are progressing and meeting these standards and to suggest how they can be supported to improve outcomes. The results are also being used as part of system evaluation

DEVELOPING TEACHERS' ASSESSMENT CAPACITY

to identify where schools are performing well and where they may need to improve and to hold policy-makers, school leaders and teachers accountable (OECD, 2013).

If the evidence and data generated are to be used confidently as a basis for improving educational provision and learning outcomes and life chances for citizens, it is essential that educational professionals at all levels, but especially in the schools and classrooms where learning actually takes place, understand what is to be learned; how pupils learn, and how they can promote and support that learning; how best to gather evidence about learning; and how to interpret and use that evidence to plan for better learning. This, in essence, is what being 'assessment literate' means. However, some teachers have found it challenging to develop their understanding of what new curriculum and learning theories mean for their classroom practice (Organisation for Economic Cooperation & Development [OECD], 2010, 2011), especially understanding assessment as part of pedagogy (OECD, 2013). Learning and teaching are complex processes and the changes needed to develop teachers' capacity in assessment to promote pupils' learning require better understanding of the complicated and dynamic interactions among curriculum, assessment and pedagogy, pupil and teacher learning needs and the school and classroom contexts in which learning and teaching take place. School leaders, teacher educators and policy advisers, as well as teachers, need to develop this deeper understanding. Building capacities in assessment also requires teachers to understand its interrelationship with other key aspects in educational change processes, including the wider policy context and the social, cultural and professional contexts in which they work.

Three main aims are addressed in the following three sections of this paper.

1. to explore the capacities teachers need to develop in order to understand how to use assessment to promote learning, focusing on the interrelationships among curriculum, pupils' learning needs and their own pedagogical choices;
2. to consider the opportunities for building teachers' capacities in assessment through career-long professional learning (CLPL) and the challenges this process presents, in schools and in the wider education community;
3. to explore how an effective approach to CLPL based on local practice can be scaled-up, implemented and sustained across a national education system.

The development and implementation of assessment policy, approaches to teachers' professional development and curriculum and pedagogical change in Scotland provide the context to consider the challenges and opportunities associated with the three aims. Teachers have an ongoing commitment to maintain their professional expertise and they need continually to revise and enhance their knowledge and skills and teaching and learning approaches. A review of teacher education in Scotland (Donaldson, 2011) reported that there are numerous professional development opportunities for teachers but they are not always designed in ways that enable and support a coherent approach to teachers' professional learning, nor are they tailored to the individual needs of teachers and their pupils. A continuum of teacher education (spanning initial teacher preparation, the induction period when teachers begin their first job and their continuing professional learning) is required (Livingston & Shiach, 2010) which provides a comprehensive framework for organising and understanding how teachers acquire and improve their capacity to teach across their entire career (Schwille & Dembélé, 2007). The particular focus of this paper is on the professional learning of teachers at all levels beyond the initial stage of teacher education. Discussion of CLPL draws from social learning theory (Vygotsky, 1978; Wenger, 2010); adult learning theories (Mezirow, 1996, 1997); professional learning communities (Wenger, 1998, 2010); and empirical research in the field of teachers' professional learning, including peer-mentoring (Livingston & Shiach, 2013, 2014). The paper's significance is twofold. It aims to enhance understanding of the importance of developing and scaffolding quality learning conversations among teachers that support and challenge them in making meaning of individual pupils' work and in using evidence to make decisions about next steps in learning and teaching. It also emphasises the importance of a dynamic sustainable framework of CLPL that recognises the individuality of teachers' learning needs and the consequent need for tailored professional learning opportunities, with different combinations of support and challenge at school, local and national levels.

Teachers' understanding of assessment to improve pupils' learning

O'Neill (2002) argues that professionals in public services should be accountable to their stakeholders and inspire their trust because stakeholders need to rely on them to act in their interests. However, if the balance of assessment for purposes of accountability and pupil learning is perceived by teachers to be skewed towards auditing performance, this may reduce teachers' trust and limit their freedom to adapt to their pupils' learning needs. According to O'Neill, to achieve a balance in audit and monitoring requires 'intelligent accountability'. Cowie and Croxford (2007) argue that in educational settings, this implies 'trust in professionals; a focus on self-evaluation; measures that do not distort the purposes of schooling; and measures that encourage the fullest development of every pupil' (p. 1). The dependability of assessment and evaluation tools and processes, and therefore the confidence that can be placed in them, also underpin intelligent accountability (Mansell, James, 2009). Newton and Shaw's (2014) recent account of validity likewise focuses on the crucial importance of quality and fitness for purpose of assessment and evaluation strategies and methods. They emphasise that the validity of assessment and evaluation tools and processes also underpins intelligent accountability since unless they are valid in the widest sense, information and data generated will be at best worthless and at worst damaging to learners and learning. Their account of validity focuses on measurement of the quality of pupil learning, interpretation plausibility and ethical considerations relating to the outcomes and impact of assessment on learners and their communities. Assessment literacy covering all of these dimensions of assessment is needed by educators to ensure that it is fit for its different purposes and to secure intelligent accountability to support improvement planning at all levels in the education system, across policy, research and practice communities.

In common with many countries, Scotland has reformed the curriculum for schools (*Curriculum for Excellence*) and developed guidance about associated pedagogical and assessment approaches (Scottish Executive Education Department [SEED], 2006, 2007; Scottish Government, 2008, 2009, 2011a, 2011b). As in many countries, the curriculum incorporates 'twenty-first century learning' approaches and a wide range of learning outcomes, including the familiar cognitive components (knowledge of facts, symbols, rules and concepts and problem-solving skills and strategies for using and applying this knowledge flexibly) and personal and affective dimensions (such as positive beliefs about oneself as a learner and skills in monitoring one's own thinking and learning, closely connected to motivation) (Istance & Dumont, 2010). Not all of these outcomes are amenable to straightforward, conventional measurement. Nevertheless, teachers' capacity to assess all areas of pupils' learning is important in order to understand how they are progressing across the whole curriculum and to support improvements. If teachers, pupils and other relevant stakeholders are to be actively involved in making dependable judgements about learning, there needs to be shared understanding of what is valued in learning and what can be expected of pupils in terms of progression and achievement.

The starting point for decision-making and the choice of classroom pedagogies and assessment processes will change according to the context prevailing, including specific curricular and pupil learning needs. To improve their pupils' learning, teachers need to be able to assess what pupils already know and can do in relation to specific aspects of the curriculum, and what the next steps in learning should be. Assessment information is also needed to guide teachers as they make ongoing decisions about their next steps in teaching (Hipkins & Robertson, 2011; Livingston, 2015; Robinson, Hohepa, & Lloyd, 2009). Wiliam (2010) emphasises formative assessment's role in improving the quality of teachers' classroom decisions and suggests that it involves five key strategies: clarifying, sharing and understanding learning intentions and criteria for success; engineering effective classroom discussions, activities and tasks that elicit evidence of learning; providing feedback that moves learners forward; activating pupils as instructional resources for one another; and activating pupils as the owners of their own learning. Black and Wiliam argued in their seminal 1998 publication that a crucial characteristic of formative assessment is that 'evidence is actually used to adapt the teaching work to meet the needs [of learners].' (p. 2)

From the teachers' perspective, these observations about classroom assessment emphasise the interrelationship between learning–teaching and teaching–learning, which seems, on occasions, to go unnoticed by some teachers, particularly when the focus is on delivering a syllabus of content within a specific timescale (Livingston, 2015). However, alongside pupils' learning needs, teachers must also consider the curriculum: the form or type of knowledge to be learned; the most appropriate way to structure learning and teaching of the new knowledge; and the overarching educational aims to be achieved (Winch, 2013). In teachers' selection of classroom pedagogical and assessment processes, Winch suggests that consideration needs to be given to the conditions under which specific knowledge forms are acquired and produced and how those knowledge forms should be assessed.

In the wider school context, information from teachers' classroom assessments should be used to contribute to a school's self-evaluation and improvement planning; and information from self-evaluation should in turn be used by teachers to contribute to improving classroom practice, so that the two processes are inter-dependent (Hutchinson & Young, 2011). Since the overall purpose of both assessment and evaluation is ultimately to improve pupils' learning, teachers should be able to recognise the educational value of different types of assessments and evaluation practices and analyse and interpret the evidence and data they provide, in collaboration with colleagues (OECD, 2013). Simply focusing on professional learning about knowledge and skills in assessment will not adequately support teachers' understanding of the bigger picture of the inter-dependence of assessment with other key aspects in learning and teaching and the importance of shared understanding among all members of staff in school (teachers and school leaders). Further action to build these broader capacities is needed.

Challenges and opportunities of developing teachers' capacities in assessment

Building capacity in assessment to support pupils' learning has been a priority in Scottish education over several periods in the past 25 years. A national development programme for

DEVELOPING TEACHERS' ASSESSMENT CAPACITY

assessment in the pre-primary, primary and early secondary school years, the *Assessment is for Learning* programme (AifL) (Learning & Teaching Scotland, 2004) ran from 2002–2008, putting some emerging ideas about building teachers' capacity in assessment into practice. Its aims reflected the general concern to align assessment for learning and evaluation for accountability. It was

> designed to bring together the various purposes of assessment into a single coherent framework which would answer questions of accountability, standards and the monitoring of progress and performance, but which also emphasised the role of assessment in supporting individual pupils' learning in the classroom. (Condie, Livingston and Seagrave, 2005, p. iii)

It built on the work of Black and Wiliam (1998), particularly the emphasis on formative assessment. The programme sought to develop teachers' theoretical and practical understanding of assessment. It also quite explicitly set out to change the culture of assessment in the education system as a whole and to improve teachers' and public confidence in best fit professional judgements made on the basis of a range of evidence (Hutchinson & Hayward, 2005).

What made the programme particularly distinctive was its design, intended to help participating teachers understand how to transform their own learning about assessment. The design involved the Scottish Executive Education Department (SEED, now Scottish Government) in close partnership with other stakeholders in education, providing funding to local authorities and to teachers in local groups of associated nursery, primary and secondary schools to explore and develop various aspects of their assessment practice and document their experiences and learning in case studies (Hutchinson & Hayward, 2005). At the same time, a central management group of partners focused on achieving transformational change through collaborative projects and coordinating, developing and supporting local and national networks that promoted community building. Local authority and school projects were encouraged to create new projects to further deepen the programme's common purpose (Senge & Scharmer, 2001). As the programme progressed, there was increasing focus, through seminars and networking events, on supported dialogue about assessment issues, both with colleagues in the same establishment or group of schools and among partners in communities of enquiry and wider networks across Scotland.

Feedback and case studies from participants, and from external evaluation, gradually came together to identify agreed key features of assessment to support learning that acknowledged both research and practice. These features of effective school-based assessment *for, as* and *of* learning were presented as the AifL triangle depicting the school as 'a place where everyone is learning together' (Scottish Qualification Authority, Scottish Executive and Learning and Teaching Scotland, 2006, p. 1). The triangle was designed to show how the various aspects of assessment in schools formed a coherent whole, involving teachers as well as pupils and parents (all as learners) learning together through collaborative enquiry, founded on classroom interactions characterised by thoughtful questions, careful listening and reflective responses (Learning & Teaching Scotland, 2004). A policy Circular (Scottish Executive Education Department [SEED], 2005) sent to all local authorities aimed to link the policy framework with implementation of practice as intelligent accountability, involving good governance; professional freedom within a broad reporting framework; clear focus on, and engagement of, stakeholders in the processes of assessment and self-evaluation; honest reporting of strengths and development needs; and confidence in professional judgements (Cowie & Croxford, 2007). Staff in external bodies (including local authorities, schools

DEVELOPING TEACHERS' ASSESSMENT CAPACITY

inspectors, Scottish Qualifications Authority staff and policy-makers) as well as those in schools had responsibility for both formative and summative aspects of assessment and evaluation, and how information from each could be used to inform interpretation of information from the others (SEED, 2005).

An evaluation of the *Assessment is for Learning Programme* (Condie et al., 2005) identified a number of positive developments in assessment practices and procedures for the teachers and pupils involved in some local authorities and schools. These included funding provided to schools to enable teachers to engage in collaborative enquiry projects, giving them a sense of ownership and control over development and management of change; opportunities for focused staff development and engagement in supportive networks at local and national levels; and expert input at appropriate points to enable ongoing professional learning. Studies exploring the programme's impact after funding finished (Hayward, 2009; Hayward & Spencer, 2010) indicated that it had helped to embed the language and features of AifL and that participants valued having time to share experiences, recognising that their involvement supported their own professional learning (Hayward, Simpson, & Spencer, 2005). Fraser, Kennedy, Reid, and McKinney (2007) further found that transformative learning (in AifL) was facilitated 'when formal, planned learning opportunities were augmented by informal, incidental learning opportunities' (p. 165).

It might be assumed from this account of the aims, design and implementation of the AifL programme that all partners involved in promoting pupils' learning in the primary and early secondary years in Scotland now share a well-developed understanding of theory and practice in assessment, supported by a policy framework that fully integrates assessment for learning and evaluation for accountability and schools are places where everyone is learning together, sharing standards through active enquiry. However, while many ideas about what matters in assessment endured after programme funding was withdrawn, they were not fully shared by all partners or embedded consistently, particularly in respect of integrating assessment *for*, *as* and *of* learning, or synergising assessment for learning and evaluation for accountability.

A recent OECD Report, *Improving Schools in Scotland: An OECD Perspective* (Organisation for Economic Cooperation & Development [OECD], 2015), while mainly positive about the current educational reforms and recognising the 'previous bold moves in constructing assessment frameworks' (p. 18) and in establishing a wide range of assessment practices in Scottish schools, nevertheless observed that 'some schools and teachers are having difficulty in prioritising assessment tasks.' (p. 17). A lack of clarity about what should be assessed in relation to the experiences and outcomes of the curriculum was particularly identified as a challenge. These findings highlight the difficulties some teachers experience in the alignment of curriculum, assessment and pedagogy in making learning and teaching decisions in the classroom and in understanding the different uses of assessment for the development of pupils' learning and for accountability in terms of pupil/school performance overall.

The findings also confirm what had been suggested in an earlier report, which included teachers' views about the draft version of Curriculum for Excellence (Baumfield, Livingston, Mentor and Hulme, 2009). When faced with a new curriculum and revised qualifications, secondary school teachers in particular expressed doubts about whether the curriculum provided sufficient structure to scaffold the required planning, monitoring and assessment and many were reluctant to contemplate changes in their practice until arrangements for assessment and qualifications were clarified. This suggests a continuing lack of confidence about making dependable professional judgements about pupils' progress in learning and in interpreting and using assessment information for reporting. Without support to build teachers' capacities in assessment processes, some teachers may continue to think of them as separate from curriculum and pedagogy rather than integral, and focus mainly on externally provided summative assessments of what has been learned. Despite research evidence (see, for example, Stobart, 2008) and explicit policy documentation (Scottish Government, 2011c), there appears to be an enduring and pervading belief, across policy and practice communities, that measurement is an exact science and only tests and examinations can accurately identify a learner's precise point in progression through defined levels of achievement in a particular subject area.

A recently published guide entitled *Shaping career-long perspectives on teaching* (European Commission, 2015) suggests that leading and supporting pupils' learning requires every teacher to embark on a professional, social and personal journey that involves CLPL within collaborative learning environments. Addressing teachers' learning needs is identified as enabling coherence in learning throughout a CLPL continuum. Developing from social constructivist theories of learning, teachers' professional learning should build on their current understandings and support and enable them to apply theoretical knowledge in real contexts and make informed decisions about ways of developing and changing their assessment practice, appropriate to their own context. Without a deeper understanding of the specific challenges teachers face in relation to assessment, predetermined professional learning opportunities that are designed without consideration of teachers' learning needs are likely to fail to build their capacities in assessment processes. More needs to be understood about teachers as learners and the impact of changes in their learning and teaching circumstances on their professional learning needs.

Teachers in Scotland are not alone in their concerns about assessment. De Luca and Bellara (2013) point out that research suggests that despite assessment education efforts, beginning teachers continue to feel unprepared to assess pupil learning and that low assessment literacy levels among teachers continue. Korthagen (2010) draws attention to the many research studies which show the disappointing impact of teacher education on teacher learning and behaviour. He argues that teacher education has an inherent problem in meaning-making from the perspective of teachers, and that while there is greater emphasis by teacher educators on situated learning, they seem to forget that educational knowledge cannot simply be 'transmitted' to teachers in the hope it will improve their actions (Korthagen, 2010, p. 99). Even when professional development in assessment is provided, it is not necessarily effective in changing practice or securing subsequent improvement in pupils' learning (Timperley, Wilson, Barrar, & Fung, 2007).

In Scotland, there was recognition in research and from the AifL programme that in common with learners generally, teachers learn best in supportive learning environments that enable shared learning, connections to prior learning and experience, reflective thought and action and enquiry into the learning and teaching relationships (Hutchinson & Hayward, 2005; Livingston, 2012; Timperley et al., 2007). Furthermore, that professional understanding in assessment is most effectively developed through engaging practitioners in using and adapting guidance in their own classrooms and practice (Gardner, Harlen, Hayward, & Stobart, 2008). However, despite this recognition, there was a gradual shift, during the early implementation of Curriculum for Excellence, from process and engagement in professional learning back to mainly large-scale training events and provision of products in the form of guidelines and resources. Individual teachers continued to gain assessment experience and expertise through situated learning in school, producing, administering, marking and moderating national qualifications and national monitoring assessments, and producing exemplification. However, nationally provided (often web-based) staff development activities focused increasingly on a transmission model involving teaching techniques, curriculum content and external assessment and measurement, rather than developing professional understanding of theoretical ideas through participation (George Street Research, 2007).

It is also increasingly recognised that attempting to support teachers in the development of meaningful learning that transforms practice brings the challenge of uncovering their often deeply rooted personal views, on education generally and learning, teaching and assessment specifically. The way teachers (including teacher educators) understand and use new information is likely to be shaped by the extent to which it is consistent with their existing understanding and assumptions. This idea that long-held views can inhibit change in professional thinking and practice (Brownlee, 2003; Pajares, 1992) is not new; yet support for teachers to uncover and confront their prior beliefs and reflect on the impact they have on their pedagogy (including assessment) is seldom an integral element of their professional development. Insufficient attention is given to recognising them as adult learners with their own personal beliefs and experiences (Livingston, 2015). Mezirow (1997) argues that faced with new situations and educational reforms, teaching professionals bring their own 'frames of reference', structures of assumptions through which experiences are understood, 'selectively shaping and delimiting expectations, perceptions, cognitions and feelings' (p. 5). He says, 'To understand others, one must gain access to their lived experience so as to clarify and elucidate the way they interpret it.' (Mezirow, 1996, p. 160).

Building teachers' assessment capacity and their capacity to understand and adapt to specific learning needs and contexts can be seen as involving 'adaptive competence', the ability to apply knowledge and skills flexibly and creatively in a variety of contexts and situations contrasting with 'routine expertise' (De Corte, 2010, p. 45). De Corte cites the work of Bransford et al. (2006), who argue that adaptive competence is important because it involves learners in being self-regulating, willing and able to change their core competences and continually expand the breadth and depth of their expertise, through active and experiential as well as guided learning (Simons, van der Linden, & Duffy, 2000). Greater attention is needed to enable teachers to understand the way their assumptions can act as a filter or indeed as a block to adaptive ways of thinking and acting in the classroom. Adaptive competence is also important in understanding and adapting to the multiple representations of reality in the complex world of schools. Teachers' learning needs to be facilitated and supported to encourage and enable them to take an ongoing enquiry approach to their practice through purposeful dialogue, in collaboration with pupils, teachers and other partners, as part of their day-to-day professional learning in schools and across learning communities.

Experience in Scotland suggests that it is not just engaging in dialogue that matters, although the opportunities to do so are an essential prerequisite to assessment for learning. In addition, the *quality* of the learning conversations that characterise teachers' professional practice is crucial to the development of their own and their pupils' learning. In two separate studies, Livingston and Shiach (2013, 2014) researched and developed mentoring skills with a total of 53 primary and secondary school teachers in Scotland at various stages of their teaching career (including teachers and school leaders who had between 1 and 35 years experience of teaching[1]. Both studies were pilot studies commissioned by

DEVELOPING TEACHERS' ASSESSMENT CAPACITY

Education Scotland (Scottish Government Agency with responsibility for supporting and improving education) as part of the actions taken to respond to Recommendation 39 in the *Teaching Scotland's Future* report, 'All teachers should see themselves as teacher educators and be trained in mentoring' (Donaldson, 2011, p. 98). In the first study (Livingston & Shiach, 2013), the selection of 12 teachers from 5 primary schools and 14 teachers from 2 secondary schools in different regions of Scotland was made by the researchers to ensure a mix of teaching experience among the participants. In the second study (Livingston & Shiach, 2014), which had a stronger focus on the schools taking ownership and sustaining mentoring processes, the selection of 17 teachers from 2 primary schools and 10 teachers (including a deputy head teacher) from 1 secondary school was made by the school leaders according to their own school's needs as identified in their school improvement plans. In 1 primary school, 4 teachers were selected and in the secondary school, all the faculty heads were selected to engage in the training to build their capacity in leading mentoring across their schools. In the other primary school, the head teacher decided that all 13 members of the teaching staff should have the opportunity to engage in the mentor training at the same time. In both studies, the overarching aim was to strengthen teachers' professional development through mentoring, with a particular focus on developing teachers' capacities to engage in learning conversations with their peers. A secondary teacher in an interview conducted following the mentor training said that while he had conversations with his colleagues in school about teaching and learning prior to the mentor training, their conversations had not been focused and structured in a way that enabled them to identify specific evidence of the pupils' learning needs and understand more about the interactions between different forms of knowledge, assessment approaches and their own pedagogical choices. Peer-mentoring in both studies enabled all the participants to experience actively being a mentor and a mentee as they mentored each other during the training process. Designated time was then identified by the participants to engage in focused mentoring conversations with a colleague in their own school to ensure that between the four training days, all the participants were able to practise and reflect on their mentoring skills. The selection of a mentee varied according to the individual school context. Mentees selected included a colleague who had fewer, more or the same number of years experience (e.g. a newly qualified teacher, a new colleague to the school, a colleague in their own or a different department or stage of the school). The mentoring process was recognised as being responsive to the needs of the mentee and reflexive as both the mentor and mentee engaged in reflecting on learning and teaching. The teachers reported that they benefitted from taking up the roles of mentor and mentee as in both roles they had opportunities to think more deeply about their own teaching and their pupils' learning. The study participants recognised that the training developed their mentoring language skills and enabled them to focus their conversations on understanding learning and teaching and using evidence from collaborative analysis of their pupils' work in ways that had previously not been understood. They said that it was the structured support for in-depth detailed dialogue and collaborative reflection with their teaching colleagues that enabled them to develop the language of learning, teaching and assessment and helped them align their learning and teaching more closely with pupils' learning needs. It also helped them consider what the evidence from particular forms of assessment told them about what the pupil had and had not learned in relation to specific learning outcomes. Analysing pupil work and talking about learning in greater detail with their peers in school rather than making general assumptions about progress (or lack of it) also enabled the teachers to be much more confident in giving specific feedback to individual pupils and in making decisions about how best to support and improve their learning. They were then able to use their greater understanding of the pupils' learning to plan appropriate next steps in learning and teaching, a process at the heart of assessment literacy.

Livingston and Shiach (2013, 2014) concluded that peer-mentoring interpreted as structured, interactive and supported conversations as part of teachers' CLPL can provide opportunities to promote a critical constructivist perspective, enable them to articulate their thinking through social interaction, uncover their assumptions, help them develop the language of learning and teaching and develop their practice to improve pupil learning. However, the conditions that enable and facilitate meaningful teacher dialogue and build teachers' capacity in the language of learning, teaching and assessment must be understood if supportive and challenging conversations are to be valued by teachers and school leaders as part of CLPL and as means of improving pupils' learning.

Structures and conditions to develop and sustain teachers' CLPL

CLPL in schools may offer opportunities for teacher learning but the challenge lies in ensuring it is meaningful and sustainable, both locally and nationally. The evidence from research and practice reviewed above provides helpful insights into what teachers need to know and be able to do to promote pupils' learning, and how they might go about developing their knowledge and skills though supported and detailed conversations focused on evidence of pupil learning. Building teachers' capacity in assessment processes requires professional learning to be understood from both epistemological and ontological perspectives: teachers need knowledge to gain a deeper understanding of the what, when and how of assessment; and they need to change what they do (their way of being) in their own classrooms. Teachers, like their pupils, need to be able to make meaning of their practice for themselves through engagement with new learning, with each other and with their pupils in their own constantly changing context in school (James & Pedder, 2006; Livingston, 2012). If learning is embodied in actions, then classroom enquiry needs to be situated, carried out in and by the relevant learning community, with the guardians of quality within the learning community rather than outside it. To engage in reflective and challenging conversations about learning and teaching, teachers need to recognise their practice as ongoing enquiry. What makes the most difference to the quality of learning and can bring about transformative, sustainable change is building not only teachers' knowledge and skills in assessment but also their capacity to enquire and to engage in quality learning conversations involving communication, engagement, interaction and trusting relationships among colleagues in school. Such conversations can lead to learning developed through shared understanding, specific feedback and collaborative action, mediated by their distinctive values and personal prior beliefs (Livingston & Shiach, 2013, 2014; Senge & Scharmer, 2001). As Wenger (2010) suggests, teachers need to engage in a continuous process of creating and recreating 'regimes of competence' through dialogue and collaboration within and across their own practice communities (pp. 180–181).

From the education policy perspective, however, although it is relatively straightforward to commit to an improvement agenda, to recognise that assessment and evaluation have a central role in providing an evidence base for planning for improvement, and that professional capacity in assessment at all levels in the system is therefore a priority, 'scaling-up' from small-scale pilot projects to sustainable system-wide, implementation is complex and difficult. It requires strong partnerships and shared understanding, focus and identification of strengths and priorities among partners. Ingvarson (2005) observes that

> Policy makers can be quite naïve about expectations about how easy it is to bring about change, not understanding that the kinds of change that really matter in education are not structural changes but those that build teacher capacity and professional development. (p. 63)

Arresting teachers' professional learning too soon or neglecting the ongoing support needed and the maintenance and further development of emerging local and national partnerships and networks of expertise can lead to frustration and the sense of one innovation following another with limited connection to what went before.

Starting from the inside: CLPL in classrooms and schools

Wenger (2010) emphasises that no matter how much external effort is made to shape practice, what matters is the meanings arrived at by those engaged in it, through active negotiation of meaning in their own context. A facilitated community of practice that continues to encourage and stimulate teachers' enquiry into learning and teaching in their own classrooms, taking account of the complex relationship between social and personal factors of learning (Wenger, 2010), is a key part of a system, culture and practice change process. The teachers in the mentoring studies (Livingston & Shiach, 2013, 2014) indicated that mentor training was essential in enabling them to uncover and amend their own beliefs and assumptions about learning and teaching (including assessment); to know how to analyse pupil learning in depth; to think about the relationship between content and their teaching and assessment decisions; and to develop the language of learning and assessment to support and challenge their peers through mentoring conversations. Yet training for mentors that goes beyond technical or 'buddy' support is limited and often only offered as a 'one-off' course rather than seen as central to enabling teachers to learn with and from one another in school in ways that support, question and challenge learning and teaching in ongoing practice.

The teachers' engagement in the mentoring studies (Livingston & Shiach, 2013, 2014) also highlighted the importance of a collegiate culture in schools to enable mentoring and professional learning to be valued and sustained. If teachers are to change the way they approach assessment, they need to feel that they are part of a professional community that is focused on improving outcomes for learners and responsive to learners' needs (Timperley et al., 2007). They are more likely to engage meaningfully in professional learning where they feel the issues presented are real for them and the learning is focused on exploring possible solutions they can put into place in their classrooms. Wenger (1998) suggests the drivers and levers that are needed to support meaningful learning in social contexts include mutual engagement, shared repertoire and joint enterprise. He emphasises that the community does not exist by itself: 'It is part of a broader conceptual framework of thinking about learning in its social dimensions.' (p. 179). In his view, a community of practice has characteristics of systems more generally: for example, 'emergent structure, complex relationships, self-organisation, dynamic boundaries and ongoing negotiation of meaning' (Wenger, 1998, p. 180).

It is also necessary to recognise that learning and change have an emotional dimension (Illeris, 2009). A culture of teachers working together in enquiry, reflection, assessment and improvement must be nurtured and supported by building trusting relationships among staff, who feel able to share opportunities and challenges in learning and teaching with each other in school. The professional interactions in collaborative, collegial working beyond the classroom also need to involve more challenging conversations about the relationship between classroom practice and outcomes for learners that are at the heart of enquiry and improvement planning. These conversations should focus on analysis, reflection and changes in relation to real examples of what pupils say, write, make and do in response to their learning experiences. 'Talking about learning' in this way is consistent with approaches to the local moderation that was part of the AifL framework and emphasised as fundamental to effective assessment practice in the more recent guidance on assessment at all levels in the education system, including national qualifications (Scottish Government, 2011c). However, what is essential to recognise is that teachers need training and ongoing support. The teachers in Livingston and Shiach's mentoring studies (2013, 2014) indicated that they needed structured practice in developing the language of learning, teaching and assessment and the knowledge and skills to hold mentoring conversations with their peers in the context of CLPL to support and challenge practice.

Teaching Scotland's Future (Donaldson, 2011) proposed a framework for professional development that has potential to be developed and sustained over time and provide a flexible approach to CLPL in (spite of) a shifting educational policy environment. It was proposed that mentoring in schools should be the 'engine' of an integrated CLPL process to provide support for such collaborative conversations, recognising it as a way of working which engages pairs and groups of mentors and mentees in interactive learning in school, respects the value of diversity and skilful communication and takes account of individual and collective strengths, ongoing development needs and collaborative accountability. The report recommends that priority be given to developing skills in mentoring in schools so that staff at all levels have the capacity to initiate, focus and facilitate high-quality learning conversations and practitioner networking, and ensure that the climate, culture and resources of each school actively support mentoring processes. There are positive signs that some teachers are being trained in mentoring and are increasingly engaging in mentoring with their colleagues in the context of CLPL. However, the recommendation still needs to be realised across all schools.

Robinson et al., 2009 suggest that school leaders have a key role in ensuring that individual and group relationships and mentoring processes are developed collaboratively by and for all staff. Leaders should be actively involved in planning and promoting professional learning for staff, especially if learning activities take place on-site. In an integrated CLPL framework, leaders of learning need not only to provide time and opportunities for teachers to engage in focused learning conversations with their pupils and peers, but also to value mentoring and professional learning as ongoing professional enquiry processes as part of the school's learning culture, ensuring that competing priorities do not lead to fragmentation of effort or mean that learning conversations are not sustained. All staff as members of a learning community should develop leadership as well as mentoring skills. Emphasis needs to be put on developing teachers as learners and leaders of learning who are able to value the views and contributions of other teachers; help others to envisage new ways of thinking, seeing and working; show a determination towards achieving the highest standards for everyone; show initiative and actively pursue their objectives; be good listeners; and serve as models to others (Scottish Government, 2009). Leadership in this sense is about

DEVELOPING TEACHERS' ASSESSMENT CAPACITY

all learners taking responsibility for building a learning culture, where assessment supports learning and provides evidence to inform planning for improvement.

Working outwards: a national framework for CLPL

A structured framework for CLPL in schools can offer opportunities and challenges for teachers' learning that improves pupils' work, but, if it is to be effective and sustainable, attention needs to be given not only to supporting teachers' practice within school but also to change at system and cultural levels. Donaldson (2011) made a number of recommendations that would create stronger synergies among all partners in the education system with responsibility for teachers' professional development, across policy, research and practice communities. The proposals developed in response to the recommendations drew from the examples of effective practice already familiar in Scottish schools and from the characteristics of effective professional development identified by Timperley et al. (2007) and Wenger (1998, 2010). The proposals amount to a national framework for professional learning, based on and supportive of local arrangements and requirements in schools, and have potential to provide a coherent focus on assessment and evaluation to support learning.

The proposals also emphasise the need for national policy that supports a shift in the culture of education to focus on learning and provide the resources to support this shift; and for all professionals working in education to commit to recognising themselves as learners, taking responsibility for professional enquiry in classrooms and schools as central to their day-to-day practice. However, high-quality learning conversations will only become established in schools if they are recognised as a valued form of CLPL that promotes teacher and pupil learning and are supported both locally and nationally. Donaldson (2011) acknowledges that in the wider context, it needs to be recognised that school leaders are themselves learners and require support for their approach to professional learning for their staff from the wider education community. In Scotland, national standards for registration, CLPL, middle leadership and headship published by the General Teaching Council for Scotland are now based on core principles of practitioner enquiry, presenting the teacher as a professional who will

> create knowledge to enhance, progress and lead the learning experiences of all their learners and work collaboratively with colleagues … (an) adaptive expert … open to change (who) engages with new and emerging ideas about teaching and learning within the ever-evolving curricular and pedagogical contexts in which teaching and learning take place. (General Teaching Council for Scotland [GTCS], 2012, p. 4)

The Standards provide a nationally recognised framework for a process of regular 'Professional Update' for all registered teachers and school leaders that aim to support professionals as learners. Professional Update also offers opportunities for teachers to document their learning and learning outcomes, and for identifying how their professional learning and changes to practice could be supported and developed, in the context of the school's wider self-evaluation and development planning priorities. An anonymised synthesis of teachers' Professional Updates could be used by teacher educators, researchers and other professional development providers to inform local and national priorities for CLPL in assessment and evaluation, in a continuous cycle of local and national improvement, in much the same way as information about pupils' learning is used by schools and teachers for local improvement planning.

DEVELOPING TEACHERS' ASSESSMENT CAPACITY

The CLPL recommendations also recognised that to complement the Professional Update and self-evaluation process in schools, local coordination across establishments would be essential to promote partnerships among schools, education leaders, teacher educators, researchers and national agencies to make the best possible use of local professional expertise. Learning through working in partnership can help ensure that professionals at all levels engage in learning-focused professional conversations and build and participate in communities of enquiry and professional networks. However, stronger partnerships need to be developed to provide more structured and focused networking opportunities for practitioners as part of practice-based or school cluster-based learning. Acknowledgement is seldom given to the assessment expertise of teachers within and among schools that could facilitate specific areas of peer-learning. There is potential for making better use of and building capacity from the range of teachers' professional knowledge and skills already existing in schools and local authorities (for example, through their involvement in designing and using assessment resources in national monitoring and qualifications processes). Harnessing the expertise could make a significant contribution to teachers' professional learning.

In-school mentoring and engaging in professional learning communities have potential to make important contributions to building teachers' capacities in assessment. However, like all learners, teachers also need access to a range of different professional learning opportunities, according to their own needs and preferences (Timperley, 2008). Donaldson's recommendations (2011) suggested combinations of peer and group mentoring, engaging in communities of practice within school, and external professional learning opportunities, as appropriate to professional learning needs. The experience and expertise of someone from outside their immediate peer group (or outside their school or local area) may be necessary at specific times to support and challenge teachers' existing educational beliefs, assumptions and practices and offer fresh perspectives and possibilities. This in turn requires an infrastructure to enable more effective communication about existing expertise and better identification of when external support is needed. Schools and local authorities need to work more closely with universities and other agencies to identify individuals with appropriate expertise and skills in assessment and mentoring to contribute to local provision, and to ensure that support and training is available when and where it is needed.

Conclusion

There is no single answer to building teachers' capacity in assessment. Teachers as individual learners are likely to have different understandings of assessment in relation to their pupils' learning needs, the curriculum and their own pedagogical choices. Consequently, they will need more tailored professional learning opportunities throughout their career as the contexts within and across schools change and as their own and their pupils' learning needs change. Transformational change should be recognised as a process rather than an event, and to be sustained, continuing iterative review and renewal of its processes are needed over time (Fullan, 2003). A national framework of CLPL has the potential to build teachers' capacities in assessment; however, designing such a framework to sustain ongoing meaningful professional learning remains challenging. To be sustained, CLPL needs to support and nurture teachers' professional learning in assessment and evaluation as they integrate with curriculum and pedagogy and with the teachers' and pupils' own learning needs. Teachers

DEVELOPING TEACHERS' ASSESSMENT CAPACITY

and school leaders need to be able to make meaning for themselves through quality learning conversations with peers within supportive and challenging collegiate cultures in schools.

CLPL of this kind needs ongoing training in mentoring and leadership to develop trusting relationships and build teachers' knowledge and skills in enquiry, use of evidence and engagement in thoughtful, structured conversations focused on pupils' and teachers' learning. Individuals and groups of staff in schools, local authorities and national agencies need to share responsibility for self-evaluation to inform planning for improvement and better outcomes for all children and young people. Single initiatives implemented in fragmented ways are unlikely to result in long-term sustainable and effective change. Rather, this requires professional, cultural and system changes to be conceptualised as multiple cogs and wheels that all have to be operational and interacting continuously to be effective. However, ultimately, only teachers themselves will know if their professional learning has made a difference to their pedagogy and assessment, and to individual pupils' learning in their own classrooms.

Note

1. For details of the content of the training and implementation of mentoring processes, see Livingston and Shiach (2013) and Livingston and Shiach (2014).

Disclosure statement

No potential conflict of interest was reported by the authors.

References

Baumfield, V., Livingston, K., Menter, I., & Hulme, M., with Devlin, A., Elliot, D., Hall, S., Lewin, J., & Lowden, K. (2009). *Curriculum for excellence draft experiences and outcomes: Collection, analysis and reporting of data: University of Glasgow final report*. Learning and Teaching Scotland. Retrieved from http://www.educationscotland.gov.uk/Images/GUfinalreport_tcm4-539659.pdf

Black, P., & Wiliam, D. (1998). *Inside the black box: Raising standards through classroom assessment*. London: King's College.

Bransford, J. N., Vye, N., Stevens, R., Kuhl, P., Schwartz, D., Bell, P., ... Sabelli, N. (2006). Learning theories and education: Toward a decade of synergy. In P. A. Alexander & P. H. Winne (Eds.), *Handbook of educational psychology* (2nd ed., pp. 209–244). Mahwah, NJ: Lawrence Erlbaum Associates.

Brownlee, J. (2003). Changes in primary school teachers' beliefs about knowing: A longitudinal study. *Asia-Pacific Journal of Teacher Education, 31*, 87–98.

DEVELOPING TEACHERS' ASSESSMENT CAPACITY

Condie, R., Livingston, K., & Seagraves, E. (2005). *Evaluation of the assessment is for learning programme*. Glasgow: Quality in Education Centre, University of Strathclyde.

Cowie, M., & Croxford, L. (2007). *Intelligent accountability: 'Sound-bite or sea change'*. CES Briefing No. 43, June 2007. Retrieved from http://www.ces.ed.ac.uk/PDF%20Files/Brief043.pdf

De Corte, E. (2010). Historical developments in the understanding of learning. In H. Dumont, D. Istance, & F. Benavides (Eds.), *The nature of learning: Using research to inspire practice* (pp. 35–67). Paris: OECD-CERI.

DeLuca, C., & Bellara, A. (2013). The current state of assessment education: Aligning policy, standards and teacher education curriculum. *Journal of Teacher Education, 64*, 356–372.

Donaldson, G. (2011). *Teaching Scotland's future*. Edinburgh: The Scottish Government.

European Commission. (2015). *Shaping career-long perspectives on teaching*. Brussels: European Commission. Retrieved from http://ec.europa.eu/education/library/reports/initial-teacher-education_en.pdf

Fraser, C., Kennedy, A., Reid, L., & McKinney, S. (2007). Teachers continuing professional development: Contested concepts, understandings and models. *Professional Development in Education, 33*, 153–169.

Fullan, M. (2003). *Change forces with a vengeance*. London: Routledge Falmer.

Gardner, J., Harlen, W., Hayward, L., & Stobart, G. (2008). *Changing assessment practice: Process principles and standards*. Retrieved from http://www.nuffieldfoundation.org/sites/default/files/JG%20Changing%20Assment%20Practice%20Final%20Final(1).pdf

General Teaching Council for Scotland (GTCS). (2012). *The standard for career-long professional learning: Supporting the development of teacher professional learning*. Retrieved from http://www.gtcs.org.uk/web/FILES/the-standards/standard-for-career-long-professional-learning-1212.pdf

George Street Research. (2007). *Assessment of learning evaluation. Final report for learning and teaching Scotland*. Retrieved from http://wayback.archive-it.org/1961/20100727174157/http://www.ltscotland.org.uk/aboutlts/whatwedo/research/publications/assessmentoflearning/index.asp

Hayward, L. (2009). Trust, collaboration and professional learning: Assessment for learning in Scotland. *Assessment Matters., 1*, 64–85.

Hayward, L., Simpson, M., & Spencer, E. (2005). *Assessment is for learning: Exploring programme success: The AifL formative assessment project*. Glasgow: University of Glasgow.

Hayward, L., & Spencer, E. (2010). The complexities of change: Formative assessment in Scotland. *Curriculum Journal, 21*, 161–177.

Hipkins, R., & Robertson, S. (2011). *Moderation and teacher learning: What can research tell us about their interrelationship?* Retrieved from www.nzcer.org.nz/system/files/moderation-teacher-learning.pdf

Hutchinson, C., & Hayward, L. (2005). The journey so far: Assessment for learning in Scotland. *Curriculum Journal, 16*, 225–248.

Hutchinson, C., & Young, M. (2011, March). Assessment for learning in the accountability era: Empirical evidence from Scotland. *Studies in Educational Evaluation, 37*, 62–70.

Illeris, K. (Ed.). (2009). *Contemporary theories of learning*. Abingdon: Routledge.

Ingvarson, L. (2005). *Getting professional development right*. Australian Council for Educational Research. Retrieved from http://research.acer.edu.au/professional_dev/4

Istance, D., & Dumont, H. (2010). Future directions for learning environments in the 21st century. In H. Dumont, D. Instance, & F. Benavides (Eds.), *The nature of learning: Using research to inspire practice*. (pp. 317–337). Paris: OECD.

James, M., & Pedder, D. (2006). Professional learning as a condition for assessment for learning. In J. Gardner (Ed.), *Assessment and learning* (pp. 27–43). London: Sage.

Korthagen, F. (2010). Situated learning theory and the pedagogy of teacher education: Towards an integrative view of teacher behavior and teacher learning. *Teaching and Teacher Education, 26*, 98–106.

Learning and Teaching Scotland. (2004). *'What is an AifL school? The AifL triangle'*. Retrieved from http://wayback.archive-it.org/1961/20100730123020/http://www.ltscotland.org.uk/assess/aiflschool/index.asp

DEVELOPING TEACHERS' ASSESSMENT CAPACITY

Livingston, K. (2012). Quality in teachers' career-long professional development. In J. Harford, B. Hudson, & H. Niemi (Eds.), *Quality assurance and teacher education policy: International challenges and expectations* (pp. 35–51). Oxford: Peter Lang.

Livingston, K. (2015). Pedagogy and curriculum – teachers as learners. In D. Wyse, L. Hayward, & J. Pandya (Eds.), *Curriculum, pedagogy and assessment* (pp. 325–340). London: Sage Publications Ltd.

Livingston, K., & Shiach, L. (2010). Co-constructing a new model of teacher education. In A. Campbell & S. Groundwater-Smith (Eds.), *Connecting inquiry and professional learning in education* (pp. 83–95). Abingdon: Routledge.

Livingston, K., & Shiach, L. (2013). *Teaching Scotland's future: Mentoring pilot partnership project. Final report.* Education Scotland. Retrieved from http://www.educationscotland.gov.uk/Images/GUAUMentorPilotProjectNov13_tcm4-825825.pdf

Livingston, K., & Shiach, L. (2014). *Teaching Scotland's future: Further developing and sustaining a strengthened model of professional learning through mentoring processes in the context of career-long professional learning. Final report.* Education Scotland. Retrieved from http://www.educationscotland.gov.uk/Images/GUAUMentorPilotProjectFinalReportDec2014_tcm4-845885.pdf

Mansell, W., James, M., & the Assessment Reform Group. (2009). *Assessment in schools: Fit for purpose.* Teaching and Learning Research Programme. Retreived from http://www.tlrp.org/pub/documents/assessment.pdf

Mezirow, J. (1996). Contemporary paradigms of learning. *Adult Education Quarterly, 46,* 158–172.

Mezirow, J. (1997). Transformative learning: Theory to practice. *New Directions for Adult and Continuing Education, 74,* 5–12.

Newton, P., & Shaw, S. (2014). *Validity in educational and psychological assessment.* London: Sage.

O'Neill, O. (2002). *A question of trust.* BBC Reith lectures. Retrieved from http://www.bbc.co.uk/radio4/reith2002/lectures.shtml

Organisation for Economic Cooperation and Development (OECD). (2010). *Teaching and Learning International Survey (TALIS). Technical report. Creating effective teaching and learning environments.* Paris: OECD.

Organisation for Economic Cooperation and Development (OECD). (2011). *Building a high quality teaching profession: Lessons from around the world.* Paris: OECD.

Organisation for Economic Cooperation and Development (OECD). (2013). *Synergies for better learning: An international perspective on evaluation and assessment.* Paris: OECD.

Organisation for Economic Cooperation and Development (OECD). (2015). *Improving schools in Scotland: An OECD perspective.* Paris: OECD.

Pajares, M. F. (1992). Teacher beliefs and educational research: Cleaning up a messy construct. *Review of Educational Research, 14,* 5–19.

Robinson, V., Hohepa, M., & Lloyd, C. (2009). *School leadership and student outcomes: Identifying what works and why.* Best Evidence Synthesis Iteration, New Zealand Ministry of Education. Retrieved from http://www.educationcounts.govt.nz/__data/assets/pdf_file/0015/60180/BES-Leadership-Web.pdf

Schwille, J., & Dembélé, M. (2007). *Global perspectives on teacher learning: Improving practice.* Paris: UNESCO.

Scottish Executive Education Department. (2005). *Education department circular no. 02: Assessment and reporting 3–14.* Retrieved from http://www.scotland.gov.uk/Publications/2005/06/2393450/34518

Scottish Executive Education Department. (2006). *A curriculum for excellence – building the curriculum 1: The contribution of the curriculum areas.* Retrieved from http://www.educationscotland.gov.uk/Images/building_curriculum1_tcm4-383389.pdf

Scottish Executive Education Department. (2007). *A curriculum for excellence – building the curriculum 2: Active learning in the early years.* Retrieved from http://www.educationscotland.gov.uk/Images/Building_the_Curriculum_2_tcm4-408069.pdf

Scottish Government. (2008). *Curriculum for excellence – building the curriculum 3: A framework for learning and teaching.* Retrieved from http://www.educationscotland.gov.uk/learningandteaching/thecurriculum/buildingyourcurriculum/curriculumplanning/whatisbuildingyourcurriculum/btc/btc3.asp

Scottish Government. (2009). *Curriculum for excellence – building the curriculum 4: Skills for learning, skills for life and skills for work*. Retrieved from http://www.educationscotland.gov.uk/Images/BtC4_Skills_tcm4-569141.pdf

Scottish Government. (2011a). *Curriculum for excellence – building the curriculum 5: A framework for assessment*. Retrieved from http://www.educationscotland.gov.uk/Images/BtC5Framework_tcm4-653230.pdf

Scottish Government. (2011b). *Curriculum for excellence – building the curriculum 5: A framework for assessment: Reporting*. Retrieved from http://www.educationscotland.gov.uk/Images/CfEReportingdocument_tcm4-612845.pdf

Scottish Government. (2011c). *Curriculum for excellence – building the curriculum 5: A framework for assessment: Understanding, applying and sharing standards in assessment for curriculum for excellence*. Retrieved from https://www.educationscotland.gov.uk/Images/BtC5SharingStandards_tcm4-630057.pdf

Scottish Qualification Authority, Scottish Executive and Learning and Teaching Scotland. (2006). *The assessment is for learning: Self-assessment toolkit*. Learning and Teaching Scotland. Retrieved from https://blueskyvgms.files.wordpress.com/2016/04/aifltoolkitforschools.pdf

Senge, P., & Scharmer, O. (2001). Community action research: Learning as a community of practitioners. In P. Reason & H. Bradbury (Eds.), *Handbook of action research: Participative inquiry and practice* (pp. 238–238). London: Sage.

Simons, P. R. J., van der Linden, J., & Duffy, T. (2000). New learning: Three ways to learn in a new balance. In P. R. J. Simons, J. van der Linden, & T. Duffy (Eds.), *New learning* (pp. 1–20). Dordrecht: Kluwer Academic Publishers.

Stobart, G. (2008). *Testing times: The uses and abuses of assessment*. Abingdon: Routledge.

Timperley, H. (2008). *UNESCO educational practices series – 18: Teacher professional learning and development*. UNESCO. Retrieved from http://www.ibe.unesco.org/fileadmin/user_upload/Publications/Educational_Practices/EdPractices_18.pdf

Timperley, H., Wilson, A., Barrar, H., & Fung, I. (2007). *Teacher professional learning and development: Best Evidence Synthesis Iteration (BES)*. Wellington: New Zealand Ministry of Education.

Vygotsky, L. S. (1978). *Mind in society: The development of higher psychological processes*. Cambridge, MA: Harvard University Press.

Wenger, E. (1998). *Communities of practice*. Cambridge: Cambridge University Press.

Wenger, E. (2010). Communities of practice and social learning systems. In C. Blackmore (Ed.), *Social learning systems and communities of practice* (pp. 179–198). London: The Open University with Springer-Verlag.

Wiliam, D. (2010). The role of formative assessment in effective learning environments. In H. Dumont, D. Instance, & F. Benavides (Eds.), *The nature of learning: Using research to inform practice* (pp. 135–159). Paris: OECD-CERI.

Winch, C. (2013). Curriculum design and epistemic ascent. *Journal of Philosophy of Education., 47*, 128–146.

Index

Note: **Boldface** page numbers refer to tables & italic page numbers refer to figures. Page numbers followed by "n" refer to endnotes.

Abell, S. K. 89
accountability 1; evaluation for 174, 175; intelligent 172; in Ireland 152; moderation for 135–6
Accreditation of Initial Teacher Education Programmes in Australia 133
Adamson, B. 7
adaptive competence 177
AfL *see* assessment for learning
AfLAi *see* assessment for learning audit instrument
AifL programme *see* *Assessment is for Learning* programme
Alexander, Colette 4
Allal, L. 109
Allen, A. R. 159
AoL *see* assessment of learning
APST *see* Australian Professional Standards for Teachers
assessment: competence 2; and counselling 11; domain 14–17, 19–21; factors and items in **17**; formative 8, 10, 11; in German teacher education 12; main themes of 7–8; as pedagogic tool 48–9; rating of standards **19**; summative 8, 21; *see also* student teachers' assessment competence
Assessment Expertise Rubric 88
assessment for equity: equitable outcomes 66–7; formative assessment 67; interconnected facets of practice 66; 'patterns of practice for equity' 66; Project RITE team 66; *see also* preservice teachers, assessment learning
assessment for learning (AfL) 2, 11, 67–8, 151; continuous professional development 160; engagement framework 158; *Literacy and Numeracy Strategy* 155; Norwegian context 3, 45; 'part of a comprehensive system' 152; as pedagogic tool 50; policy development 154;

professional development in 160; site-based professional development 157; status quo in 152–5; in teacher education programme *see* Master of Education programme, assessment education in; teacher professional development 152
assessment for learning audit instrument (AfLAi) 152, 154, 156–7, **167**; data for hillside 158–9; development of 160; engagement framework 158; Irish-speaking schools 157
Assessment is for Learning (AifL) programme 174, 176; design and implementation 175; evaluation of 175; features of 175; framework 181
assessment literacy 27–9, 85–6; dimensions of 89, 102; gauging 100–1; importance of 1; for pre-service and novice teachers 86; *see also* data literacy
Assessment Literacy Inventory 85–6
assessment of learning (AoL) 45, 53
AsTTLe 81n2
attitudes toward mathematics 35
Australia 4, 131; inter-agency collaboration in 130; national standards 133; professional standards 148; teachers in 29
Australian Professional Standards for Teachers (APST) 131, 133, 134, 148

balanced assessment system 151
BA/MA programme 9
beginning teachers 1
Bellara, A. 1, 29, 176
Bennett, R. E. 67
Berry, R. 7
Big Five model 13, 23n5
Biggs, J. 45
Black, P. 23n1, 44, 59, 174
Blikstad-Balas, Marte 3
Bloom, B. S. 108
Bodensohn, Rainer 2
Breslin, C. 47
Brevik, Lisbeth 3
Burry-Stock, J. A. 121

INDEX

CA *see* constructive alignment

Cady, J. 111

Campbell, C. 78, 85

Canton of Geneva, primary teachers in 121n8; dimensions of assessment practice 119; limitations 119; method 113; professional controversy in 115–17; project design 120; social moderation project 111–12

Canton of Vaud, secondary teachers in 112; curricular alignment project 112–13; dimensions of assessment practice 119–20; limitations 119; method 113–14; professional controversy in 117–18, 127–9; project design 120–1

capstone submissions 142

career-long professional learning (CLPL) 5, 171, 172; assessment is for learning 174–6; classrooms and schools 180–2; collaborative learning environments 176; meaningful learning development 177; national framework for 182–3; peer-mentoring 178, 179; recommendations 183; Scottish Executive Education Department 174; teachers' professional learning 176; *see also* pupils' learning

Carless, D. 161

CFA, *see* confirmatory factor analysis

Cheng, B. H. 159

Chick, H. 29, 38

Clot, Y. 110

CLPL *see* career-long professional learning

Coburn, C. 159, 161

Cochran-Smith, M. 44

collaborative research 110–11

COmpetence and STAndard Orientation in Teacher Education (KOSTA) project 12–14; aims 13; assessment competence, research questions 15–16; previous findings from 14–15; quality of teaching 23n4; student teachers' competence, evaluation of 12–14, *14*

competence assessment *see* student teachers' assessment competence

confidence, in assessment 47, 60

confirmatory factor analysis (CFA) 17–18, 20

constructive alignment (CA) 45

'constructive controversy,' pedagogical model of 110–11

continuous professional development (CPD) 152–5

Cooper, Beverley 2–3

counselling competence 17, 23n8

Cowie, Bronwen 2–3

Cowie, M. 172

CPD *see* continuous professional development

Croke Park agreement 162n3

cross-disciplinary engagement 161

Croxford, L. 172

curriculum alignment model 112–13 *see also* Canton of Vaud, secondary teachers in

Curriculum for Excellence 175

curriculum maps 31

Daniels, H. 48

data analysis procedures 17–18

data literacy 3; assessment literacy *vs.* 27–9; definition of 28; focus on 28; New Zealand context 3, 30–1; pan faculty approach 40; school leaders' views of 37–8; *see also* mathematical-statistical literacy

day-to-day professional learning 177

DBIR *see* design-based implementation research

De Corte, E. 177

DeLuca, C. 1, 7, 8, 22, 29, 47, 60, 176

Denzin, N. K. 114, 115

Department of Education and Skills (DES) 153

design-based implementation research (DBIR) 152, 159–61

Direction générale de l'enseignement obligatoire (DGEO) 112, 115, 126

Donaldson, G. 182, 183

Drechsel, B. 21

Dreyfus, H. L. 88, 89

Dreyfus, S. E. 88, 89

Dublin geographical bias 157

e-asTTLe 30

Education (Queensland College of Teachers) Act 2005 133

educational assessment, landscape of 1

educational change process 171

Education Council Aotearoa New Zealand 31

education domain 10, 14–15, 17

Edwards, A. 49, 50

Edwards, Frances 3

effective learning 2

'effective pedagogy' 30

effective school-based assessment 174

empirical structure, of assessment competence 16–17

engagement of stakeholders across stages **138**; development of shared understandings 138; expert moderation 139–40; ITE-led moderation 138–9; preparation of evidence reports 139; provision of institutional feedback 140–1

Engelien, Kirsti 3

examination-focused education systems 151

Expert Panel Feedback Reports 142

external evaluation 21, 22

Figari, G. 111

Fishburn, Deanne 4

Fishman, B. J. 159

formative assessment 8, 10–11, 74, 174; advocacy for 2, 27; definition of 59; emphasis on 47, 50; information, use of 67; purpose of 49, 57; teachers' use of 87

INDEX

Fraser, C. 175
French-speaking Switzerland 4, 109, 111
frequency of application 15, 17–18
Fullan, M. 134, 135
Furlong, J. 132

Gaelscoileanna 157
Gal, I. 29
Galligan, L. 35
generic submissions 142
Germany: education curricula, assessment element in 12; pre-service programme in 2; teaching profession in 9
GLoSS 81n1
Gradual Release of Responsibility Model 61n4
Graduate Teacher Performance Assessment 145
Graduating Teacher Standards 31, 71
Groulx, L.-H. 112–13
Guidelines on assessment in the primary school in Ireland (2007) 154

Hall, K. 154
Hasting, J. T. 108
Hill, Mary 3
Hillside school: case of 157–8; feedback in **168**; learning intentions and success criteria **167**; peer- and self-assessment **168–9**; questioning and classroom discussion **167–8**
Hislop, H. 153, 154
Hutchinson, Carolyn 4–5
hypothetical submissions 142

Improving Schools in Scotland: An OECD Perspective 175
Ingenkamp, Karlheinz 10
Ingvarson, L. 180
initial teacher education (ITE) 85, 130, 131, 144, 145n3; academic programme 131, 143; curriculum 144, 149–50; ITE-led moderation 138–9; monitoring of 137, 142; programmes 86, 90; Provider Evidence Reports 142; review of 131; targeted feedback relation to 140
innovative domain 10, 14–15, 17, 19, 23n9
in-school mentoring 183
insufficient attention 177
intelligent accountability 172
Ireland 4; accountability in 152; continuous professional development 154, 155; education development 155; and PISA data 153; primary teachers in 157; supported primary schools in 156
Ireland's education and training sector: Overview of service delivery and reform 152
Irish National Teachers Organisation 162n3
ITE *see* initial teacher education

Johnson, D. W. 110–11

Kavanagh, L. 153
Kavanagh, V. 154
Kennedy, A. 175
Klinger, D. A. 29, 47, 60
KMK, *see Kultusministerkonferenz*
knowledge of assessment 4
Korthagen, F. 176
KOSTA II sample, The 16
KOSTA project, *see* COmpetence and STAndard Orientation in Teacher Education project
Kultusministerkonferenz (KMK) 9; assessment domain 21, 23n7, 23n8; assessment competence 10–13, 22n2, 23n7, 23n9; standards of teacher training **10–11**

Länder legislation 9–10, 12
LaPointe-McEwan, D. 7
large-scale assessments 21–2
Lasater, K. 87
Latent Change Models (LCM) 15, 17, 19
latent variable 17–18, *20*
Law, D. Y. K. 161
LCM, *see* Latent Change Models
learning and teaching 171; language of 178, 179
Learning Intentions and Success Criteria (LISC) 156
learning to assess 5
lecture notes, and formal assessments *55, 58*
Leighton, J.P. 21
Lessard, C. 110, 121
lesson plans, and R&D reports 56–8, *57*
Leydens, J. A. 92
LISC *see* Learning Intentions and Success Criteria
Literacy and Numeracy Strategy 153, 155
Livingston, K. 177, 179, 181
Livingston, Kay 4–5
Looney, A. 131
Lopez, Lucie Mottier 4
Luhanga, U. 7
Lyon, E. G. 88, 89
Lysaght, Z. 4, 154

Madaus, G. F. 108
MARKITE study *see* Mathematical Thinking and Reasoning in Initial Teacher Education study
Master of Education (ME) programme, assessment education in 3, 61n2; assessment as pedagogic tool 48–9; assessment component 46; assessment education 46–8; assessment terms 53; in Canada 47; competence 60; confidence in assessment 47, 60; data collection 50; division of responsibility 60; explicit assessment courses 47; feedback practices 49, 60; formal assessment situations 46; formative assessment 47, 57, 59; importance of 60; integration of lectures, workshops and seminars 52–6, 59; key principles and terms 53–4; lecture

INDEX

notes and formal assessments 55, 58; lesson plans and R&D reports 56–8, *57*; limitations of study 52; overview of 44–5; PLATO criteria 53, 54; quadrant model 49–50, 53; research participants 50; research question 45, 50; self-assessment principles 45, 52, 58, 59; steps of analysis 50, **51**; students feedback during teaching 57; student teachers, assessing 55–6; student work, open assessment tasks of 54–5; summative assessment 47; tightly structured tasks 54; University of Oslo 46; validity, reliability and ethics 50, 51; video-taped classroom situations 53; Vygotskian approach 48, 49

Master of teaching (M Tchg) degree 65, 69–70

mathematical-statistical literacy 28–30; data interpretation 36; design-based intervention 31; MARKITE study 31, 35; 'Maths Hub' website 31; New Zealand Curriculum 30; numeracy competency 31

mathematical thinking 31–2; attitudes towards mathematics 35–6; embedding, notion of 33; lecturer views of 32–5; mentors 36; and reasoning 32; student teachers 35–7

Mathematical Thinking and Reasoning in Initial Teacher Education (MARKITE) study 31, 35

'Maths Hub' website 31

McKinney, S. 175

McMahon, Paula 4

Meier, S. L. 111

mentoring process 178; group relationships and 181; and professional learning 180; training 180

Mertler, C. A. 85

Mezirow, J. 177

Millar, D. 153

model fit parameters **18**

model for science teachers' assessment literacy (MSTAL) 89

Moskal, B. M. 92

Moss, C. 108

Mottier Lopez, L. 109

MSTAL *see* model for science teachers' assessment literacy

M Tchg degree *see* Master of teaching degree

National Certificate of Educational Achievement (NCEA) 87, 90, 96, 101

National Council for Curriculum and Assessment (NCCA) 153, 160

National Curriculum for Teacher Education (2013) 46

NCCA *see* National Council for Curriculum and Assessment

NCEA *see* National Certificate of Educational Achievement

'new self-evaluation model' 153

Newton, P. 49, 172

New Zealand 3; diverse context in 69; Education Council Aotearoa New Zealand 31; education policy 87; formative assessment 30; Graduating Teacher Standards 31, 71; 'high achievement, low equity' 69; Ministry of Education 65, 69; National Standards 30; primary schools and teachers 37; priority learners in 65; rubric in 3–4; schools 30; teachers summative assessment processes 87

New Zealand Curriculum (NZC) 30, 87

New Zealand Qualifications Authority (NZQA) 87

Nicol, D. 47

Norway: educational assessment 46; students in 61n1

Norwegian Education Act 46

Norwegian Ministry of Education and Research 46

Norwegian Social Science Data Services 51

numeracy competency 31

NZC *see* New Zealand Curriculum

NZQA *see* New Zealand Qualifications Authority

Odom, S. L. 159

O'Leary, M. 4, 154

O'Neill, O. 172

Organisation for Economic Cooperation & Development (OECD) 9; case study 67; evaluation and assessment framework 154; *Improving Schools in Scotland: An OECD Perspective* 175; *Synergies for Better Learning: An International Perspective on Evaluation and Assessment* 170

Orrill, R. 40

orthogonal factors 17

Oser, F. 12

Overall Teacher Judgment (OTJ) 30

PaCT *see* Progress and Consistency Tool

Pasquini, Raphaël 4

PATs *see* Progressive Achievement Tests

Patton, M. Q. 114

Pedagogical Diagnostics 10–12

pedagogic tool, assessment as 48–9

peer-mentoring 178, 179

Penuel, W. R. 159

PER curriculum *see Plan d'études romand* curriculum

Pierce, R. 29

Plan d'études romand (PER) curriculum 111, 116–18; mathematics organisation in 111, 125

PLATO *see* Protocol for Language Arts Teaching Observation

political submissions 142

Popham, James 1

Practising Teacher Criteria 90

practising teachers 1–2

Prenzel, M. 21

INDEX

pre-service and novice teachers: assessment literacy for 86; development 88; radar charts for *99*; teachers' development patterns 97–100; *see also* Summative Assessment Literacy Rubric

pre-service assessment education 2

preservice teachers (PTs), assessment learning 65; assessment preparation 68; assignments 74, **74**, 76; AsTTLe 81n2; campus-based summer school courses 69; confidence in assessment 71, **71**, 73, 79; content analysis 72; conventional teacher education programmes 78; in cultural programme 69; electronic questionnaire 71; entry and exit surveys 73, **73**; equity and fairness issues 76; facet 4 indicators 73, **74**, 76, 78; facets of practice for equity 70; feedback, importance of 75; focus group interview 72; formative assessment 67, 74; GLoSS 81n1; guiding principles 67–8; implications 80–1; interviews with 76; involvement in courses 77; Likert-type items 71, 72; Master of teaching degree 65, 69–70; mathematics and literacy courses 70; moderation processes, use of 76; monitoring acticities 78; negative effects of assessment 76; New Zealand context 69–70; observations and reflections 70; open-ended questions 71, 77; prior teaching experiences 79; research participants 72; study findings 78; summative assessment 74, 79; teacher preparation 69, 78; theoretical ideas 77

priority learners 65

professional competence 8, 15, 18–20, 22

professional development (PD) 152; continuous 152–5; framework for 181; opportunities 171; site-based 157, 160, *160*

professional learning 171; day-to-day 177

Professional Standards Committee (PSC) of QCT 134

Professional Standards for Queensland Teachers 133

professional standards for teaching 132

'Professional Update' 182, 183

Programme Approval Guidelines 133

Progress and Consistency Tool (PaCT) 30

Progress in International Reading Literacy Study (PIRLS) 153

Progressive Achievement Tests (PATs) 30

Project Rethinking Initial Teacher Education for Equity (RITE) 66

Protocol for Language Arts Teaching Observation (PLATO) 49; criteria 53, 54

PSC *see* Professional Standards Committee

pupils' learning 178; accountability and 172; assessment and evaluation tools 172; decision-making 173; development of 175; needs 173; O'Neill, O. 172; primary and secondary years 175; quality of 172; in Scottish education 173; and teaching 178, 179

QCT *see* Queensland College of Teachers

QDEF *see* Queensland Deans of Education Forum

quadrant model 49–50, 53

Queensland 4; ITE programmes 133

Queensland College of Teachers (QCT) 131, 133, 138, 145n1; Analysis and Feedback Tool 140, 149; expert moderation stage 139–40; ITE programmes 133–4; Professional Standards Committee of 134; regulatory presence 134; review cycles 133

Queensland Deans of Education Forum (QDEF) 137–9

Questioning and Classroom Discussion (QCD) 156

Quinn, J. 134, 135

radar charts 101; for assessment literacy development *99*

'regimes of competence' 179

Reid, L. 175

Remaud, D. 111

research-based teacher education programmes 44

Resource Teaching/Learning Support 154

Rich, B. S. 111

rubrics 87–8 *see also* Summative Assessment Literacy Rubric

Sabelli, N. 160

SALRubric *see* Summative Assessment Literacy Rubric

SA principles *see* self-assessment principles

scaffold learning, using evidence to 66–8

scale reliabilities 17

'scaling up' 159–61, 179

Schneider, Christoph 2

Schools Excellence Fund 155

Scotland 4–5; curriculum and pedagogical change 171; different regions of 178; experience 177; General Teaching Council for 182; teacher education in 171, 176

Scottish Executive Education Department (SEED) 174

SEB, *see* self-efficacy beliefs

SEED *see* Scottish Executive Education Department

self-assessment (SA) principles 45, 52, 58, 59

self-efficacy beliefs (SEB) 15

SEM, *see* structural equation modelling

Shaping career-long perspectives on teaching 176

Shaw, S. 172

Shiach, L. 177, 179, 181

Shiel, G. 153

Siegel, M. A. 89

site-based professional development 157, 160, *160*

social constructivist theories 176

social moderation project 111–12 *see also* Canton of Geneva, primary teachers in

sociocultural approach 48

standards-based education 4

Standards for Qualified Teacher Status (QTS) 132

INDEX

Standards for Teacher Training in the Educational Sciences 10

Standards Project, The 130, 145; Core Activities 137, 138; data in overview 137–8, **138**; evidence of standards *vs.* standards of evidence 143–4; evidencing enacted curriculum 142–3; Focus Area 5.4. 133, 137, 140, 141–2, 144, 149–50; methods used in 137; moderation as professional accountability 135–6; practice-informed policy 134–5; professional standards for teaching 132; Queensland College of Teachers 133–4; results of 144; risk-based regulation 134–5; teacher education 131–3; *see also* engagement of stakeholders across stages

Standing Conference of the Ministers of Education and Cultural Affairs of the Länder in the Federal Republic of Germany, the 9

statistical literacy 29

structural equation modelling (SEM) 15

student teachers' assessment competence: binding standards for teacher education 9–10; data analysis procedures 17–18; development in German university 12–14; domain *14*, 16–17; empirical structure of 16–17; German teacher education system 9, 12; implication of findings 20–2; within KMK's standards 10–12; KOSTA II sample 16; KOSTA project 14–15; latent change model *20*; limitations and directions for further research 22; research questions related to 15–22; results of 18–20; teaching profession in Germany 9

summative assessment 8, 21, 47; preservice teachers 74, 79; purpose of 49; for system monitoring 1

summative assessment, controversies between teachers 4, 108; collaborative research 110–11; curricular alignment project 112–13; professional judgement 109; social moderation project 111–12; triangulations 114–15; *see also* Canton of Geneva, primary teachers in; Canton of Vaud, secondary teachers in

Summative Assessment Literacy Rubric (SALRubric) 3, 88, 103; application of 97; average scores for teachers *100*; deductive development 89–90; development and refinement 89–92; dimensions 90, 92; draft dimensions for 90; Elizabeth's case 99; implications for teacher education 102; inductive observations 90, **91**; Jane's case 98–9; levels of competence in **92**; levels of expertise **93–5**; limitations 102–3; patterns of teachers' development 97–100; quality and 92–6; reliability of 96; Ryan's case 99–100; scoring with 96–7; teacher's scores using **98**; use of 86, 101, 102

Swiss Conference of Cantonal Ministers of Education (EDK) 111

Switzerland 4

Synergies for Better Learning: An International Perspective on Evaluation and Assessment 170

teacher candidates, perceptions towards assessment learning 2

teacher education 131–3; assessment development in 47, 60; binding standards for 9–10, **10**; curriculum 12, 171; German context 9–10; implications for 102; initial stage of 171; knowledge acquisition 44; National Curriculum for Teacher Education (2013) 46; preservice teachers 68; *see also* initial teacher education

Teacher Education Ministerial Advisory Board 131

teacher education programme 9, 10, 12–14, 16, 19

teacher preparation: in assessment 78; programmes 69

teacher professional development 111, 152; *see also* professional development

teachers domain 10, 14–15, 17, 23n9

teaching experiences 75, 79, 177–8

Teaching Scotland's Future report 178, 181

TEQSA *see* Tertiary Education Quality Standards Authority

Terhart, E. 10

Tertiary Education Quality Standards Authority (TEQSA) 136

Thomas, G. 35

Thomson, A. 47

transformative learning 175

Trends in International Mathematics and Science Study (TIMMS) 153

triangulations 114–15

Tsui, A. B. M. 161

Tveit, S. 46

'twenty-first century learning' approaches 172

United States: schools of education in 29; teachers 29

University of Oslo, Norway (UiO) 45 *see also* Master of Education programme, assessment education in

Volante, L. 47

Vygotskian approach 48, 49

Ward, J. 35

Watson, J. 29

Weinert, F.E. 12

Wenger, E. 179, 180, 182

White Paper (1995) 153

Whole School Evaluation (WSE) 157, 158, 162n2

'whole system reform' 153

Wiliam, D. 44, 45, 59, 174

Wiseman, A. W. 152

WSE *see* Whole School Evaluation

Wyatt-Smith, C. 4, 131

Zhang, Z. 121